Mervyn Stockwood
A Lonely Life

Mervyn Stockwood
A Lonely Life

Michael De-la-Noy

MOWBRAY

Mowbray
A Cassell imprint
Wellington House, 125 Strand, London WC2R 0BB
127 West 24th Street, New York, NY 10011

© Michael De-la-Noy 1996

First published 1996

British Library Cataloguing-in-Publication Data
A catalogue record for this book is available from the British Library.

ISBN 0-264-67410-3

Typeset by Keystroke, Jacaranda Lodge, Wolverhampton
Printed and bound in Great Britain by Redwood Books, Trowbridge, Wiltshire

Contents

For Tim Beaumont
(The Rev. Lord Beaumont of Whitley)
A catalyst of the 1960s, and in gratitude
for much kindness

A bishop . . . is necessarily a lonely person.
And it is not easy for a lonely man
to carry such a burden for twenty years.

Mervyn Stockwood, *Chanctonbury Ring*

An introduction

I never knew Mervyn Stockwood, but I knew of him, of course. From the moment he was consecrated, in 1959, until he resigned the see of Southwark 21 years later, he was seldom out of the news. This is one reason why, within a fortnight of his death, I was invited to write his biography. How often in future years will a publisher be so quick off the mark following the death of a bishop – and a bishop, moreover, whose last 13 years have been spent in retirement? Mervyn Stockwood became the sixth Bishop of Southwark in only 54 years. Being so recently created, his diocese was virtually unendowed, and by the time he arrived it was already creaking with those seemingly intractable inner-city problems due to beset so many industrialized areas of the Church of England. Eminently mimicable, a man about whom anecdotes abound, and at times prelatical in the tradition of the medieval prince bishop, Mervyn Stockwood stamped the force of his personality upon his diocese, making it the most talked about, and for ordinands the most sought after, diocese in the Church. Mervyn Stockwood was appointed before the Church of England had got around to demolishing its liturgy and choosing bishops in committee; a big man in every way, for better or worse no bishop is likely to have the opportunity in future to make his mark in the way that Mervyn Stockwood was able to. And this is one reason why so many people were so anxious to talk to me about him.

There is a danger inherent in writing about such an anecdotal person as Mervyn Stockwood, for with the best will in the world, people sometimes find it difficult to disentangle the anecdotal from the apocryphal or, indeed, from pure fantasy. The occasion on which the witty Bishop of London chided Mervyn Stockwood for wearing formal episcopal garb has been set in the garden at Buckingham Palace, at a bishops' meeting at Lambeth Palace, and in half a dozen other locations as well. More seriously, I was reliably informed, by someone who should have known better, that during the 1968 Lambeth Conference, Dr Stockwood entertained only English bishops. If this was the case, there have been a lot of very clever forgeries in his visitors' book. I can only say that I have discarded any story of whose truth I was not as sure as I could be.

I say I never knew Mervyn Stockwood. I did however meet him twice, but to claim on the basis of one lunch and one interview to have known Mervyn Stockwood would be absurd. There are people who shared his ministry or worked with him in one way or another for years who would tell you they never really knew him; at best, that they only knew one aspect of his personality. And it is because his was such a complex character that he presents a formidable challenge as the subject of a biography. Often unpredictable, he was even more frequently unfathomable. There were few tints or shades. He could be immensely kind and considerate, cruel and rude; by turns funny and exasperating, pompous and humble. The advantage of writing about him with what to some may seem indecent haste is that memories still remain warm, and to a large extent I have availed myself of first-hand personal testimony. Dr Stockwood's autobiography has all the hallmarks of one written without enthusiasm, and poses far more questions than it answers. He never wrote a serious book from which it would be profitable to try to cull the essence of the man; most of his slim volumes are merely collections of sermons. In fact, he left very few traces of his life other than in his pastoral work, much of that by its nature ephemeral; hence my unabashed reliance on personal recollections.

And yet part of the paradox of Mervyn Stockwood's life is that he wanted a biography; not necessarily one written by myself, but a wish to be memorialized in some way was consistent with his egotism. He asked in his will for the greatest possible economy to be observed with regard to his funeral, yet he requested also a Requiem Mass at the reincarnated Anglo-Catholic church of his childhood (the original building had been bombed in the war), and he would surely have been mortified had not at least one former Archbishop of Canterbury and eight other bishops appeared robed in the sanctuary. A note was discovered disclaiming any desire for a memorial service, but this his executors tactfully ignored. 'Well', one can so easily hear him drawling, as he always did, from the corner of his mouth, 'if there *must* be a tablet in the cathedral, just a small one.' There was nothing false about his self-regard, and it is actually rather an endearing side to his many-faceted nature.

Less entrancing was his ability to reduce grown men to a quivering mass of jelly. Yet this was the same person who prayed all his life for every priest he had ordained, and whose Boy Bishops and servers kept in touch with him until, quite literally, the day of his death.

The two occasions on which I met Mervyn Stockwood were separated by 30 years, and it was only as I was about to leave his house in Bath following the second meeting, in 1989, when I was researching a memoir of Michael Ramsey, that he rather shyly said 'You know, we have met before'. I had in fact been desperately hoping he would not remember. It was shortly after his consecration that I saw a photograph of him sporting a bow tie; I was a foolish young man of 26 at the time, and imagined I knew how other people ought to behave, so I wrote to the new bishop to complain about his sartorial appearance. Somehow our correspondence, entirely charitable and forbearing on his part, developed into an exchange of limericks. The press got hold of the story (I have an extremely uncomfortable feeling I probably gave it to them, so conceited was I at the thought of being in communication with a bishop), and headlines appeared like 'Bow Tie Bishop Breaks Into Verse'. Mervyn Stockwood ended up inviting me to luncheon at the Athenaeum. I should probably have had some difficulty finding the place, but when the press rumbled our meeting the venue was switched anyway, to a restaurant in Victoria Street, where I found Mervyn Stockwood ensconced behind an enormous screen. I was extremely disappointed that no one could see me eating with a bishop; I am equally ashamed to admit I do not recall a single word of his conversation, save for his parting remark on the pavement. 'If you want to discuss spiritual matters any time, come and talk to me again.' I never did, although I have no doubt the invitation was entirely sincere.

It may be wondered why, although I was a member of the Church Assembly from 1965 to 1967, and served as press officer to the Archbishop of Canterbury from 1967 to 1970, I never met Mervyn Stockwood in any official capacity. The answer explains a great deal about Mervyn Stockwood. He quite simply – and quite understandably – avoided Church House like the plague.

The choice of an appropriate method of referring to one's subject can be a dilemma for a biographer. Although in life I claim no intimacy of any kind with Mervyn Stockwood, I have not hesitated to call him Mervyn. He was the first bishop to address his fellow prelates by their Christian name; he invited his chaplains to call him Mervyn in private; even before he retired, the Orthodox custom of addressing bishops and clergy as Bishop Mervyn or Father Dominic was gaining widespread acceptance in the Church of England; and such is the sense of shared knowledge about, or friendship with, Mervyn Stockwood, that all those who have had anything to do with him refer to him automatically as Mervyn. This is not a sign of over-familiarity, but of affection. It reflects too the way in which he progressed with remarkable ease through a social sea-change; in his youth the use of surnames among men of his background was *de rigueur*.

Those who have helped me, to whom in many cases I owe an enormous debt of gratitude, are legion, and include especially Mervyn Stockwood's sister Miss Marion Stockwood, and his executors, Mrs Diana Cooke, Miss Mary Cryer, Canon Peter McCrory and Mr Ivor Seager. Without their initial encouragement and later whole-hearted support this book would certainly not have been written, and I can only hope it does not fall too far below their expectations. Copyright material is reproduced by permission of the executors.

An extract from 'The Diocese' by Sir John Betjeman is reproduced by kind permission of Candida Lycett Green. I am also particularly grateful to the following: Mr Paul Bailey, Mr Denis Ball, the Rt Hon. Tony Benn MP, Mrs Mary Bevan, Bishop John Bickersteth, the Rev. Tony Binns, the Rev. David and Mrs Brecknell, the Rev. David Bubbers, Bishop Colin Buchanan, Mrs Barbara Bunce of the Churches' Fellowship for Psychical and Spiritual Studies, Dame Barbara Cartland, Lady Elizabeth Cavendish, Mr Martin Cawte, Mr Dick Chapman, Mr Hubert Chesshyre (Norroy and Ulster King of Arms), Mr John Clement, Mr Roy Cleverly, the Rt Rev. and Rt Hon. Lord Coggan, Mr John Collins, Canon Martin Coombs, Mr Graham Cooper (Tavistock Secretary, Old Kelleian Club), the Rev. Tony Crowe, Mr Tam Dalyell MP, Mr J. S. Dearden (curator, Bembridge School), Mr Clive Edwards of The Canterbury Press, Mr Munir Elhawa, Mr David Faull, Miss Livia Gollancz, Mr John Gough, the Rev. Giles Harcourt, Mr Blair Harrison, the Rev. Andrew Henderson, Mr Christopher Hirst (formerly headmaster, Kelly College), Canon Michael Hocking, Mr John Holroyd (the Prime Minister's secretary for appointments), Canon Robin and Mrs Howard, Canon David Hutt, Mrs Elizabeth Inglis of Sussex University library, the Very Rev. Murray Irvine, Canon Eric James, the Rev. Charles Lansdale, the Hon. Mrs Rupert Legge, Canon Francis Longworth-Dames, Mr James Macpherson (headmaster, The Downs School), Canon Gervase Markham, Bishop Michael Marshall, the Very Rev. Michael Mayne, the Rev. Michael Miller, Major General Viscount Monckton of Brenchley, Bishop Hugh Montefiore, Lord Napier and Ettrick, Canon Paul Oestreicher, Dr Bernard Palmer, Dr Richard Palmer (librarian, Lambeth Palace), the Rev. Donald Reeves, the late Canon Douglas Rhymes, the Rev. Michael Roberts (Principal, Westcott House), Mrs Ruth Robinson, Canon Roger Royle, Miss Betty Saunders, Mr Steven Shakespeare, Miss Teresa Shepherd of the Law Society, the Rt Rev. David Sheppard (Bishop of Liverpool), Mr Ned Sherrin, the Rev. Bill Skelton, the Rev. Lord Soper, the Rev. David Sox, the Rev. Nicolas and the Hon. Mrs Stacey, Mr Richard Storey (archivist, Modern Records Centre, University of Warwick), the Rt Rev. Keith Sutton (Bishop of Lichfield), Mr David Tankard, Lord Taverne QC, the Rt Rev. James Thompson (Bishop of Bath and Wells), the Rev. Arthur Valle, Canon Dominic Walker OGS, the Rev. David Watkins, Mr Francis Wheen, Mr J. S. Williams (Bath city archivist), the Rt Rev. Robert Williamson (Bishop of Southwark), Bishop Kenneth Woollcombe and Dr David Wright of St Martin's Hospital, Bath.

Michael De-la-Noy
Hove, 1996

List of plates

Chapter 1

A very solemn boy

The most important event in the childhood of Arthur Mervyn Stockwood – perhaps in his life – occurred when he was three. His father, John Arthur Stockwood, a solicitor by profession, but now, thanks to the Great War, a sergeant in the Rifle Brigade, was killed, on 3 September 1916, at the Battle of the Somme. He was 37. He had been educated at Cowbridge Grammar School, and was admitted to the Supreme Court of England and Wales in 1903, practising for the next eleven years on his own, first at Cowbridge and later in Bridgend, Glamorganshire.[1] With the outbreak of war Arthur, with two of his friends, one a barrister, had tried to enlist in the Welch Regiment,[2] but was rejected on the grounds of age. The Rifle Brigade proved more easygoing and it seems that after initial training he was offered, but declined, a commission.[3] In August 1916 Arthur was due for home leave, and had actually reached the French coast and was about to sail when he and his comrades were recalled to the trenches, to take part in one more 'big push'. He was also, apparently, at this time about to have his commission gazetted, having realized, no doubt, that the war was not going to be 'over by Christmas', and that the pay of a subaltern, never mind his pension as one should he be killed, would be well worth the extra responsibility. Neither he nor his family were ever to benefit.[4]

Mervyn's paternal grandfather, a solicitor too, had also been baptized John, which was why Mervyn's father was known as Arthur; Mervyn, in his turn, was given his father's name Arthur, but his parents called him Mervyn from the start, and he always seemed more than content to use a Christian name with such a magical Welsh flavour to it. In later life Mervyn made astute use of what might be called his Celtic flair; it seems to have furnished him with a native cunning, an intuitive understanding of how people ticked which, had he been an intellectual, he might not have possessed. In his autobiography,[5] Mervyn claimed that he could recall the arrival, dreaded daily by so many families, of the telegraph boy bearing the news of his father's death. His mother, Beatrice Ethel Naunton Davies, who was always known as Ethel, had become a widow at 36. She had three young children and very little money. Her daughter, Ethel Marion, was just two days short of her tenth birthday when her father was killed, and into her first week at boarding school. To avoid confusion with her mother, she was known as Marion, and in fact she had been so named in memory of her maternal grandmother, who had died when Marion's own mother was only four. Alick, Mervyn's elder brother, was five.

When, in retirement, Mervyn came to write his autobiography, he stretched his childhood memory even further back than to the death of his father. He said his earliest recollection was of riding on his father's back when he was two, in search of cockles at Bridgend market. It was at 54 Park Street, Bridgend that Mervyn had been born, on 27 May 1913. And it was here that Arthur Stockwood maintained his wife and three young children 'in modest comfort'. It was not too difficult before the Great War to live in modest comfort as a solicitor. The house 'seemed large', the garden 'was a source of delight', and there was a servant called Bessie, who took the boys for afternoon walks. Unfortunately her favourite route went past the local lunatic asylum, and when the inmates emerged in crocodile formation, Mervyn was so terrified that his mother told Bessie to choose a different location. So now the boys were led by a river bank, and out of the river, so Bessie averred, a big fish would leap and then eat them if they misbehaved. Her dismissal and replacement can have been no great misfortune. In the garden at Park Street, Mervyn, Alick and their friends fought imaginary battles, and Mervyn, being the youngest, 'was expected to represent the Germans and to suffer defeat'. This, he also tells us, 'will doubtless give the psychologists several clues to my subsequent complexes and inhibitions'. But what Mervyn thought those 'complexes and inhibitions' were he does not say.

For better or worse, his father's death removed from Mervyn's boyhood the influence of a sporty type, a man who loved cricket, tennis, golf and football. At none of these 'manly' pursuits did Mervyn excel, although at school he did play fives, and at Cambridge he took up rowing for a time, until told it was bad for his heart. But by and large he disliked competitive games, for he disliked competition. Whether, as a result of being left fatherless so young, he actively sought, in his boyhood or adolescence, some father substitute is not clear; no one except possibly a parish priest in Clifton readily comes to mind, although he was undoubtedly drawn more towards his teachers than his peers. But in adult life he certainly assumed the role of a father figure, on two occasions to schoolboys. He scarcely knew his father and could not have missed a specific person, but being orphaned very possibly led to his heightened religiosity. Mervyn accepted that his father had been 'little more than a stranger' to him, but at the time of Arthur's death he also recalls 'looking out of the bedroom window . . . with my chin cupped in my hand, feeling I had lived for years and years and was steeped in the agonies and sufferings of the world and always would be'. He described it as 'a curiously vivid impression that has never left me, a blend of sorrow and loneliness. Perhaps the hallmark of my life.'

The adoption of a romanticized attitude towards his father's death was at all events a prelude to his imminent adoption also of religion. By the age of four, according to his sister,[6] he had made up his mind he was going to be ordained, and it certainly does seem as though for Mervyn (as for many clergy) ordination and allegiance to the Church were synonymous; life as a faithful layman was never seriously contemplated. A model altar was set up on the tuck-box in the bedroom he shared with Alick, and visits to All Saints' at Clifton in Bristol, a shrine of Anglo-Catholicism, provided the certitude and glamour missing as a result of the loss of his father and a reduction in the family's standard of living. There was no evangelistic piety involved. For the whole of his life, Mervyn's mind and body contended between God and good living. While strongly attracted to the secular, he could also be said to have had religion on the brain. No matter how worldly his outward appearance, he was always fully reconciled to the Faith. He delighted in theological and ecclesiastical discussion. Someone has said he liked his friends better than his family,[7] which was undoubtedly true when he was grown up, but he liked religion best of all, and the father substitute he sought when his father was killed, to whom, if only in his own idiosyncratic manner, he stuck closest all his life, was surely God.

No holiday visit to the Mendips, still a paradise of small, isolated village communities between the two World Wars, each with its separately maintained parochial community, would be complete

3

without excursions led by Mervyn to the parish church. When Alick and Marion got bored and rebelled, Mervyn's mother would patiently keep him company. As a small boy, Mervyn regularly read his Bible and said his prayers. His mother's church affiliations were loosely based, and sometimes she took Mervyn to a Unitarian church, to hear the sermons preached by a minister who was universally admired. The contrast with All Saints' could not have been greater, and Mrs Stockwood's action was more significant than she could have realized, for when Mervyn was a parish priest in Bristol he was to initiate ecumenical experiments far ahead of their time.

Mervyn's mother was a resourceful woman. She had been educated in Germany, spoke German and French, was good at tennis and played hockey to county standard. Although it was unusual for a girl to leave a comfortable home and take a job, Ethel Davies, before her marriage, joined the resident staff of The Downs School at 8 Upper Belgrave Road, Clifton (it was not until 1927 that the school moved to Charlton House, Wraxall), to teach small boys modern languages and English grammar and composition. She also gave piano lessons. The school had been founded in 1894, with just eight boarders and eight day boys. Five years later a new headmaster, Hugh King, was appointed, and it was by him that Ethel was hired. When she left to get married she kept in touch with Mr King, and in 1917 he introduced her to a Miss Whitmore, headmistress of a girls' school in Alma Road, Clifton.

On her hopelessly inadequate pension of £3 a week, even though it was supplemented by wages earned at the Admiralty office in Avonmouth, Ethel Stockwood was only too glad to be taken in by Miss Whitmore as a lodger in an annexe to her school, in Hanbury Road. Some of the teaching staff slept there, and there was a sitting-room Mrs Stockwood shared. It was in Hanbury Road that Alick and Mervyn now lived, joining in Miss Whitmore's morning lessons, and being taken in the afternoon for walks by another war widow, a Mrs Skinner.

Clifton was (and still is) that sedate quarter of Bristol in such marked contrast to the city's poverty-stricken East End, where 19 years later Mrs Stockwood's younger son was to begin a spectacular ministry among the poor and dispossessed. But Clifton, it should also be remarked, has a notoriously damp climate prone to cause, or at least to exacerbate, asthma. Its most remarkable feature, however, as far as the young Mervyn Stockwood was concerned, was All Saints' Church, and it seems that Mrs Skinner was of a High Church persuasion, for it was she who steered her youthful charge into the incense-charged interior of All Saints'. These were the days when it was unheard of for a church to be locked during the week. It was also a time when churchmanship was clearly demarcated, between Evangelicals, Central Churchmen and Anglo-Catholics – and when Anglo-Catholicism, the result of the early nineteenth-century Oxford Movement launched by John Newman, later a Cardinal, Canon Edward Pusey of Christ Church and the saintly John Keble, meant bells and smells, men and women segregated on opposite sides of the nave, birettas, Benediction, a daily Mass and the Blessed Sacrament reserved, usually (and strictly illegally) on the High Altar.

The liturgical glory that was All Saints', the church that provided Mervyn with his earliest religious impressions, is now quite rare. In all but a handful of staunchly defended strongholds, Anglo-Catholicism as he knew it when he was a boy has been watered down to a more uniform brand of catholicism, incorporating much of what used to constitute Central Church worship. And in any case, in 1940 the church became a victim of the blitz. So we must rely on Mervyn's own description of the building he knew before the Second World War. It was, he tells us, 'a large and magnificent building, quite different from the smaller church that took its place thirty years later', where, in 1995, Mervyn's funeral service was to take place. All Saints', he says,

was sometimes called the Anglo-Catholic cathedral of the West Country. It attracted vast congregations, and was constantly used by many people, often hundreds, throughout the week. The lofty roof, the imposing high altar, the great sanctuary lamps, the multiplicity of stained glass, the graceful side-chapels, the priests moving up the aisles in cloaks and birettas, combined to produce an atmosphere of mystery and awe. I cannot imagine anybody talking above a whisper, or entering without kneeling to say a prayer. My earliest religious impressions date from these afternoon visits. I enjoyed them; I felt at home in the church; I began to develop a sense of mystery and worship.

He also, without a doubt, envisaged himself as one of those priests 'moving up the aisles in cloaks and birettas'.

When Mervyn was five he developed a severe attack of colitis, a dietary disorder involving inflammation of the colon, a part of the large intestine. This, he tells us in a book he published in 1955, *I Went to Moscow*,[8] left him with a weak stomach, and on his visit to Moscow in 1953 he found the rich Russian fare, which included goose and sucking-pig, hard to swallow. Having recovered sufficiently to become a boarder, in May 1919, two or three weeks before his sixth birthday, Mervyn was first enrolled at The Downs School in Bristol, the school where before the war his mother had been a teacher. It seems a heartless age for a fatherless boy to have begun boarding-school life, and Mervyn has said he could not understand why his mother should have sent him away. 'I remember', he wrote in his autobiography, 'as though it were yesterday, the sense of gnawing despair which gripped me as she walked out of the front door. I cried myself to sleep, thinking I was the most pitiable creature in a cruel world.' In defence of her mother, Marion Stockwood has commented that 'Mervyn was too young to understand *her* despair. But when, as an oldish man, he came to write his life story, it might have occurred to him to mention it.'[9]

Whatever view one takes of Mervyn's distressing initiation into boarding-school life, it would appear that his first day at The Downs was not to be his worst. 'It is a very tedious book', one of Mervyn's chaplains has commented about *Chanctonbury Ring*, 'and reveals nothing about Mervyn whatsoever.'[10] One thing it certainly does not reveal, which Mervyn confided late in life to at least two friends,[11] was that while a pupil at The Downs he was mercilessly teased and actually forced to drink another boy's urine. The trick of peeing into a bottle and inviting someone to drink it, pretending it to be lemonade, is a standard prep school prank, and unless Mervyn was physically compelled to drink from such a poisoned chalice he must have been a true innocent to fall into a trap like this. His sister does not believe he would have been bullied into drinking. 'Once over his colitis', she has written, 'he was again a sturdy child, quite pugnacious, with a hot and hasty temper (which he afterwards learned to control). He was wilful, and liked to have his own way.'[12] In whatever manner the incident came about, the outcome must have had a searing effect on Mervyn, as it would on any boy. Miss Stockwood doubts whether there would have been much physical bullying at The Downs, but the truth is, no mother or sister in those days ever knew anything more about what went on in a boys' school than their son or brother cared to tell them. As a bishop, Mervyn was quite capable of wielding a heavy hand, episodes of his disciplinarianism amounting to what those who experienced it regarded as a form of adult bullying, and bullies are almost invariably those who have been bullied themselves.

In 1915 Hugh King had been appointed chairman of the Association of Preparatory Schools; in September that year an old boy, aged 19, had been killed in Flanders, and his parents had presented a cup 'to encourage others to follow a good example'. Now Mervyn's arrival in May 1919 coincided with the appointment of new headmasters, brothers called Wilfrid and Aelfric Harrison. The number of boys had risen to 41, and that winter the school had its first stab at producing a Shakespeare play – a great favourite with young boys, *Julius Caesar*. Sports loomed large. Although he had lost an arm in the war, Aelfric Harrison captained Gloucester at hockey, and both brothers played cricket for Dorset. Wilfrid Harrison's son, David, had died in the influenza epidemic which spread like wildfire through Europe in the aftermath of the Great War, and Mervyn, the youngest boy in the school, has recalled that Wilfrid and his wife Dorothy gave him David's toys to play with, and told him fairy stories to comfort him in his homesickness.[13] He has recalled too, with less than wholehearted enthusiasm, that in the summer terms 'we had three compulsory periods of cricket': half an hour before lunch, an hour in the middle of the afternoon and another 45 minutes of fielding and batting after tea.[14] There were, 'for the enthusiastic', yet another couple of voluntary periods of cricket, before breakfast and after prep. With no attempt at understatement, Mervyn says 'I detested the game'.

Religion was as strictly observed as sport, and on Sunday mornings, having studied the Collect for the day, the boys were marched off to St John's Church, Clifton, 'for an immensely long and boring service of Matins, lasting an hour and a half. For this penance, we wore Eton suits and top hats.'[15] In later life, Mervyn, who became very much a kind of free-wheeling Anglo-Catholic, surprisingly sympathetic to Evangelical worship and worshippers, used to say of the liturgy 'I don't mind if it's High Church or Low Church as long as it isn't Long Church'. One can well imagine the impatient lad longing for the colour and security of High Mass at All Saints'. A conformist at heart, he became the first boy at The Downs School to wear a straw hat, and felt 'greatly insulted'. Wilfrid Harrison was apparently 'a deeply committed Christian', the kind of deeply committed Christian who has no compunction about thrashing little boys. 'Discipline', Mervyn Stockwood remembered when looking back on his childhood, 'by today's standards, was severe. We had a system of set marks, and any boy who lost more than fourteen in a fortnight was severely caned on a Monday morning.'[16] Nevertheless, it seems the boys had considerable freedom. On Saturdays they were at liberty to wander round Clifton spending their pocket money, and those boys with bicycles were allowed to explore the countryside. But the food, thanks to post-war rationing, scarcely matched up to Mervyn's later gastronomic standards. Three days a week tea consisted of bread and margarine; the rest of the week there was bread and jam. Like many children of his generation, Mervyn was nine before he savoured the delights of butter or sugar. According to a son born later to Wilfrid Harrison, 'Food at the school was basic but adequate. On Mondays boys referred to lunch as YMCA – Yesterday's Muck Cooked Again.'[17] But this description of the school's catering almost certainly owes more to the inventiveness of eight-year-olds than to the ineptitude of the cook, and recalls several stories concerning Mervyn and initials. At Bishop's House in Southwark, for instance, a chaplain trying to arrange a confirmation spotted in Mervyn's diary 'SSNT' against the name of a certain parish priest. It transpired that on a previous visit to confirm, the incumbent had invited Mervyn into the vicarage 'for a drink', and had then enquired 'Which would you prefer, my Lord, tea or coffee?' The initials on this occasion were to remind Mervyn to 'Send Suffragan Next Time'.

In April 1923, shortly before Mervyn's tenth birthday, he was whisked away from The Downs for a couple of terms, and the sole reason for Mervyn crossing the Solent was because his mother had been offered a new job, matron to the junior school at Bembridge, on the Isle of Wight. Bembridge School stands upon the most prominent headland on the east coast of the Isle, and Mervyn served as one of the founder's guinea pigs. The school had only been in existence four years when Mervyn arrived, to enjoy briefly what all who remember the place in its early years have described as an enlightened and progressive atmosphere. The headmaster, John Howard Whitehouse, who had been born in 1873, prided himself on being something of an educational pioneer, and had the humility to call himself the Warden, not the Headmaster – for all he possessed in the way of academic teaching qualifications was an honorary Oxford MA. His real passion was for architecture, and he was a Fellow of the Royal Society of Architects. Unfortunately he thought it quite unnecessary to call upon the services of professional architects to supervise the proliferation of school buildings that arose during his 35 years as Warden, with the result that a number of them gave every appearance of being on the point of falling down.

Whitehouse had previously dabbled in good works (from 1905 to 1908 he was secretary of Toynbee Hall). In politics he served briefly as a Parliamentary Under-Secretary of State, and his Liberal sympathies appealed to Isaac Foot, patriarch of the famous political family, two of whom, Dingle and John, were sent to Bembridge. He was also a devotee of Ruskin, and in 1932 he became president of the Ruskin Society. Like so many hearty idealists of his time, he was a firm believer in the outdoor life, and in 1911 he had written a book called *Camping for Boys*. Indeed, he ran summer camps at Yellowsands before he founded Bembridge School, and to one of these camps the former cabinet minister C. F. G. Masterman repaired during the war to try to recoup his strength and spirits. In typical *Boys' Own* idiom he wrote to his wife to say 'I have been slaving like a rat, though all pleasant work, taking bathing parades, tea, etc., getting up footer and tip cricket and generally stirring things up. It's quite a lark . . . I am sure these boys are a better cure than any "restcure" or even grown up golf.'[18]

Masterman would return to the Isle of Wight after Whitehouse had opened his school, to give uplifting talks to the boys, and Mervyn got to know him, for he used to visit his widow, Lucy, when she was in her eighties and living in a flat in Overstrand Mansions, Battersea. Another of Whitehouse's influential friends, and a visitor to the school, was William Inge, Dean of St Paul's from 1911 to 1934. The Dean, Masterman, Isaac Foot and the painter Christopher Nevinson became Governors of the school. One of Whitehouse's many interests was American history, and this, most unusually, found its way on to the curriculum, along with current affairs, then called 'civics'. Alan Marlow, who was at Bembridge with Mervyn, has written: 'The academic standards may not have been high but the boys were encouraged to be responsible, independent in thought, and to develop their potential to the full in their chosen subjects. The range of subjects was wide and included many handicrafts.' He remembers that the school was 'considered very progressive at the time. The Warden . . . was able to attract staff of similar views, the general atmosphere was excellent, and the site was, and still is, superb.'[19]

Mervyn's mother was matron in the junior school during the summer and Christmas terms of 1923, and Alick, too, became a pupil at Bembridge. The three of them remained at the school during the summer holiday, and Marion Stockwood remembers 'There was a quiet little beach just below the school. There was a nice matron in the senior school who would join them on picnics and outings.' Two of the attractions were 'the little island railway' and a cinema at Sandown, where the family saw *The Prisoner of Zenda*.[20] At the end of the summer term there had been an exhibition of school work, and Mervyn's contribution had been an essay on photography, for which he was awarded two marks – out of how many history does not record. Shortly after becoming Vicar of Great St Mary's, Cambridge, in 1955, Mervyn travelled to St Margaret's, Westminster to preach at a memorial service for John Whitehouse, whom he had got to know properly 27 years after leaving the Isle of Wight. He recalled vivid memories of the sermons Whitehouse himself used to preach. He thought, on reading them when they were published, they had been 'masterpieces of English prose, noble illustrations of what addresses to boys should be'. One homily Mervyn especially remembered contained an admonition to the boys to find themselves at the end of each day 'divinely athirst'. He said Whitehouse 'helped to turn me into a young crusader' when he delivered an address about slum conditions in Manchester.

In some ways it seems a pity that Mervyn did not stay longer than two terms under the benign influence of John Whitehouse. He thought Whitehouse 'in the best and fullest sense of the word' a Liberal. At Whitehouse's memorial service in 1956 he said

In an age of mediocrity and mass production, he valued individual worth, reverenced individuality, and encouraged individualism. His critics may say, perhaps justly, that he did not attach sufficient importance to academic standards in so far as they affect examinations. If this is true, it was because he refused to look upon a school as a factory for cramming facts into unappreciative heads. He preferred boys to develop along their own lines and to hold a balanced, a discriminating and an independent view of life.

As to the religious affiliations of the man whose sermons had so inspired him, Mervyn told the congregation at St Margaret's

Howard Whitehouse was not an orthodox Christian and I should be guilty of hypocrisy if I were to suggest that at this service we were saluting a devoted son of the Established Church. Organised religion meant little to him though he was careful to respect the feelings of people like myself to whom it means much.

Mervyn returned to Bembridge on 11 July 1969, when by this time he was Bishop of Southwark, to preach at celebrations to mark the school's half-century. He admitted his knowledge of the school was slight; he had, after all, spent just two terms there. But he had become one of the school's most distinguished old boys. Only Robin Day was as well known to the public. He said he doubted whether in the early days the school had struck the right balance between freedom and authority, between discipline and licence, and he said he was removed 'and sent to a more orthodox school' because 'it was thought that I required a greater knowledge of the three Rs, to say nothing of the idiosyncrasies of Greek and Latin grammar and of the irregularities of French verbs'. Perhaps intending to be tactful, at Whitehouse's memorial service he had earlier told the congregation he left 'for domestic reasons', which also happened to be true, for his mother gave in her notice as matron, and it was to The Downs School in Bristol that he was returned, in 1924, and where he stayed for the next two years, earning an early reputation as a raconteur; after lights out he 'regaled the dormitory with hair-raising stories'.[21]

Following the death of David, another son, Blair, had been born to Wilfrid and Dorothy Harrison in 1921, and it was at a very tender age indeed that Mervyn developed his astonishing capacity for remembering other people's anniversaries. Seventy-four years later Blair Harrison wrote to the current headmaster of The Downs School to tell him 'Mervyn was in the school on the night that I was born and he remembers my birthday to this day!' Alick, too, who had caught scarlet fever soon after the family's arrival in Clifton and then developed pleurisy, and had started life as a 'delicate, nervous child',[22] became good at keeping in touch with people. He corresponded with his old headmaster, Wilfrid Harrison, until the end of his life, and went to see him in his retirement. Unlike Mervyn, Alick preferred maths to Latin, but a more solid reason for the lack of any strong fraternal links in later life was because after being at The Downs School together the two boys attended different public schools, and in 1932 Alick left for Canada. When he was 13, Alick was sent to an early sixteenth-century foundation, King's School, Bruton, in Somerset, and on leaving school he was taken on by an old established Bristol firm of printers, E. S. and A. Robinson. Told that prospects of promotion would be quicker if he transferred to the firm's new plant in Toronto, he decided to emigrate. He had been living at home, 'a thoughtful, practical young man', according to his sister, 'and a companion who would have been a great loss to his mother'.[23] Eventually Alick became a director of the Toronto branch of the firm, married a Canadian, Anne Trafford Jones, and provided Mervyn with two nephews and a niece.

The school chosen in 1926 for Mervyn was what snobs would regard as another 'minor' public school, Kelly College. It had been founded in 1877 at the behest of the splendidly named Admiral Benedictus Marwood Kelly, who in fact died in 1867 (he had been born when the eighteenth century still had 15 years to run). Kelly left about £150,000 to establish a school in the West Country for the education of 'lineal descendants of the Kelly family [they are called Foundationers], sons of officers in the Royal Navy and other gentlemen'. Mervyn was presumably accepted on the grounds that solicitors are gentlemen. Twenty acres of land about a mile outside Tavistock were presented to Admiral Kelly's trustees by the eighth Duke of Bedford (his senior courtesy title was Marquess of Tavistock), and Charles Hansom, who had already built two public schools, Clifton and Malvern, and whose brother had gained immortal fame as the designer of the Hansom cab, was hired as architect.

An ecstatic description of the site and its subsequent purpose-built school has been left in the College's Golden Jubilee Register.

Standing on the Terrace one realises how marvellously well the Architect, or whoever it was, chose the site of the College. The fine buildings cleverly set back into the slope of the hill; the steep grassy slope down the leat bank and that splendid expanse of green sward below; opposite, the heavy verdure of Mount Tavy clothing the whole hillside up to the Downs; a gleam of the river rushing through the valley; and, presiding over all, the granite-covered slopes of Cox Tor. These are some of the attributes that entitle us to claim that we have one of the loveliest schools in England.

The college opened with a dozen boys, eleven of whom were Foundationers, so the Admiral had no shortage of 13-year-old lineal descendants. Of the 350 old boys who fought in the Great

War, more than 60 received decorations for gallantry. In 1921 the college was admitted to the Headmasters' Conference, and Mervyn's arrival in September 1926, by which time there were 180 boys, coincided with the appointment as headmaster of the Rev. Norman Miller, a Classical Scholar of Queens' College, Cambridge and a former housemaster at Haileybury. His abilities and qualifications must have been formidable, for he was chosen from over 100 applicants for the post. Today the college is coeducational, and has established a reputation for its prowess at swimming; in Mervyn's day, although it was against school rules, the boys used to swim in the River Tavy. Tavistock itself was out of bounds, so an appearance in chapel on Sunday by the bursar's daughter provided one of the few glimpses of a female face the boys enjoyed from one holiday to the next, and their life was basically monastic. But they were allowed to go for walks on the moors, and it was generally remarked that whereas most of the boys went for walks in small parties of three or four, Mervyn invariably went by himself.

Mervyn has written of his four years at Kelly 'I endured it rather than enjoyed it'. Denis Ball, however, the headmaster appointed in 1972, reports Mervyn as saying that he 'loved Kelly (and Dartmoor) & was very pleased when I made immediate contact on becoming HM of Kelly'.[24] That same year Mervyn accepted an invitation to return to his Alma Mater, returning again in 1977 to preach at the centenary celebrations, taking as his text 'Remember now thy creator in the days of thy youth'. He was back yet again to preach on Founder's Day in 1985. He took a great shine to Mr Ball's young wife, and it was entirely typical of Mervyn that in 1987 he travelled from Bath to the Balls' retirement home near Canterbury to give her communion before she died of cancer at the tragically early age of 34. He must have formed a very warm attachment to the Balls, for he stayed with them at Ickham five times – always signing their visitors' book in purple ink.

But Mervyn had a liking for pedagogues, and with his own headmaster, Norman Miller, he formed such a close relationship that in 1946 he stood as godfather to his son Michael. Michael Miller remembers that Mervyn was 'a very attentive godfather' whom he saw regularly throughout his childhood.[25] Dr Miller asserts that Mervyn was given a place at Kelly College 'on the strong recommendation' of his father, 'who enjoyed seeking out intelligent youngsters and giving them opportunities'.[26] Apparently Mervyn often spoke to Michael Miller of 'the profound influence' his father had had on him, 'allowing him to think for himself and encouraging him to do so'.[27] A contemporary of Mervyn's, John Hadley, has testified also to 'the very strong influence in his early days that Miller had upon [Mervyn] – and it was certainly an influence for good'.[28]

Another contemporary, John Clement, recalls Mervyn as 'a loner', as a 'very solemn boy who seldom smiled'.[29] Mervyn served at communion in the college chapel, and before long he was known to the other boys – although not in any derisory way – as the Bishop. It came as no surprise to Mr Clement when Mervyn was ordained, and as even less of a surprise when he really did become a bishop. It was probably in 1927, when he would have been 14, that Mervyn was confirmed, by George Nickson, formerly suffragan Bishop of Jarrow and since 1914 Bishop of Bristol. There was, at Kelly, no tradition of fasting before taking communion, which was just as well, for Holy Communion was sometimes celebrated in the middle of the morning, by which time growing schoolboys might have been fainting with hunger. But back at All Saints' in Clifton the Anglo-Catholic discipline of fasting was strictly observed – so strictly that one of the parish clergy told Mervyn that if he continued to receive communion at school after having eaten breakfast he would withhold absolution when he next sought to make his confession. Mervyn the budding polemicist pointed out there was no rule in the Prayer Book about fasting. The argument reached the ears of Nickson, who let it be known – quite rightly – that the matter was one for an individual's conscience. This left relations between Mervyn and the Clifton curate permanently ruptured, and sowed in the future bishop distrust 'of ecclesiastical regulations and legalism'. With the incumbent at Clifton, Canon M. P. Gillson, Mervyn continued, however, to enjoy a cordial relationship. This is strange in a way, for Mervyn says that Gillson ruled the congregation with a rod of iron, and that he could not imagine anybody daring to argue with him. But Canon Gillson, rather a remote and awesome figure, 'remarkably handsome, and, in the strict sense of the word, an aristocrat', seems to have become a role model. In the holidays Mervyn was often round at the vicarage, was invited to meals, sometimes stayed with Canon Gillson, and one year joined a party led by Gillson to see the Passion Play at Oberammergau. Gillson remained in touch with Mervyn by letter during termtime, taking a keen interest in his educational progress. He impressed Mervyn particularly with his 'loathing of emotion and undignified behaviour'.

Religion at Kelly, Mervyn has recalled, 'was treated seriously, but without emotion'. The school day began with a short service in the chapel, and usually on Sunday there was an early celebration of Holy Communion and later a Sung Matins. It was exactly what one would have expected in such an establishment. There was little intellectual stimulation, and it was left to Mervyn, during a divinity lesson, to question the Virgin Birth. He served as chapel monitor, responsible for 'visiting preachers, seeing to their robing and generally being "on hand" to see to their wants'.[30]

Although John Clement's mother had known the Stockwood family in Bridgend he says that Mervyn was not easy to get to know at school. At 14 'he was a fine, big-built boy, but a loner'. There were only two boarding-houses, and Mervyn had been assigned to School House, where his headmaster was also the housemaster. He shared a large dormitory with 19 boys, and fagged for a senior boy. Following the fashion of the time (the plan was to dampen sexual ardour) he was compelled to take a cold bath every morning, and endured 'an average standard' of school food. As for his abilities on the sports field, they were, John Clement recalls, 'Nil!' He enjoyed tennis but opted out of cricket, hockey and rugby, and was therefore compelled instead to go on four-mile cross-country runs – an occupation ideally suited to a 'loner'. It was the solitary aspect of Mervyn's nature that left the overriding impression on those who knew him at Kelly. 'I used to feel sorry for him', Mr Clement says. 'He always seemed to be on his own.' Despite his dislike of organized games, Mervyn's physical capabilities could not have been insignificant. In their report on Founder's Day and Prize Giving in 1930, when Mervyn was 17, the *Western Morning News* recorded 'the cup for the best physical training instructor' being presented to A. M. Stockwood. Academically, Mervyn impressed his contempories by being placed in a form two ahead of them, and he generally came out near the top of a Latin test administered once a month to the entire school. In September 1929 he gained the School Certificate with a modest four credits.

In his autobiography, Mervyn makes the usual criticisms of public school life in his day, objecting to the emphasis on sport ('when I reached university it was like passing from Sparta to Athens') and to the failure of the system 'to take into account the development of the sexual instincts. Human nature being as it is', he wrote, 'a boy is likely to form a romantic attachment to a member of his own sex if he cannot fall in love with a girl. This is not necessarily bad, in fact it may be good, but it should be faced realistically and not brushed under the carpet.' These are fairly innocuous platitudes, and give no indication as to whether he was writing from a generalized standpoint or from personal experience. Mr Clement has said he was quite unaware of any sexual liaison between Mervyn and any other boy, but as he was not in School House he might not have observed it had it occurred. At all events, Mervyn seems to have reserved plenty of energy for academic pursuits, for it must have been while at Kelly and involved in the school curriculum that he found time to study for ecclesiastical examinations, being admitted as a lay reader at the very unusual age of 18. By this time also he had been appointed a school monitor, with the privilege of sitting at top table.

Mervyn made occasional contributions to the Debating Society, proposing, in January 1929, that 'In the opinion of this House, civil-isation has benefited as a result of scientific research'. Apparently his speech 'contained good material and showed evidence of classical training', although it was 'marred to some extent by over-frequent reference to his notes'. Nevertheless the motion was lost by 17 votes to 12. In May 1930, at the half-term concert, Mervyn trod the boards in a play entitled *The Cat and the Cherub,* when the part of 'Hoo King, the sorely worried father of the child' was 'well played by Stockwood'. Perhaps rather more surprisingly, Mervyn reached the rank of corporal in the Cadet Force, and distinguished himself by gaining a Cert A proficiency award.

It was while still a schoolboy that in 1929 Mervyn met the famous Evangelical clergyman Bryan Green – during a mission conducted by Green in Clifton. It says much for Mervyn's broadminded attitude to religious experience that while rejecting some of Green's methods he admitted 'the freshness of his approach', and he says that from Bryan Green he learnt many things about personal religion which helped to mould his future ministry. Meanwhile, he had to give serious consideration to a career. He says he thought both of ordination and schoolmastering, perhaps even of combin-ing the two vocations as a school chaplain, but John Clement says that Mervyn did not strike him as a natural schoolmaster; he had no doubt that Mervyn would carve a career in the Church, and indeed, by January 1933 it was being reported back to Kelly from Christ's College, Cambridge that A. M. Stockwood had proved 'rather elusive to run to earth', although there was 'little doubt that he is now in the front rank of theological pundits in this place

– a veritable mine of information upon all matters ecclesiastical'. But before Mervyn had been able to go up to Cambridge it had been necessary for him to earn and save some money. These were the days when impoverished graduates and even non-graduates were welcomed on to the staff of prep schools, and the fewer qualifications they had the more warmly they were welcomed, for the less it was thought necessary for them to be paid. Readers of Evelyn Waugh's semi-autobiographical novel *Decline and Fall*, published in 1928, will recall with what ease Paul Pennyfeather obtained a teaching post as 'junior assistant master' at Dr Augustus Fagan's dubious educational establishment, Llanabba Castle, at the princely salary of £90 a year – but in his case the fee had been reduced from £120, for Dr Fagan was under the mistaken impression (as was Paul himself!) that Paul had been sent down from Oxford for indecent behaviour. Hence there was nothing too exceptional in the fact that in order to save enough money to study at Cambridge, at the age of 18, without formal qualifications of any kind, Mervyn obtained a post as a master at a boys' preparatory school.

Notes

1 Information supplied 31 May 1995 by the Professional Standards and Development Directorate of the Law Society.

2 Amalgamated with the South Wales Borderers in 1967 into the Royal Regiment of Wales.

3 Information supplied by his daughter, Marion Stockwood.

4 Ibid.

5 *Chanctonbury Ring* (Sheldon Press and Hodder & Stoughton, 1982) (and throughout).

6 In conversation with the author.

7 Mary Cryer, in conversation with the author.

8 The Epworth Press.

9 Information supplied by Marion Stockwood.

10 Donald Reeves, in conversation with the author.

11 Mary Bevan and Tony Crowe.

12 Information supplied by Marion Stockwood.

13 *The Downs School 1894–1994: A Century of Achievement* (The Downs School, Wraxall, Bristol, 1994).

14 Ibid.

15 Ibid.

16 Ibid.

17 Blair Harrison, letter to the author, 16 March 1995.

18 Lucy Masterman, *C. F. G. Masterman: A Biography* (Frank Cass, 1968).

19 Letter from Alan Marlow to the author, 2 March 1995.

20 Information supplied by Marion Stockwood.

21 Blair Harrison, letter to the author, 16 March 1995.

22 Information supplied by Marion Stockwood.

23 Ibid.

24 Letter from Denis Ball to the author, 23 March 1995.

25 Michael Miller: memorandum dated August 1995. Mervyn also stood as godfather to a son of Patrick and Pamela Fedden and to John and Ruth Robinson's son Stephen.

26 Ibid.

27 Ibid.

28 John Hadley, in a letter to the author, dated 9 April 1995.

29 John Clement, in conversation with the author.

30 John Hadley, as above.

Chapter 2

The most loving
community

In 1931, when Mervyn Stockwood was 18, Ramsay MacDonald formed his National Government, and although Mervyn had joined the staff of a preparatory school in Shrewsbury called Kingsland Grange, he found time to campaign for his local Conservative candidate. Nothing had yet occurred in his life to upset the political convictions with which someone from his middle-class background was virtually born. Having a professional father and being educated at a public school were good enough reasons for voting Tory. Mervyn was at this time entirely conventional; in many ways, he always remained so. The only working-class boys he had ever encountered lived in Devonport. They were patronized by Kelly College, who occasionally condescended to send a coachload of toffs to play table tennis with them. On one such visit Mervyn and his friends had been warned not to accept invitations to dance with local girls for fear they might be infectious, and on the return journey the master in charge of the outing had stopped the coach and made all the boys take deep breaths of Dartmoor air 'in order', so Mervyn later recorded, 'to rid ourselves of the germs that we might have picked up in "the slums"!'

Now he had moved from one conservative stronghold, Kelly College, to another, for many of the boys at Kingsland Grange, founded in 1899, were destined to go on to Shrewsbury. Mervyn has written that although Kingsland Grange had no official connection with Shrewsbury School, 'we lived under its eye and adopted some of its customs'. A martinet called W. B. C. Drew was headmaster when Mervyn arrived, a man who, like Wilfrid Harrison, thought the best way to instil Latin and Greek into the minds of little boys was by thrashing their backsides. He was replaced by an altogether more civilized headmaster ('kind and charming but not very forceful', in the opinion of one of Mervyn's colleagues[1]), the Rev. P. C. West, with whom Mervyn got on well and who was not afraid to show affection and respect towards his pupils. They numbered about 80, half of whom were boarders, and part of Mervyn's responsibilities involved keeping an eye on the dormitories. Mervyn taught English to boys between about ten and 13, some of whom he liked sufficiently to photograph for an album he kept all his life. Aged about eleven, Jimmy Hough posed for Mervyn in shorts held up with a belt, his tie askew and his socks falling down. 'The Four Sergeants', on the other hand, aged about 13, smartened themselves up for the camera in grey suits and school caps.

As is customary when prep school boys encounter a new, young master, on his first night Mervyn was interrogated by a lively lad who wanted to know if he was married. 'No', said Mervyn, 'I'm not married.'

'Are you engaged?' the boy enquired.

'No', said Mervyn, 'I am afraid I am not even engaged.'

Still in hot pursuit of information about the new beak, the boy had no hesitation in asking 'How many children have you got, Sir?'

Mervyn told this story in years to come, always with a chuckle. Nothing is more natural than for a young boy to probe the marital status and sexual inclinations of his teaching staff, but it is extraordinary how, many years after Mervyn had quite obviously settled into the role of a bachelor cleric, adults would not hesitate to make what they were pleased to regard as an amusing reference to his chances of still getting married. It has been intimated[2] that when he was about 13, Mervyn informed the daughter of a Bristol clergyman that when he was grown up he was going to marry her, but that need not be regarded as anything more than a youthful shot at gallantry. To all intents and purposes, Mervyn was not the marrying kind.

Kingsland Grange would be described today as Stockbroker Tudor. There was no school chapel and Mr West escorted the boys to the local parish church, where it seems almost certain that Mervyn preached his first sermon. He kept a school exercise book in which the first sermon preserved, delivered on 10 July 1932, began 'I don't know what's come over Tom lately but ever since he left school he's never been to church'. The reasons Tom stayed away seem to have been that 'church was so dull', 'Mother always made me go against my will', and 'church is so boring'.

Mervyn kept in touch with a number of masters and boys at Kingsland Grange. One of the boys Mervyn taught was Alan

Groves, who returned some years later as headmaster. Mr Groves remembers Mervyn, when he was 18 or 19, looking older than his years.[3] 'He was not everyone's cup of tea. He could be a bit dry with some of the boys, but he came across as obviously intelligent and well read for his age.' Unfortunately, in addition to a dislike of sports Mervyn had acquired an aversion to bridge, so that his life in the common room was not as sociable as it might have been. Instead, using a bicycle for transport, he went dancing, for ballroom dancing was an almost obligatory accomplishment for a young man of his generation. More importantly, perhaps, as his aim was to go to university, he availed himself of every hour torn from the demands of small boys to read, devouring fiction, he tells us, biography, travel, history and philosophy. During term-time he sometimes escaped from the Grange for weekends, for his uncle, Charles Stockwood, Archdeacon of the Isle of Man, had an old-fashioned Evangelical friend near by, James Chitty, Rector of Yockleton, who made Mervyn welcome at his rectory. It was Mr Chitty who had persuaded the Bishop of Hereford to license Mervyn as a lay reader. It was Mr Chitty too, far keener on horticulture than ecclesiastical gossip, who introduced Mervyn to the solitary pastime of fishing.

After a year of teaching and saving, Mervyn left Kingsland Grange in July 1932. In August he went on holiday to Llandudno, where he had himself photographed in a most unbecoming swimming costume, writing on the back of the photograph 'When I was a dashing "seventeen"', although he was in fact already 19. And then he entered Christ's College, Cambridge. Originally founded in 1448 by Henry VI, Christ's was refounded in 1505 on its present site on a triangle between St Andrew's Street (in which is situated the entrance to the college through Great Gate), Hobson Street and the open space of Christ's Pieces. Its sixteenth-century benefactress was Margaret Beaufort, mother of Henry VII. The beautiful First Court, containing the chapel, with its 1705 'Father' Smith organ, the Master's Lodge and the library, dates from the fifteenth century. Those who studied here before Mervyn included Darwin and Milton, and in the garden is a mulberry tree reputedly planted in 1608, the year of Milton's birth.

Mervyn was at Christ's College for three years. He read history in his first year, taking a Second Class in 1934, and then he switched to theology, in which he again graduated with a Second. It was a respectable but not a brilliant academic achievement. He seems also

to have left less than a startling impression on some of his contempories. 'I was up at Christ's at the same time as Mervyn but
I have no recollection of him as an undergraduate', the honorary
archivist of the college has written.[4] Others remember him better.
'One could hardly not be aware of someone with Mervyn's style
and panache', Dean Norman Rathbone has written.[5] 'Mervyn
and I went up to Christ's in the same term and he was even then
something of a presence in the college.' But it is interesting how
even the earliest impressions of Mervyn differ to a marked degree.
Canon Geoffrey Young recalls Mervyn as being 'something of a
rebel (no harm in that) but I thought that he could be mannerless
and even cruel with it. He had no great distinction, academic,
athletic or social, but he always had a following, which I found
hard to explain.'[6] The Rev. John Mowll writes 'I think that the
most remarkable thing about him prior to his ordination was the
amazing influence that he had on so many colleges when he was
an undergraduate at Christ's'.[7] Mervyn's disciples were known as
'The Mervyn Crowd'. Apparently there were 'a number of young
people whom Mervyn wished to be trained as evangelists' and they
got marched off to Pembroke College. Mervyn 'could not stand
the chaplain [at Christ's], a man called Frank Woolnough', Canon
Michael Hocking recalls, 'and thus he had little to do with the
college chapel. Instead he became very friendly with the Dean of
Pembroke, and they arranged a weekly communion service in
Pembroke with breakfast afterwards.'[8]

The Dean of Pembroke was Edward Wynn, who in 1941 was
consecrated Bishop of Ely. And it was Bryan Green, with whom
Mervyn had remained in touch since meeting him in 1929, who
inspired Mervyn to round up other eager young Christians for talks
from Wynn. In 1933 Mervyn took a party of undergraduates
to Bournemouth to help run one of Green's missions, and he joined
up with Green in Coventry the following year. Canon Francis
Longworth-Dames, a year younger than Mervyn and destined to
become a lifelong friend, makes the point that in those days it was
most unusual for Evangelicals and Anglo-Catholics to rub along
together, and very early on he spotted Mervyn's personal brand of
Broad-Churchmanship, his feeling equally at home preaching the
gospel while celebrating the sacraments.

Longworth-Dames was himself the product of Irish Protestantism,
and although he later veered towards the catholic wing of the
Church of England, when he first met Mervyn they seemingly had

little in common. But Longworth-Dames was one of those instantly swept up by Mervyn's enthusiasm for missions. To Mervyn, Longworth-Dames represented a creature from another planet, and before long he was accepting invitations to visit the family home in Ireland, not immensely grand by Irish ascendancy standards but the Longworth-Dames employed three maids, three more than Mervyn had ever been used to. In Ireland too, while staying with Longworth-Dames, who was later to become one of his parish priests in Southwark, he had the chance to practise trout fishing, and so hooked did Mervyn become on the sport that at one time it featured as his only recreation in his entry in *Who's Who*; but eventually even this was dropped. He enjoyed teasing Longworth-Dames about his Low Church background, escorting him on one occasion into a Roman Catholic church in Ireland, where Mervyn cross-examined an Irish labourer about the origins of the building. He made the point to Longworth-Dames that no casual worshipper in an Anglican church would have quite unselfconsciously conversed about the building, and more to the point, about a statue which had caught Mervyn's eye. Mervyn made it plain that if he had been born in Ireland he would have found it quite natural to be a Roman Catholic, an indication of the importance he attached to the 'established' nature of any national Church, whatever the Church's obvious imperfections. At university he gave a wide berth to Nonconformists.

Mervyn seems to have entertained a youthful contempt for most of the dons at Cambridge. 'The supervisors and lecturers, with few exceptions, were intolerably dull', he has written, 'and I suspect that many of them had relied upon the same notes for thirty years.' But things must have looked up when he began to read theology, for like so many young men more or less of Mervyn's generation, he fell under the spell of Charles Raven, whose fictional *alter ego* can be found in C. P. Snow's *The Masters*. Raven was a biologist as well as a theologian – Regius Professor of Divinity, in fact. Mervyn reckoned he could 'electrify his audiences', and he says that Raven's 'liberal and scholarly approach' made an immense impact upon him. But so far as Mervyn was concerned, at Cambridge in 1934 Canon Raven was the exception to the rule. He thought the position worse, if anything, than it had been while he was reading history. 'The other lecturers', he claims, 'were indescribable.' Apparently one of them 'spent the greater part of a lecture arguing that St Paul was let down a wall at the time of his escape in a sack and not a basket'. One wonders if perhaps when he was writing his autobiography Mervyn had overlooked the lectures given at Corpus Christi by the dean, Edwyn Hoskyns, an engaging Anglo-Catholic and a baronet, whose discourses on biblical theology were eagerly attended by undergraduates from colleges other than his own – among them Mervyn, according to the recollections of Francis Longworth-Dames.[9] In fact, when, during the war, Mervyn came to write his first book, *There Is a Tide*,[10] he included a tribute to Hoskyns, among others, admitting that the dons 'taught me so much when I was at the University, either by their lectures or their books'.

Like most sensible undergraduates, Mervyn did not confine his time at university to study. He seems to have had a lunch, tea or dinner engagement every day, and this comes as no surprise when one considers how gregarious he was, dependent on company, conversation and, hopefully, enjoyable fare. There were picnics on the Granta, and visits armed with his camera to inevitable ports of call like Trinity College and King's. The courts of his own college, the Backs and friends called Reggie and Peter were all duly snapped. And within days of his arrival at Christ's he was busy recruiting for the Conservative Party. This led to an invitation to dine at Corpus Christi to meet members of the Government, but Mervyn was disillusioned when he actually encountered them. Hunger marches were beginning to stir his conscience, but the process was a slow one, for, as he says himself, his generation of educated young men were 'woefully unaware of historical, social and economic trends'. His own history syllabus had stopped short at the end of the nineteenth century. 'Of America and Russia there was scarcely a mention.'

Although many people assert that Mervyn could not stand his college chaplain, Mervyn says that he attended his college chapel on Sundays. Nevertheless King's College became his liturgical home. And it was certainly to the Dean of Pembroke's rooms, along with many other appreciative undergraduates, that Mervyn made his way both for convivial company (Wynn was, he says, a delightful host with 'a fund of amusing stories and an infectious laugh') and for spiritual advice. In fact, Edward Wynn became Mervyn's confessor, and it was he who in 1955 was to institute him to the living of Great St Mary's in Cambridge, for Cambridge is in the diocese of Ely. But as for his own college chaplain, Mervyn somewhat uncharitably described him as 'a creeping opportunist and a schemer'.

Having graduated and been photographed resplendent in gown, with his mortar-board in his hand, Mervyn moved in July 1935 across to Jesus Lane to study for the priesthood at Westcott House Theological College. On the staff as vice-principal was L. John Collins, later destined for a canon's stall at St Paul's and fame as a leading campaigner against nuclear weapons. The Principal was Canon B. K. Cunningham, and among Mervyn's contempories as an ordinand was George Reindorp, later to become Provost of Southwark and then successively Bishop of Guildford and Salisbury. The chaplain at Westcott House, Gerald Hawker, had the grace in later years to admit 'We never thought much of Stockwood and Reindorp at Westcott'. John Mowll remembers at Westcott Mervyn's 'very abrasive nature', evidence of which emerged one day when Mervyn became irritated by some fellow ordinands who were playing table tennis when he thought they ought to have been working. He was much in demand as a preacher while still an ordinand, according to a contemporary whose name, by coincidence, was Philip Westcott.[11] Mervyn's early admission as a lay reader and his brief experience as a prep school master would have appealed to the Principal, who was ahead of his time in liking ordinands to have gained some 'experience of the world' between university and theological college; Mervyn's experience, limited as it was, had even more unusually been gained before going up to Cambridge.

In Mervyn's year at Westcott (theological training was quite brief in his day) there were about 40 men, all but two of them bachelors, the two married ordinands having served in the army. Mervyn always used to say that George Reindorp 'looked after him wonderfully at Westcott', that Reindorp 'had been a great friend to him'. And they seem to have been the two who stood out as 'characters'. But they were very different, Mervyn being 'the more unexpected in his opinions and the way he expressed them'.[12] Yet the only impression he made on a future Mirfield monk, Fr Alexander Cox, was that 'he wore a curly brimmed hat which I thought gave him an over-dressed look'.[13] It was to John Collins that Mervyn was almost instantly attracted, and in 1939 he was to assist at Collins's wedding. (Forty-three years later, Mervyn conducted Canon Collins's funeral service at St Paul's Cathedral.) Meanwhile, together with like-minded ordinands like Michael Hocking, Mervyn would spend 'hours in John's room putting the Church and the world right. John was a great rebel and he had a great influence on Mervyn.'[14] John Collins had been hired – in 1934

– as a theologian, recruited by Canon Cunningham who had been Principal when Collins was an ordinand. One of Collins's innovations was the dispensing of sherry before dinner; Mervyn's approval can be taken for granted, but he responded also to the fact that by this time Collins seemed to the students to be a man of the world, a radical thinker and an important New Testament scholar. Collins's widow, Diana, believes that at Westcott, Mervyn was probably the vice-principal's closest friend, and in her biography of John Collins she records him saying 'If ever a master owed more to his pupil than the pupil to his master, I was that man'. But Diana Collins perceptively notes that Mervyn, 'for all his ability', was not a very rewarding pupil, for he was not really interested in theology. 'And he was one of the few who realised that theology was unlikely to remain John's chief interest either.'[15]

Mervyn was virtually tone-deaf and musically illiterate, something of a disadvantage for a priest whose liturgical preference would lead him to intone the prayers and sing High Mass. At Westcott, a student designated Minstrel was supposed to accompany the services in chapel, and Mervyn's inability to hit the right note was commented on more than once. A student one year ahead of Mervyn, Canon Squire Heaton-Renshaw, reminded Mervyn at a retirement party in 1980 that he had been known 'as the man who could not strike the right note. You would say "Heaton, are you sure that *is* the right note?" I would say "Yes, listen", but you seldom got it right. I remember once in exasperation playing B flat to you. You sang something near F sharp and we were in business, but it was always very dicey.'

In a book recording ecclesiastical witticisms, the definition of a psychiatrist as a man who goes to the *Folies Bergères* to look at the audience has been attributed to Mervyn, but Canon Heaton-Renshaw claims that it was from him that Mervyn pinched the story.

On his arrival at Westcott House Mervyn was still a Tory. By the time he left he had been converted to socialism. Diana Collins says that he and John Collins 'made the transition from the Tory to the Labour party more or less together', Collins having seen the light on a visit to Porth in South Wales at the invitation of the son of a Nonconformist minister. On his return to Cambridge, Collins would have regaled Mervyn with his impressions of the squalor and wretchedness of so many poor people's lives, and by the time Mervyn arrived in his own downtown Bristol parish to serve his title only a few months later the seeds of socialism would have been firmly planted. Yet again John Collins gave the credit for leadership to Mervyn. 'It is certainly to him', he wrote, 'more than anybody else, that I owe my first attempts to relate the Gospel to social and political matters.' It is not however too surprising to discover that Collins, at Westcott, regarded Mervyn as his equal. Mervyn had already acquired an aura of *gravitas*. Canon John Hargreaves thought of his fellow ordinand, Mervyn Stockwood, as 'considerably older than me, whereas I now discover that he was a year younger'.[16] Canon Hargreaves sees Mervyn

vividly as a member of a trio. There was the Vice-Principal, John Collins, mildly high-church, teaching New Testament from a 'modernist' point of view, with a hesitant giggle escaping at intervals (with no hint whatsoever of what he would later become); second in the trio was George Reindorp, a swashbuckling extrovert, & Mervyn. I see this trio tripping gaily out of the college gate while the rest of us settled down to work in the library, confidently assuming that the trio were playing billiards after a visit to the pub.

With a pleasant whiff of self-mockery, yet another of Mervyn's contempories, Canon Gervase Markham, has written 'What an *admirable* set of young men we were!'[17] He makes the point, which may come as a surprise to modern ordinands drawn from almost every sphere of life, that 'almost all of us were Public School and Oxbridge graduates'. Indeed, before the Second World War hardly any attempt was made to encourage vocations to the priesthood in working-class parishes; it was automatically assumed that missions conducted in public schools would produce the kind of 'leaders' required as future bishops at home and missionaries overseas. Canon Cunningham himself, 'an impenitent snob' in the opinion of Mervyn, once said, 'half in jest', that his job was to provide a gentleman in holy orders in every parish, and it was considered axiomatic that public school-educated clergy should preside over working-class parishes. Canon Markham continues:

We worked hard, attended lectures regularly in the House or in the university. We wrote essays: we composed sermons. We practised pastoral visitations: we went on Student Missionary Campaigns; we learned how to pray in the daily services in the chapel, & were deeply moved by the devotional addresses at Friday night Complines. We did not use 'bad language': we practised no secret vices that I ever heard of. Many smoked, and drank a glass of beer at dinner in Hall where food was plain but plentiful. We played football & cricket with zest against similar small colleges, & were slightly baffled by the practice of Oak Hill Theological students who would hold a prayer meeting on the pitch before a game: we felt this was a rather underhand and unsporting way of asking the help of the Almighty for success in sport.[18]

Alas many did smoke, among them Mervyn. Like so many young men of his generation, he knew nothing of the dangers and no doubt felt that a pipe or a cigarette (he smoked both, heavily) would somehow enhance his masculinity. Like converts to so many causes, when Mervyn gave up smoking (he suffered from bronchitis anyway) he did so with a vengeance, and became fanatically opposed to smoking, banishing anyone who wished to smoke to the garden. The only time ashtrays ever appeared at Bishop's House were when Princess Margaret was coming to dinner.

Canon Markham remembers life at Westcott House in 1935 as

great fun, in the sense that we were living with our contemporaries who shared our background, our interests, our intellectual habits of thought, our slang, our jokes. We shared a common assumption that we were called to serve in a Church that we took for granted as the backbone of the nation. We knew we should be accepted everywhere as clergymen, entitled to respect wherever we went. It was before the days when the media took it for granted that the Church of England was a comic & fatuous institution, riddled with vice, hypocrisy and heresy.

We knew that there were hundreds of other well-educated young men in other theological colleges going through the same sort of course as ourselves, about to be ordained to serve as the clergy of the future, a highly respected part of the life of every community in the country. We did not expect to be paid very much [as vice-principal, John Collins was on £250 a year], none of us was in it for the money. But we knew we should have a 'job for life' somewhere, if we did not lose our faith and drop out.

Whereas Mervyn had been almost unrelentingly critical of his university dons, he has left some endearing recollections of his theological college Principal. Known to the students as 'the professor', or simply by his initials, B.K., Cunningham, although kind and generous on occasions, seems to have found it impossible to eradicate his innate Scots instincts where money was concerned. He once invited Mervyn to his rooms for a glass of whisky, the bottle having been given to Cunningham by a friend, but as Cunningham began to open the bottle he had second thoughts, and 'putting it on the table, remarked, "It's too expensive, boy; we'll have some tea instead"'. On a visit to a London theatre, B.K. said that he intended sitting in the stalls but Mervyn was to buy his own ticket and sit where he liked. 'But it was impossible to be offended', Mervyn has written, 'because I knew that, had I been in distress, he would have given me a hundred pounds or more without turning a hair. As indeed he did, when shortly before my ordination I had to go into hospital for an operation.' Only too typically, Mervyn fails to say what the operation was for. It may have been the first of several he underwent throughout his life for sinus trouble. There have been conflicting theories to explain why he habitually spoke out of the corner of his mouth; he is variously believed to have suffered a mild stroke, to have taken to imitating the way Charles Raven spoke until it quite literally became a fixation, and to have undergone some sort of dental surgery that went wrong. If the third hypothesis is correct, this may have been the misfortune over which Cunningham came to the rescue in 1936. At all events, Mervyn's health was marked down in his Westcott House records as poor, which indeed it was.

Mervyn pays a considerable tribute to Canon Cunningham. He says he insisted on charity in personal relationships, expecting his students to refrain from unkind and negative criticism of one another, which was why 'Westcott was the most loving and caring community in which I have ever lived'. And with an almost audible sigh of resignation he went on to record 'I could wish that all clergy had had the experience, for soon after ordination it did not take me long to realise that a weakness, perhaps a curse, of the clerical profession is gossip and scandal-mongering. It was, perhaps, the major cause of unhappiness in my episcopate.'

Mervyn pinpoints precisely his disillusion with the National Government: 3 October 1935, the day he read of Mussolini's invasion of Abyssinia. The Hoare–Laval pact, 'which set out to carve up [Ethiopia] to Mussolini's advantage', only served to undermine Mervyn's allegiance to all the conservative instincts with which he had been brought up. When Lord Halifax, a great favourite of the future king and queen, partly because he was a fervent churchman, became Foreign Secretary, Mervyn felt convinced he at least would do something in defence of liberty; but when Halifax toasted the

King of Italy as Emperor of Ethiopia, Sir Stafford Cripps, another
devout Anglican and soon to become a firm friend of Mervyn's,
remarked 'The trouble with Edward is that as he enters the doors of
the Foreign Office he hangs up his bowler hat on his crucifix'. Halifax
was later to say he found Göring 'frankly attractive', likening him to
the head gamekeeper at Chatsworth. Mervyn and his generation
were entering the world of the Appeasers, and he says it was the
'challenge to priorities' that hastened his political development. He
cites as a good example of digression from the essentials – war in
Abyssinia, the rise of Hitler and unemployment – 'the fuss and the
near hysteria' over the abdication of Edward VIII.

After enjoying holidays at Portmeirion in north Wales and
County Donegal in Ireland Mervyn left Westcott House in
December 1936, and it was, he laconically records, 'a few days after
the Abdication I put on a clerical collar and was ordained in Bristol
Cathedral'.[19]

Notes

1 Bill Hammond.
2 By Mrs Dorothea Coles.
3 Alan Groves, in conversation with the author.
4 To the author, 22 February 1995.
5 Dean Norman Rathbone, letter to the author, 14 March 1995.
6 Canon Geoffrey Young, letter to the author, 17 March 1995.
7 Rev. John Mowll, letter to the author, 3 March 1995.
8 Canon Michael Hocking, letter to the author, 28 February 1995.
9 Canon Francis Longworth-Dames, in conversation with the author.
10 Mervyn Stockwood, *There Is a Tide* (Allen & Unwin, 1945).
11 Letter to the author from Philip Westcott's niece, Mrs Marigold Lamin,
    17 March 1995.
12 Undated letter to the author from James Lovejoy.
13 Fr Alexander Cox, letter to the author, 1 March 1995.
14 Michael Hocking, as above.
15 Diana Collins, *Partners in Protest: Life With Canon Collins* (Gollancz, 1992).
16 Canon John Hargreaves, letter to the author, 28 February 1995.
17 Canon Gervase Markham, letter to the author, 3 March 1995.
18 Westcott House does not adhere to any rigid form of churchmanship, for
    most of its ordinands are Cambridge graduates, but the ethos is broadly

catholic, whereas Oak Hill in Southgate caters exclusively for Evangelicals.

19 Edward VIII abdicated on 10 December 1936. It was to the diaconate that MS was ordained in December 1936. He was ordained priest on 21 December 1937.

Chapter 3

Induction by fire

All his life Mervyn Stockwood exercised a happy knack of keeping in touch with people. On 18 December 1936, on the eve of his ordination as a deacon, he received a letter from P. C. West, his headmaster at Kingsland Grange. West wrote, from an address in Isleworth:

Dear Friend and Brother, Thank you for your letter. If I have in any way helped you to realise your great heritage & opportunity, it is indeed a reward.

I want to send you one last word. It often happens that in the long Service of Ordination, from sheer exhaustion of body & spiritual strain, that one's mind begins to wander, & some fresh thought is a help.

He went on to write of Love and Charity, but his own thoughts are not too easily discerned; it seems he may have been ailing at this time, for he concludes: 'I am more than sorry I can't be there. But I find I have so many pleasures to forgo now – if only – if only – I could do what I always planned to do – help all round and feast on good things, how happy I should be. But instead I have to learn to submit.'

Mervyn was ordained deacon in 1936 by Clifford Woodward, Bishop of Bristol since 1933, and priested by Woodward on 21 December the following year. He could hardly have imagined that on 21 December 1977, the fortieth anniversary of his ordination, he would be entertaining Princess Alexandra and her husband to dinner to celebrate. In 1945, having been narrowly passed over as Bishop of London on the grounds of age (he was by then 67), Woodward was translated to Gloucester, a good example of the sort of pointless episcopal shuttlecock so often indulged in before the days when bishops were compulsorily retired. 'Shrewd and sagacious' is how Bernard Palmer has described Woodward in his entertaining study of the making of bishops,[1] and it was indeed a shrewd move on Woodward's part to send Mervyn off to an impoverished working-class parish in which to serve his title. The bishop might however have been astonished had he known at the time that Mervyn would remain in that same parish, first as assistant curate and then as incumbent, for 19 years.

The parish chosen by Bishop Woodward for Mervyn's training was St Matthew, Moorfields, Moorfields being on what Lady Bracknell would without hesitation have described as the unfashionable side of Bristol. It more or less approximated to the East End of London. Poverty, unemployment, lack of family planning, poor housing and tuberculosis were endemic. And it was to the most impoverished portion of the parish, served by a mission church, St Saviour's, that the parish priest, Thomas Hayter (he had been inducted only the year before), assigned his new assistant curate. Mervyn had no private income, his stipend would have been a pittance, and he knew what it was to be relatively poor by comparison to the boys with whom he had been at school and the young men he had known at Cambridge. Nevertheless the conditions he encountered at Moorfields were an eye-opener, not least the numbers of deformed children. Although for a year, until ordained priest, Mervyn could not of course celebrate Holy Communion, he says he was given responsibility for some 2,000 parishioners. The mother church of the parish, St Matthew, may have been an unlovely Victorian edifice, but St Saviour's, 'an ugly concrete building', was hideous. It doubled during the week as a rehabilitation centre for the unemployed, and provided somewhat spartan accommodation for Mervyn: a living-room that served as a study, a bedroom and a small, rather grandly designated, dressing-room; there was really only space to hang up cassocks. Downstairs at 30 Chapter Street (the whole area had an ecclesiastical ring to it: Dean Street, Proctor Street, Canon Street, Bishop Street) was

a tiny kitchen and bathroom. In the bathroom were two baths, served by gas geysers, standing on a bare concrete floor, and a washbasin. The local football teams used it after games on Saturday. To use the toilet meant walking through this bathroom into the chancel, past the organ, through the folding doors into a corridor off the main hall which led to a yard. There was no private toilet for the curate, only those used by the public.[2]

These quarters Mervyn shared with a black and white cat called Seagull.

From his study window Mervyn

looked out on to a row of red brick terraced houses, and a corner shop. He saw life as he had never seen it before. He witnessed poverty and observed people in plight. Trying to write sermons he had to contend with constant interruptions of his doorbell ringing. 'A penny for the gas, please mister', or, 'Mr and Mrs Somebody are nearly murdering each other'. A family which lived opposite with a lot of children were nearly always squabbling, screaming or crying. It was much worse on summer evenings when all the doors were open and families brought out the kitchen chairs to sit in the sun, and the tin baths to bathe the children.[3]

It was not until she was evacuated during the war that Mrs Pearl Hughes, whose first-hand recollections these are, experienced the luxury of electric light and a bathroom. In 1939 her mother, Maud Pocock – Mrs P. to Mervyn – became housekeeper and caretaker to the mission church. Her housekeeping, thanks to the primitive conditions and Mervyn's gastronomic tastes, could be a bit hit-and-miss. 'One memorable time', Mrs Hughes recalls, 'was when he swept in with a shopping list.' Mervyn wanted salad, which he was going to prepare himself, a cold chicken and mulligatawny soup,

something we had never heard of and our local shops did not sell. One persevered for Mervyn, so I walked into town and eventually tracked some down. On returning home I found Mum worried because she did not know how to cool the chicken in time. Neither Mervyn nor we had a fridge. After the football team had finished with the bathroom we cleaned it up and put the chicken on to a plate with a net over it & stood it on the concrete floor to cool from the draught between the two doors!

Mrs Hughes's sister, Mrs Yvonne Grimsley, remembers that at St Saviour's 'where there was a lot of poverty & not much employ-ment, where men gambled on street corners', there was something going on each evening.[4] On Wednesday evenings there would be a dance in the hall, 'packed to the door'. On Friday afternoons 'an infant welfare clinic was held in the hall, the Lady Chapel became the weighing room and the vestry would be turned into the doctor's surgery'. To these little girls, Mervyn, 'so tall and dark with his cape over his cassock', seemed 'larger than life. Everything about him was powerful and positive; his large strong features, piercing dark eyes and thick black wavy hair. When he threw back his head and laughed the room seemed to shake.'[5]

St Saviour's was known as the mission church because, like many poor parishes, Moorfields had established links with a public school, whose mission it was to help support the parish financially. This led also to visits from the public school boys, who were supposed to learn about the economic conditions of the poor and to lend a practical helping hand – with sports activities, decorating and any other occupation the parish priest deemed a useful tool for building bridges between the privileged and those less well off. Amazingly, the altar, lectern, choir stalls, pews and portable font at St Saviour's were all made by visiting public school boys. Missions of this nature were regarded not as patronizing but as a natural social responsibility; for many years summer camps for public school and working-class boys were run by the Duke of York, and were only curtailed in 1939 by the outbreak of war.

Moorfields' twinned public school was Blundell's at Tiverton, and the curate in charge of St Saviour's was always made Missioner to Blundell's. Hence part of Mervyn's duties, perhaps the least onerous of them, was to visit Blundell's, stay the night in one of the boarding houses, occasionally preach in the school chapel and arrange for parties of Blundell's boys to visit Moorfields. The headmaster, Neville Gorton, an engaging and saintly eccentric, was a former chaplain at Sedbergh, and, no doubt meaning well, had excited one of his Yorkshire pupils, Brendan Bracken, with discourses on ecclesiastical history. As a result, Bracken, who became an unlikely and somewhat dubious crony of Winston Churchill, took it upon himself, while Churchill was prime minister, to attempt to influence appointments to the episcopal bench. When Bracken pushed for Neville Gorton to go to Coventry as bishop in 1943, Mervyn attended Gorton's enthronement, amid the ruins of the bombed cathedral, as his chaplain.

Mervyn served as Missioner to Blundell's for five years, until in fact he was appointed Vicar of St Matthew. When boys from Blundell's arrived in the parish for a visit they would bed down on the floor of St Saviour's, and join in by day in whatever parish activities Mervyn had managed to organize under the tutelage of an indolent incumbent. One of the vicar's gravest sins, in Mervyn's eyes, was his unpunctuality. He even turned up late for Mervyn's first celebration of Holy Communion after he had been ordained priest. No wonder Mervyn found consolation by travelling 70 miles to Blundell's once a week, far more frequently than duty dictated, even though the school did supply half his salary. He says he found Neville Gorton 'one of the most exciting men I have had the joy to know'. What appealed to Mervyn was the maverick in Gorton. He was, he says, a law unto himself, disregarding 'most public school conventions'. So fond of Gorton did he become that he even seems to have forgiven the fact that his sermons were incomprehensible, preached as they were from jottings on the back of cigarette packets, 'most of which he dropped on the steps as he mounted the pulpit'. Mervyn prepared many of the Blundell's boys for confirmation, even though the school had a resident chaplain, albeit a muscular Christian of the type Mervyn frankly abhorred. The chaplain served as a major in the Officers' Training Corps, had no hesitation in dragging a boy out of one of Mervyn's confirmation classes to beat him for some minor misdemeanour, and issued dire warnings about the evil consequences of masturbation. Gorton, on the other hand, would pay a visit to the local workhouse rather than meet some visiting general, and there can have been little competition between the two of them for Mervyn's admiration.

Mervyn's connection with Blundell's led to invitations to preach at other schools, including Eton, whose headmaster, Sir Robert Birley, was alerted by Gorton to Mervyn's potential; and this led to Etonians being sent to St Matthew to join its annual mixed public school weekends. Mervyn was rather partial to public schools, and would not have been displeased to find three, Dulwich College, Alleyn's and St Paul's, in his future diocese. In his autobiography he tells a strange tale about Blundell's. Apparently two boys had been caught in bed together, and the headmaster had decided to expel the elder of the boys. Mervyn offered to mediate, and invited the boy, whose name was Peter, to tea. Peter told Mervyn his affair with James 'had been the most wonderful experience in his life', but now that everyone had been so foul about it he was contemplating suicide. Mervyn said to Peter, 'I apologize for the question, did you have it off with James?'

'Of course not', he replied.

'Silly ass', says Mervyn. 'If you are going to be hanged, why not for a sheep rather than a lamb?'

The story is strange for a number of reasons. Mervyn could not, surely, have been so naïve as to imagine two adolescent boys went to bed merely for a chaste cuddle; if these were indeed his words at the time, he was quite clearly encouraging Peter to consummate his schoolboy crushes in future, a pretty risky thing for any member of staff to do; and he was revealing all too clearly that distinct streak of voyeurism upon which so many of his friends came to comment. When Mervyn reported the outcome of the tea-party to Gorton, Gorton appointed Peter head prefect! Under Gorton's headmastership Blundell's certainly seems to have been a progressive institution, and there can be no doubt that a good deal of Neville Gorton's nonconformity was to influence Mervyn's own approach to parochial and diocesan life. He came to believe that Gorton was in fact a genius, and that in his day Blundell's was a school of unusual achievement, 'alive and brimful of ideas'. Among the visitors roped in by Gorton to widen the boys' horizons was Eric Gill. Under Gill's directions the boys carved the four stone sides of an altar placed in the middle of the chapel chancel, such a revolutionary siting at the time that Gorton's successor as head-master had it removed. On the staff was Stephen Spender, 28 in 1937 and married originally to Agnes Penn. The marriage ended in divorce, and when in 1941 Spender was married again, to the pianist Natasha Litvin, Mervyn did not hesitate to officiate.

In the parish, as at Blundell's, there was no shortage of eccentric characters to help enliven the drudgery and sometimes depression of routine parish work – so depressing that like many a young curate before and since, Mervyn thought of chucking the whole thing in, and perhaps going back to teaching. One such was an old lady called Sophie Vowles, who supplied Mervyn with meals to compensate for those prepared by his mother – 'a very bad cook' in the opinion of Mrs Vowles's granddaughter, Patricia Hocking.[6] Mrs Hocking has recalled that as her grandmother was old, Mervyn could tease her 'and say outrageous things with impunity. They both *loved* this banter.' To celebrate the end of the Second World War Mervyn organized a ball, at which he danced the polka with Sophie, who treasured a photograph of Mervyn in his clerical collar and a grey pullover, which, most unusually for Mervyn, for he prided himself on sartorial exactitude, revealed a dropped stitch.

Mrs Hocking has also recalled that in addition to St Saviour's there was a daughter church in the parish, St Chad's, long since closed, which backed on to her grandmother's garden at 17 Herbert Street, and that after celebrating Holy Communion at St Chad's, Mervyn would clamber up a ladder and call to Sophie 'to see if she had finished baking date cakes', a culinary speciality of Sophie's to

which he was particularly partial. Mrs Hocking's most vivid
memory of Mervyn, however, is of

his great love of Jesus. You can have ministers who understand
intellectually the Scriptures, but fail to love Jesus in their lives. Mervyn
was the exception. He was intellectual, but he 'knew' Jesus from within
his heart. That was what made Mervyn so special. He transmitted this
love of Jesus in his politics, in home visits, in social events, and the
church services were exciting, compelling and filled with the Holy
Spirit. St Matthew, Moorfields was always packed, whether Mervyn
was preaching or not. He brought everything alive through his deep
beliefs.

When Mrs Hocking was married at St Matthew, in 1954, by her
cousin, Sophie Vowles's grandson Peter Vowles, Mervyn, in his last
year in the parish as it transpired, gave the address.

Mervyn had not been at Moorfields many months before politics
began to impinge on his social conscience, and a visit to the nearby
church hall at All Hallows', Easton, where Sir Stafford Cripps
was booked to speak, finally tipped him into the Labour camp. He
has said, in fact, that this meeting was the determining event of
his life. Cripps has often been depicted as a dour and insincere
– because wealthy – socialist, even sometimes as being a little
mad. When Labour came to power in 1945 Cripps, who served as
Chancellor of the Exchequer from 1947 to 1950, was a favourite
butt of derision among fogey Conservatives, as much a hate-figure
as Aneurin Bevan. He was in fact an intellectual, and a deeply
committed Christian who believed 'that religion and politics were
closely linked and that hard work and dedication to duty were the
privilege rather than the burden of mankind'.[7] On 27 September
1942, while Cripps was serving as Lord Privy Seal in the wartime
coalition government, Mervyn managed to secure him to preach at
St Matthew. It has been said, with some justification, that Mervyn
tended to make a beeline for the rich and famous, but the sincerity
of his affection for friends like Sir Stafford and Lady Cripps cannot be in doubt. And it mattered little which side of the political
divide such people happened to be on. Once Sir Walter Monckton
had become MP for Bristol West in 1951, Mervyn was on familiar
terms with another well-connected patrician politician; it had
been Monckton, when he was Attorney General to the Duchy of
Cornwall, who had acted as trusted mediator between Baldwin and

Edward VIII during the abdication crisis. Mervyn became a guest at Monckton's home, Priors Court in Worcestershire, but it was Monckton's deeply religious attitude to life (he regularly went into retreat at Mirfield) that appealed to Mervyn as much as his money and influence. Mervyn was concerned too that since his divorce in 1947 Monckton had 'gradually given up practising his religion'.[8] Monckton was unwell but in a hurry to return to the sacraments, and it was Mervyn who married him, in his sickroom, to Bridget, previously Countess of Carlisle. She was to become one of Mervyn's closest women friends. She died in 1965, a few months before Lord Monckton (he received a viscountcy in 1957), who was himself 'seen through his death' by Mervyn.[9]

At Stafford Cripps's memorial service in 1952 Mervyn placed Monckton in the same pew as the Labour chief whip, Attlee and Churchill having previously asked Mervyn to take flowers on their behalf to the clinic in Switzerland where Cripps was dying. In his biography[10] of John Robinson, later Bishop of Woolwich but at one time Mervyn's curate in Bristol, Eric James recalls an occasion, supposedly while Robinson was on Mervyn's staff and was due to preach, when Robinson was slipped a note that read 'Sir Walter Monckton is in the congregation – so no reference to the Government!!!' But unless the tale is entirely apocryphal the event must have taken place on a return visit to the parish by Robinson, who had left Moorfields before Monckton came on the scene.

Within a few months of hearing Cripps speak, Mervyn had joined the Labour Party; equally swiftly, along with his mentor, he was expelled, for Cripps, the Member of Parliament for Bristol East since 1931, had advocated the formation of a united popular front to combat Hitler and the threat of fascism. The idea appealed to Mervyn, but not to the Labour Party Conference. The old jibe that the Church of England was the Tory Party at prayer was perfectly apt as far as the clergy were concerned, and for a curate to make no bones about joining the Labour Party was almost akin to heresy. Even before Mervyn stood for election to Bristol City Council as a Socialist candidate in 1946 his politics were public knowledge, and in the opinion of many, a cause for scandal. Today the clergy appear to have moved, almost *en masse*, to the left of centre, but Mervyn's espousal of Labour principles, and his desire to try to work out a social gospel, were, like so much of what he did, in the vanguard of clerical conduct. With commendable courage, he would hike three miles there and back on Sunday evenings to join fellow

Christian socialists at open-air meetings on Clifton Downs, there to be heckled, as is customary on such occasions, and also to lay himself open to hostility from other clergy in the deanery. Even though his bishop offered moral support it was hardly the action of a young clergyman ambitious for speedy preferment.

In his autobiography, Mervyn explicitly states that these open-air meetings were held 'under the auspices of the Socialist Christian movement of which Cripps and [George] Lansbury were supporters'. This is not strictly true, but in 1982 Mervyn was writing in a sort of convenient shorthand, and it is certainly a fact that long before the Movement was set up officially, the concept of 'Christian Socialism' was a reality; as an undergraduate, Mervyn would go to Thaxted 'to be thrilled by Conrad Noel's "sermons on Christian Socialism"'. The Christian Socialist Movement, which Mervyn never joined, did not, however, come into existence until 1960. It was the Socialist Christian League, founded in 1931, to which Mervyn (and George Lansbury, Leader of the Labour Party in 1931) belonged. In 1941 a conference was held in Malvern, attended by Mervyn, as a result of which in the following year a new organization, calling itself the Council of Clergy and Ministers for Common Ownership, was established. This cumbersome title was later changed to the Society of Socialist Clergy. Its president was Alfred Blunt, the Bishop of Bradford who in 1936 had almost unwittingly alerted the nation to the pending Abdication crisis by telling his diocesan conference he wished the King would give more positive signs of his awareness of the need of God's grace. At the 1941 Malvern Conference a paper was read by Kenneth Ingram which called on the Church to be 'fearlessly revolutionary' and to 'provide the nucleus of those who will lead the vanguard in the social-political-religious struggle', sentiments which were approved by Mervyn. It was as a result of a merger in 1960 between the Socialist Christian League and the Society of Socialist Clergy that the Christian Socialist Movement came into being. In an obituary of Mervyn written for the *Christian Socialist Magazine*, Dominic Walker, who served as chaplain to Mervyn for three years, wrote: 'He believed Christian socialism to be the pattern of the early Church where common ownership, Eucharist and care for the poor characterised their lives.'

In 1942 a number of Socialists, disillusioned by the Labour Party's pre-war acquiescence in appeasement, and unimpressed by the wartime political truce, which had resulted in the formation of a coalition government with the Leader of the Labour Party serving as deputy prime minister, set up a new party, socialist in doctrine, called the Common Wealth Party. It was rather an ill-judged title, for it can only be safely differentiated from 'the Commonwealth' when written down, and although the party fought by-elections during the war, acquiring in 1944 its third Member of Parliament, its active life was brief. It lasted only until defeat, in the 1945 General Election, for all but one of its candidates drove the founder, Sir Richard Acland, MP for Barnstaple since 1935, and most of his followers back into the Labour Party. But officially the Common Wealth Party remained in existence until it was wound up by a rump in 1994. Acland was an influential educationalist, and became an early political associate of Mervyn's. They met at the 1941 Malvern Conference, and once the Common Wealth Party had been set up, Mervyn became an active member of the Bristol branch, and was elected to the National Appeals Tribunal, a rather hollow honour as it transpired, for the Tribunal was never called upon to hear any appeals. Recalling those days in 1965, for someone preparing a thesis on the Common Wealth Party, Mervyn said the Bristol branch included several 'very able' civil servants and a good many working-class members from his own parish, although it was not characterized by any particular religious outlook.[11] A Jewish family and one or two Roman Catholics signed up, together with neighbouring countrymen who would formerly have voted Liberal. There was a by-election in Bristol Central in 1943 when Jennie Lee, the wife of the future Labour Minister of Health, Aneurin Bevan, stood, unsuccessfully, as an Independent candidate with Common Wealth Party support, and Mervyn served as chairman of her election committee. He was later to attribute her co-operation, together with the involvement in Common Wealth of other socialists like himself, to 'the depth of feeling there was among socialists that the Labour Party had really deserted the cause'.[12] They still felt betrayed, in fact, by Ramsay MacDonald's action in August 1931 in agreeing to lead a coalition.

In his autobiography, Mervyn quotes with approval Jennie Lee's remark in *her* autobiography,[13] 'That was the most enjoyable election I ever fought', but he drew a veil over the none too flattering picture she went on to paint of his efforts on her behalf.

He was with me on the night before the poll. We had no loud-speaker equipment then, all we had was a barrel-organ that we trundled from street to street to alert the surrounding populace that we were in the area. As the evening wore on Mervyn's speeches grew shorter and shorter. A vote for Jennie Lee was a vote on the side of righteousness. A vote against her was a vote for the devil. Of course these were not the words he used, but that was the gist of it. Under my breath, I was thinking, 'Please, Mervyn, put in a few conditional clauses.'

Those who helped in Jennie Lee's campaign included Michael Foot, Tom Driberg and Victor Gollancz, who had enjoyed the dubious distinction of being sacked from Repton by the future Archbishop of Canterbury, Geoffrey Fisher. According to a letter of condolence Mervyn wrote to his widow when Gollancz died in 1964, he first met him 'in the days of the Spanish Civil War'. He claimed, in fact, 'a friendship of 30 years', and recalled that he and Gollancz 'often met in Bristol during the War', but he does not seem ever to have established a relationship of any intimacy with Ruth Gollancz, signing his letter 'Mervyn Southwark'. He told Lady Gollancz her husband was invariably 'propounding some new idea or sponsoring a fresh cause, or initiating an act of kindness'.[14] Thirty years was perhaps a bit of an exaggeration. A 'National Spain Conference' was held at the Queen's Hall in London on 23 April 1938, and it is quite likely that this was the event that marked the first meeting of Mervyn Stockwood and Victor Gollancz. It seems equally likely that both supported the Republican cause; Gollancz, 20 years Mervyn's senior and already by 1938 an established left-wing publisher, did so, if not with great enthusiasm, and Mervyn would have regarded him from the outset as a man of mature judgement.

Another of Mervyn's wartime political activities, for which he found time in addition to teaching Scripture at St George's Grammar School, involved membership of something called the People's Convention, although Stafford Cripps had advised him against getting too involved. The Convention, Mervyn has recalled, 'attracted the sort of people like myself who were extremely Socialist. We felt so frustrated in the war. This was a time when I worked more closely with the Communists than at any other.'[15] One Communist he had worked with, whether or not he knew he was a Communist, had been Tom Driberg. Was Mervyn himself ever a Communist? He was certainly to enjoy the fruits of Communist hospitality and to make some ill-considered judgements about the alleged benefits of Communist discipline. John Bickersteth, who began his distinguished ecclesiastical career as one of Mervyn's curates, is certain that Mervyn was a member of the Communist Party 'for about 18 months. He thought the ideal, that we should share everything in common, was right, but he denounced the iniquities of Stalin.'[16] Bishop Bickersteth did not, however, meet Mervyn until 1950, so his evidence cannot be taken as positive proof, although it is perfectly possible it is based on something Mervyn told him; there is, at all events, no reason not to suppose that at the very least Mervyn flirted with Communism. Many people at this time saw international politics in terms of black and white, believing the only way to combat fascism was by supporting Communism. It seems, at any rate, that Mervyn rejoined the Labour Party at the same time as Cripps was reconciled, late in 1944, although during the 1945 election campaign Mervyn still spoke on Common Wealth Party hustings.

Soon Mervyn was to come to rely not only on the moral support of his diocesan bishop but on that of the Archbishop of York, William Temple. Already a legend in his lifetime, Temple was staying on holiday at Lower Weacombe, near Bicknoller in Somerset, in August 1941, and had been told by Clifford Woodward that in a sermon preached in Cambridge at the invitation of the Student Christian Movement Mervyn's passionate indignation aroused by sales of British zinc to Japan had spilt over into an incitement to the workers to strike. Hence Conservative critics of Mervyn's open-air tub-thumping had seized on an excuse to demand that he be refused permission any longer to preach in the Bristol diocese, or to prepare boys for confirmation at Blundell's. One of the school's governors and an old boy, the redoubtably named Sir Lionel Goodenough Taylor, even descended on Mervyn in person, but Mervyn managed to charm Sir Lionel into submission, and ended up with Sir Lionel as one of his wealthiest and most generous patrons until his death in 1963. (Taylor had been Sheriff of Bristol and Master of the Society of Merchant Venturers of Bristol.) Quite why Woodward involved Temple with rumours that even the police were taking an interest in Mervyn's seditious opinions is a bit of a mystery; as Archbishop of York he exercised no jurisdiction in the matter, but the upshot was a letter, followed by a telephone call, from Temple, inviting Mervyn to meet him at Bicknoller.[17] (In time-honoured tradition, when the Archbishop rang, Mervyn assumed it was a fellow cleric, in this case Charles Claxton, later Bishop of Blackburn, pulling his leg.) Thus was founded a firm but all too brief attachment between Mervyn and

Temple, whose tragic death in 1944 after only two years at Canterbury changed the fortunes of the Church of England in a multitude of ways. Some can obviously only be surmised, but it is safe to say that had Temple lived, Mervyn would not have remained on the sidelines in Bristol as long as he did. Temple was a fellow socialist, quite as fearless and adventurous as Mervyn, and like Mervyn, adept at talent-spotting. His book *Christianity and Social Order*, published in 1942, sold 139,000 copies, and is said to have contributed significantly to the election three years later of a Labour Government. Temple was less than enchanted by the established nature of the Church, and he and Mervyn were obvious soulmates who were destined never to work together. Temple died on 26 October 1944, and was writing to Mervyn in September to say he had been 'laid up all this month with a fabulous attack of gout', hardly the kind of letter to prepare Mervyn for the shock of his death.

By the time Mervyn first met William Temple he had served as an assistant curate to an uncongenial incumbent for four and a half years, and even by 1939 it would have been perfectly reasonable for him to begin to consider a move to pastures new. As it happened, in March that year the Warden of Lincoln Theological College, Eric Abbott, later a renowned Dean of Westminster, invited Mervyn to join the staff as chaplain. Nothing came of this, however, for with the outbreak of war numbers of ordinands began to fall, and the post was put in abeyance. John Collins had left Westcott House at the end of 1937, and rather surprisingly, perhaps, for Mervyn had not been one of the Principal's favourite students, two years later, Mervyn says, Canon Cunningham invited him to become vice-principal. But nothing came of this either, for apparently Cunningham was overruled by the College Council, perhaps because they too had disapproved of Mervyn's recent Cambridge sermon on the subject of exporting zinc to Japan. The man who now attempted to come to Mervyn's rescue, by offering him a chance to consolidate his gifts among poor parishioners by running a parish of his own, was Leslie Hunter, who had just been consecrated Bishop of Sheffield and whose outstanding ministry in that sometimes unfortunately led diocese remains a magical memory to this day. But the war was to intervene again. Bristol, a vital port, with access to the Atlantic from the Avon and the Bristol Channel, became an early target for German bombers. On the eve of Mervyn's departure by train to visit his prospective new downtown parish in Sheffield and to meet Leslie Hunter, the first raid on Bristol took place. Roads were blocked. Trains were cancelled. Obviously another appointment could have been made, but both Mervyn's parish priest and his fellow curate chose this moment to accept new jobs, and, no doubt in some desperation, Woodward asked Mervyn to stay on, to run Moorfields as parish priest. He could hardly say no.

Mervyn would have endured the blitz had he gone to Sheffield, but it would not have been more devastating than the bombing he and his parishioners were now subjected to in Bristol. Whole streets were obliterated overnight, and in addition to his new parish duties Mervyn now enrolled in the Civil Defence, as a member of the Shelter Wardens' Service. He and his fellow 'executive officers', among them two other clerics, donned dark blue uniforms and collars and ties, and Mervyn's deputy was none other than Wilfrid Harrison, the headmaster at whose feet, 22 years before, he had sat as his youngest pupil at The Downs.

When he took over the parish it meant that Mervyn could move out of the dingy flat attached to St Saviour's, where he had been looked after by Mrs Pocock, whose daughter Pearl has good reason to be grateful that Mervyn did stay on. 'He did things for me', she has written, 'for which I shall be eternally grateful.'[18] Someone else with cause to be grateful is a parishioner Mervyn married in 1939. He said to her after the ceremony 'You will notice I didn't ask you to say obey in the wedding service. I don't believe in brides telling lies on their wedding day.' Mervyn also did not believe in shop-keepers taking advantage of his parishioners, poor enough in any event, and did not hesitate to read out from the pulpit the names of retailers he thought guilty of overcharging, a fairly hazardous thing to do as he might well have been sued for slander. The local news-paper was naturally delighted, and ran a story with a photograph of Mervyn, and a caption that read: 'It has come to my notice that several local shops are heavily overcharging.'

But the Germans did their best to make sure the curate who cared never lived to become vicar. On the night of Good Friday Bristol suffered a devastating air raid, with bombs missing strategic targets and falling instead on the parish. One of the youngsters from the boys' club was critically injured, St Matthew caught fire, and as Mervyn raced across St George's Park 'the Germans dropped a stick of bombs within a few yards'. Fortunately he was revived by an Evangelical clergyman from a neighbouring parish who retained a bottle of whisky 'for medicinal purposes'. By the time he reached St Matthew the fire was under control but the roof was badly damaged, and when Mervyn was inducted on 23 April 1941 the service was accompanied by the smell not of incense but of charred timbers.

Notes

1 Bernard Palmer, *High & Mitred: Prime Ministers as Bishop-Makers 1837–1977* (SPCK, 1992).

2 Letter to the author from Mrs Pearl Hughes, 1 May 1995.

3 Ibid.

4 Mrs Yvonne Grimsley, letter to the author, undated.

5 Pearl Hughes, as above.

6 Mrs Patricia Hocking, letter to the author, 7 March 1995.

7 Philip Ziegler, *Wilson: The Authorised Life* (Weidenfeld & Nicolson, 1993).

8 Letter to the author from Major General Viscount Monckton of Brenchley, 4 June 1995. On a train journey in December 1956 Sir Walter Monckton told Tony Benn that Mervyn had been very kind to him and that he thought 'Stockwood should certainly be made a Bishop and had personally urged this on Clem and Eden'.

9 Lord Monckton, as above.

10 Eric James, *A Life of Bishop John A. T. Robinson* (Collins, 1987).

11 Sussex University archives.

12 Ibid.

13 Jennie Lee, *Life With Nye* (Cape, 1980).

14 Letter from MS to Lady Gollancz, 10 February 1964, in the Modern Records Centre, University of Warwick library.

15 Sussex University archives.

16 Bishop John Bickersteth, in conversation with the author.

17 On 2 March 1994 MS gave all but one of his letters from William Temple to the library at Lambeth Palace.

18 Letter to the author from Mrs Pearl Hughes, 26 February 1995.

Chapter 4

Bright and glowing colours

The first problem Mervyn Stockwood faced in his new role as Vicar of St Matthew, Moorfields was recruiting clergy to assist him. The bombing had been so terrifying that two curates withdrew because their wives declined to face the danger. And he was impatient for help because he had already formulated some revolutionary plans, the most revolutionary of which was to anticipate ecumenical parish co-operation by about a quarter of a century. He had already made friends with Ronald Spivey, the local Methodist minister, and he and Mr Spivey laid the foundations for what became known as the Redfield United Front, consisting eventually of two Anglican parishes (St Matthew and St Leonard's), three Methodist churches, a Baptist congregation and a Congregationalist church. In those days it would have been unheard of for a Roman Catholic parish to have become involved, and no Anglican would have been invited even to pray with Roman Catholics. But allowing for the inevitable lack of Roman Catholic participation, the Redfield United Front was still a radical ecumenical experiment, and Mervyn had to tread carefully. The bishop made it clear that although non-Anglicans were welcome to receive communion from him if they wished, no Anglicans were to reciprocate at the altar. Nevertheless they all met together one day a week, first of all for communion, celebrated by Mervyn or one of his curates, and then, as the curate who arrived in September 1950, John Bickersteth, remembers with a shudder, boiled eggs. 'We always had boring boiled eggs. It put me off boiled eggs for life!'[1] A two-hour meeting would follow, which included bible study, and the drawing up of plans for the week's joint activities, which, to an extent hardly dreamed of today, consisted of regular and systematic parish visiting. A youth centre with its own 'parliament' was set up, public discussions were organized in one of the local parks in the summer, and in factories in winter. 'Impossible to overestimate the excitement created by [Mervyn

Stockwood's] "reign" at St Matthew, Moorfields', one former parishioner has written. 'As a postgraduate researching the place of grammar school pupils in local youth clubs I was greatly impressed by the ecumenical enthusiasm of the Youth Club associated with the Redfield United Front.'[2]

Mervyn wrote to William Temple, still at York, for a contribution to *The Redfield Review*, the magazine launched by the United Front. He elicited from the Primate of England an impressive imprimatur:

I send my very best wishes for the success of the united magazine. This seems to me an admirable method of presenting to the world the united front which Christians ought to show. There are differences among Christians which loyalty to truth as we see it forbids us to deny; and loyalty to truth is a primary duty. Moreover some of these difficulties are of such a kind as to keep us apart in some most important ways. But when all is said the differences between Christians are as nothing compared with the differences between all sincere Christians on one side and all non-Christians on the other. So even if we cannot yet unite in all things let us show the world that in what matters most we are united, namely that in Jesus Christ 'God hath visited and redeemed His people.'

Temple's approval was again sought when Mervyn drafted a communion service in which it was intended that all the clergy, Anglican and Free Church, should say the prayer of consecration together. The Archbishop said he welcomed that kind of experiment personally but could not give it his official approval. What he was hoping for was eventual joint ordination. But Mervyn received full backing from Temple for a form of baptism which Temple told him in a letter dated 6 October 1942 he liked exceedingly. 'I think you have done a great service in compiling it. We must, before long, revise our present service.'[3] In ecumenical matters William Temple, like Mervyn Stockwood, was years ahead of his time, and regarded with dismay the opposition of hidebound Anglo-Catholics to the Free Churches on the grounds that their ministries were invalid. He described a debate in the Canterbury Convocation on the topic as 'quite abominable' and told Mervyn he fully recognized the reality of the Free Church ministries 'as authenticated by their fruits – which seems to me a sound Scriptural principle to go by'. But he was also convinced they did not represent the permanent tradition of the Church, a situation which would not be put right until 'the consecration of some leading Free Churchmen to the episcopate'.[4]

In 1944 the United Redfield Front held a synod, and in retirement, Mervyn looked back upon the 14 years of co-operation he experienced in Bristol 'as a golden age'. The Front was to form the basis for lifelong friendships. A Methodist minister, Arthur Valle, who joined the team in 1948, was invited to lunch by Mervyn 46 years later. He remembers that Mervyn was

a great believer in forging links as close as possible with the local schools ... He was very good at establishing friendly relationships with all their heads. It was arranged that a minister from the United Front should visit each school for their morning prayers (always held in those days!).

In the summer there was always an open air meeting in St George's Park after the evening service. This was more of a Marble Arch type of meeting, with questions and heckling, than of a hymn singing–sermon type. Mervyn was in his element here; the rest of us were so useless in comparison that there was a wholly welcome tendency for him to take over, and we were more than content (relieved, most of us) to leave it to him. With his gift for ready and forthright repartee he was adept at taking on an east Bristol crowd.[5]

Guest of honour at the tenth anniversary of the United Front in 1951 was George MacLeod, leader of the Iona Community. In view of the friendship and hospitality extended by Mervyn in later years to the Roman Catholic hierarchy in Southwark, it is interesting that Mr Valle recalls that in Moorfields, Mervyn 'evinced a very strong dislike for, and distrust of, the Romans. The strength of his antagonism to them was something I never really understood.'[6]

Arthur Valle has provided a sympathetic yet penetrating portrait of Mervyn from his days in Moorfields.

For all his apparently extrovert nature, he was, I believe, an essentially lonely man beneath the surface. For all his seeming arrogance, he was humble and even self-distrustful deep down. For all his man of the world appearance, inside he was deeply spiritual. For all his enjoyment of the good things of life, he was in fact very self-disciplined. For all his seeming assurance, he was not without his doubts and uncertainties. And there is no doubt that right inside him was a kind and compassionate heart. I can hardly support these judgments with objective facts, they are simply the impressions of one who worked very closely with him for six years. He was not always in good health, and

I sometimes wondered how he managed to accomplish so much. One secret was that every day, after lunch, he went to bed for half an hour.[7]

Mervyn did not restrict his pastoral care to members of denominations committed to the Front. On the afternoon of his first Christmas Day as parish priest he rang the door bell of a recently widowed Quaker, whose two daughters were away. 'I thought you might be feeling lonely', he said. 'May I come in for a cup of tea?'[8] One female parishioner remembers how Mervyn 'charmed, infuriated and bullied' them all, and how they 'disagreed and argued violently with each other' and would end up dancing the conga – one of Mervyn's favourite group activities; he once repeated the performance during a visit to the Holy Land. At a more serious level, he broke with the common concept that only the clergy knew how to run a parish, and therefore had to be responsible for every activity, by training the laity to act in positive ways during the week, and eventually he involved the laity in the liturgy too.

But he moved slowly, for although he had clear goals in mind he sensed that no innovative parish priest can fill his church with regular worshippers unless he has their confidence, and advances at the pace of the slowest. 'There can be no short cuts in pastoral work', he was to write. 'Gimmicks may attract the crowds for a few weeks, but they drift away. Nothing can be a substitute for the hard slog of establishing personal relationships.' Initially, with no curate to assist him, Mervyn was in any case more than usually dependent on co-operation from the laity, and by dint of ceaseless pastoral visiting he got to know a core of his parishioners at a deep personal level. An additional problem was that after five years at St Saviour's he scarcely knew the people centred on St Matthew, nor they him; the two congregations were fairly separate. He never tried to know every parishioner personally; there were, as is usually the case in any urban parish, just too many for that to be possible, but his aim was to encourage those who formed a nucleus committed to himself to communicate that commitment to others – much as the early Church had radiated from a central band of Apostles.

With the vicarage requisitioned, Mervyn moved from the dreary environment of Chapter Street to the equally dismal environment of St Matthew, to rooms at 94 Church Road above a former off-licence on the corner of Morse Road. There was space for an office and room for a secretary – Miss Joyce Banwell – and once the

Common Wealth Party had been established, it was from these premises that the Bristol branch was run. It was of course from here as well that Mervyn organized his new parish. He soon realized he had virtually two potential congregations to cater for. There were people happily wedded to the Anglo-Catholic ritual, who expected a High Mass on Sunday morning; and there were as yet unchurched parishioners to whom the Eucharistic liturgy was not much more than an unintelligible mumbo-jumbo, and who no doubt equated much of what went on with activities in the Church of Rome. Candles, incense, vestments, confession remained alien to a large proportion of the population, who were either obliged to worship in a more moderate parish or would more probably stay away from church altogether. Hence Mervyn hit upon the second – and at the time revoluntionary – strand to his ministry in Bristol. In addition to a monthly service of spiritual healing, for prayer and the laying on of hands, for those who valued the symbolic ritual of High Church worship he arranged the best regimented and orchestrated parish communion on Sunday morning that he could devise and produce. And in the evening, instead of sung Evensong, which would have been quite usual in a parish like St Matthew, he instituted what became known as the People's Service, a non-liturgical occasion consisting of hymns, prayers and a bible reading centred upon a sermon. The contrast with the morning Mass was so startling that were it not for the church furnishings one might have imagined the People's Service to have been taking place elsewhere entirely. Mervyn preached looking like a Presbyterian, wearing just a black gown and white tabs. He might prepare a course on the Faith; later he elaborated on the social implications of the Gospel. Visiting preachers were advertised. Mervyn himself, in the opinion of John Bickersteth, was 'a stunning preacher. He was full of stories, he held people, he was a teacher. He never appeared to be reading his sermons, and he taught his curates always to use eye contact with the congregation.'[9] Yet every sermon was in fact meticulously written out in longhand, in a series of notebooks which he kept all his life.[10] They weigh several hundredweight.

Mervyn set tremendous store by preaching, and whereas in the early days of his ministry most of the clergy were polarized between extreme emphasis on either the Sacraments or the Word, as a kind of Anglo-Catholic Evangelical Mervyn was equally at ease celebrating High Mass or in the pulpit.[11] While he insisted on punctilious observance of ritual – and woe betide any curate who entered the sanctuary with the servers 30 seconds after ten o'clock had struck – he was equally strict about checking his colleagues' sermons. They had to be handed in on Thursday night for perusal by the Vicar, who occasionally wrote some rude comment in the margin, but generally contented himself with the advice 'to learn to leave out churchy stuff'.

The success of the People's Service, which suddenly took off after about six months and began to appeal to so many that for 14 years 'the church was usually packed, often with chairs in the aisle', was in large measure due to the reservoir of 'non-churchy' people, of all denominations and lay as well as clerical, who accepted invitations to preach. Sir Walter Monckton, Sir Stafford Cripps and Victor Gollancz were established figures, and among rising stars Mervyn alighted on a future Speaker of the House of Commons, Lord Tonypandy, a future Bishop of Lincoln, Simon Phipps, and friends from Westcott House, like John Collins and George Reindorp, both destined for outstanding careers. But the People's Service was so strongly disapproved of by those who served at Mass that none of them – and there were about 25 – ever attended. On the other hand, some of the evening congregation began to show a greater interest than before in the sacraments, so Mervyn astounded his critics by giving them communion. Until well after the end of the Second World War a sign of extreme Evangelicalism would have been an evening celebration of Holy Communion; by the time Michael Ramsey, an Anglo-Catholic primate, celebrated the fortieth anniversary of his ordination to the priesthood in 1969 he did so by celebrating Holy Communion in the evening in Westminster Abbey. Criticism of Mervyn's pioneering on this score fired, he says, 'the hatred of petty ecclesiasticism and pharisaic legalism which was to be a characteristic of my episcopate'.

Mervyn's determination to involve the congregation in worship and organization extended to the Sunday School, renamed by him the junior church. As soon as he became vicar he renewed an ancient custom, in medieval times most commonly centred on the cathedral, of having a boy elected annually on 6 December, the Feast of St Nicholas, Boy Bishop. The election was carried out by the other children, and the boy chosen by his peers was duly enthroned and vested. One of his tasks was to maintain some semblance of discipline and, more remarkably, to organize and conduct the children's service. It may be thought mildly sacrilegious to dress up a boy of 12 or 13 in the cope, mitre, pastoral staff, pectoral cross and episcopal ring of a bishop, but there seems to have been no shortage of candidates for the post, and in 1980, 14 of Mervyn's Boy Bishops reassembled for a party in Southwark. Sometimes their non-episcopal duties would extend to accompanying a guest to the cinema while Mervyn busied himself with parish affairs, but by and large their dressing up and bossing about was seen as a prelude to eventual membership of the parish church council and even to assisting with confirmation classes. Oddly enough, although Mervyn laid on this form of fun and games for the Moorfields boys, he forbade them membership of the choir, preferring men and women choristers. One explanation that has been offered is that Mervyn simply dismissed boy choristers as too disruptive. A former member of the congregation has suggested that, coming from a working-class parish, the boys felt too embarrassed to sing, but this has scarcely been the experience of Anglo-Catholic parishes in the East End of London. It may be that Mervyn just failed to appreciate the beauty of boys' voices. Music was not exactly his forte. There was at Moorfields, says John Bickersteth, a wonderful organist 'who was driven up the wall by Mervyn'.

There were occasions, however, when Mervyn provided musical entertainment himself. At Evensong on his birthday he would always play the piano. This would have been an aspect of his love of drama and theatre. At their first communion, the children were given a posy of flowers to carry. The parish pantomime was said to compare favourably with the professional show laid on at the Bristol Hippodrome. Arthur Valle recalls how St Matthew, a 'rather uninspiring Victorian Gothic building', was 'transformed by the use of bright and glowing colours'. He remembers 'most vividly the midnight masses at Christmas and Easter, all the colour and movement and drama, the incense and the banners'.[12] The parish of St Matthew had been formed by an amalgamation of St Mark, Easton and St George, and the church building was built and consecrated in 1873. To describe St Matthew as 'rather uninspiring' is an act of considerable charity. It is in point of fact a product of High Victorian ugliness. Mervyn had the pitch-black pews stripped, but the building retains its hideous windows and even more hideous overhead lights. It is a miracle that anyone devoted to ritual could ever have succeeded in bringing such a dreary building to life but, by all accounts, Mervyn did.

While busy with experiments at local level, Mervyn was becoming increasingly involved in the task, renewed by every generation, of church reform nationally, joining John Collins, Stafford Cripps, Richard Acland, a future Archdeacon of Hastings, Guy Mayfield, and the prophetic Bishop of Chichester, George Bell, in meetings of the Church Reform Group. In her biography of her husband, Diana Collins says that John Collins was always impressed by Mervyn's contributions to discussion, 'which were radical but practical and down to earth'.[13] Mervyn, apparently, was all for encouraging the clergy to take part in local politics, but he found Acland's insistence as a criterion for membership of the Group, that one should let it be known publicly that private ownership of the great productive resources was evil, too alarming to support.

Although it is perfectly true that on many occasions Mervyn experienced difficulty relating to women, one should take with a pinch of salt his alleged reaction to the idea that The Church Reform Group should include more women: 'I suppose we must have a hag or two. I know a couple of dames in Bristol.'[14] One of the dames he had in mind may have been a parishioner who became so convinced that she and Mervyn should marry, and equally impatient for him to pop the question, that she purchased a ring, put it on her finger and informed Mervyn that they were engaged. Alas, she remains a spinster to this day. 'Mervyn was', says another member of the congregation, 'very wary of unmarried women!'

There are too many recorded instances of Mervyn's pastoral concern for women to write him off as a hopeless misogynist. A woman came to him one Saturday afternoon in Bristol and asked for half an hour of his time. 'No', said Mervyn, 'I shan't give you half an hour. I shall give you as much time as you need.' 'Like a master builder', she later recalled, 'for the next two and a half hours he rebuilt my life.'[15] Another of Mervyn's female parishioners has written:

I was a member of Mervyn's church during the war. He and my father, Arthur Moody, a teacher at Carlton Park School, used to organise our street parties, when the tables were laden with whatever goodies the Mums were able to manage. We even had a piano. He was always available. He was very forthright and fair, and a kindly man. I suspect there are many who have cause to bless his name. Apart from other matters, he gave me my wedding service and the hall for the reception as a wedding present.[16]

Such was the charisma of Mervyn's personality that one woman used to undertake a 20-minute walk and two bus rides to teach at his Sunday School.

It was probably in 1943 that Mervyn came to know Joseph McCulloch. Ordained in 1931, in 1965 he gained permanent remembrance by initiating the famous dialogue sermons at St Mary-le-Bow in Cheapside. McCulloch had been pushing passionately for disestablishment, a cause to some extent espoused by William Temple through a movement he supported called Life and Liberty. Now that he was at Canterbury, Temple's view was that the actual mechanics involved in disestablishing the Church were not worth the effort, an attitude his future biographer, F. A. Iremonger, in 1943 Dean of Lichfield, regarded as tantamount to betrayal. In a letter to Mervyn dated 27 March 1943 and marked 'Confidential', Temple rather oddly refers to McCulloch's 'movement'. It was written after McCulloch had spent – so he claimed in his autobiography, *My Affair With the Church*[17] – a day with Temple at Lambeth Palace, but an interview lasting an hour would have been a generous allocation of an archbishop's time. Temple told Mervyn:

I have read some of McCulloch's books [probably *The Faith That Must Offend* and *We Have Our Orders*] and have had one fairly long talk with him. I like him though I was less forcibly attracted than I had expected after what I had heard from Iremonger, who thinks *very* highly of him. I am sure he is sincere; but I think he is a little superficial, and rather convinced that the time is critical and something ought to be done than overpoweringly convinced that just *this* (whatever it is) ought to be done. So I do not hope for a great deal as a result of any movement which he leads. But he can write, and if his movement finds its real function, he will be a first class propagandist.

I think it very desirable that you should meet him – and he you. So I rather hope you will go to his meeting; but if so, I think you should say that you come quite unpledged – that you have a very exacting job on hand, and cannot actually join up with any 'movement' unless you are quite convinced that it is needed and is so conceived as to give good hope of effective result; in other words, just as the movement should not start except under an impulse of the spirit, so you should not join in it unless you feel that you are personally called to do so.

But I think enough of McCulloch to say that I think you should give him and his friends the chance to convince you. Yours sincerely, William Cantuar:

The meeting to which the Archbishop referred may have been one in the Albert Hall addressed by Sir Stafford Cripps, at which Cripps took the opportunity to say 'If privilege is to be ended, then we must be prepared to give up our privileges with the rest, not excluding the privilege of endowment and establishment for the Church'.[18] It does not seem, however, that Mervyn and McCulloch ever really got together; neither mentions the other in his autobiography, and the reason that prompted the Archbishop to write to Mervyn on the subject of Joseph McCulloch remains unclear. It is of considerable interest, however, for here was the Archbishop of Canterbury informing an unknown parish priest aged 30 about his views on another cleric, and the implication can be drawn that Temple's opinion of Mervyn was very high indeed.

With the war over, junior church outings were organized to Weston-super-Mare, and it was in 1945 also that Mervyn accepted an invitation to conduct a quiet day at his old theological college. It turned out, for the Church at large, to be a momentous occasion, so the actual date is worth recording. It was 15 May. Among the students was a disconcertingly shy young ordinand by the name of John Robinson, product of an ecclesiastical background (his elderly father had been a residentiary canon of Canterbury Cathedral), who had taken a First in theology at Jesus College, Cambridge and was possessed of one of the most remarkable intellects of any undergraduate of his generation. But it was not Mervyn who initially alighted on Robinson; Robinson asked Mervyn if, after ordination as a deacon, he might join his parish as an assistant curate. Mervyn probably doubted Robinson's ability to rub along with the semi-educated working-class poor of Moorfields – not because he thought John Robinson a snob or upper-crust, but simply because it was quite obvious he was destined for a life of scholarship, and he was before all else an intellectual, academically far cleverer than Mervyn but possibly lacking the common touch that Mervyn undoubtedly possessed. At all events, he invited John Robinson to spend a weekend at St Matthew. The result was the offer of a job from Mervyn, release by the new Archbishop of Canterbury, Geoffrey Fisher, from any obligations to the Canterbury diocese, and ordination in Bristol Cathedral on 23 September 1945. Thus began a partnership between Mervyn Stockwood and John Robinson that lasted in effect until Robinson's death from cancer 38 years later. Between them they were to stamp their personalities on the most interesting, and for many the most exciting, decade of Church life this century. But whereas Mervyn's name is for ever synonymous with 'South Bank Religion', John Robinson's influence, largely thanks to Mervyn's insistence on his being made a bishop, was to attain an international dimension.

The danger of John Robinson joining Mervyn's team was easily spotted by the dean of his college, Percy Gardner-Smith, who wrote to Robinson to say

I hope Moorfields is not a purely working-class district, for your gifts and attainments would find more scope in a parish where there were a good many educated people. The theory, popular among the heads of theological colleges, that only cottagers have souls, that the upper classes ought to be neglected, and that to associate with educated people is unworthy of the zeal of a young clergyman, seems to me great nonsense.

He warned Robinson that in a town parish he would find his time pretty well occupied 'with little things', and he hoped he would 'still be able to open a book occasionally and perchance to write'. The most famous (or infamous, as some would have it) book Robinson was eventually to write was *Honest to God*.[19]

Having also been warned by Gardner-Smith that he would find preaching 'a tax', for preaching 'comes harder to the scholar and thinker than to the mass-produced product of the seminary', John Robinson faced his début at the evening People's Service just one month after being ordained. He automatically succeeded Mervyn as Missioner to Blundell's, which would certainly have afforded an opportunity to meet intelligent boys and masters, but he was less well cut out to cope with parish activities like whist drives and barn dances – meat and drink to Mervyn. He arrived just in time for a broadcast of the Sunday parish communion, only the second such broadcast ever undertaken by the BBC. Although Mervyn would have looked over John Robinson's sermons on a Thursday evening, Robinson's biographer, Eric James, says his sermons 'were sometimes at this stage in content above the heads and in length beyond the endurance of the congregation, but were mostly listened to attentively and frequently aroused discussion'.[20] There was soon however an indication of the sort of risk Mervyn had taken in having Robinson on his staff (a risk he was happily to repeat in Southwark 15 years later), for there was an almost holy *naïveté* about John Robinson; he could see an intellectual argument as clear as daylight without perceiving how more mundane humans might react. During the Week of Prayer for Unity Robinson was a guest at one of the local Methodist chapels, where he preached on the redemptive work of God. At communion, Methodists consecrate unfermented wine because they think alcohol an evil, and Robinson suggested it might be more appropriate for them to use fermented wine 'since the purpose of a sacrament is to express the redemption of all that is sinful'. The Methodist minister, Donald Rose, who had succeeded Ronald Spivey in 1942, was not amused. More alarming from Mervyn's point of view were Robinson's amateur assaults on the Mendip potholes accompanied by eager but less than brilliantly supervised members of St Matthew Scout Troop, aided only by dim and hopelessly inadequate bicycle lamps.

But John Robinson's three years at Moorfields added a valuable dimension to the life of the parish that Mervyn could never supply. Robinson had a wife and, after February 1948, a baby son. He and Ruth Robinson certainly exploded the myth that to work with Mervyn it was essential to be a bachelor. Mrs Robinson has said 'Bristol was a marvellous parish, as no one had any expectations of the role of a curate's wife. It provided a splendid training for John, who learned at Moorfields how to communicate. And Mervyn gave his curates a job to do and then left them to get on with it.'[21] Eric James has written that while part of the credit for John's maturing while at Moorfields must go to his wife, 'without a doubt it was Mervyn Stockwood who at this stage was the major influence upon John, teaching him his "craft" as a priest'. It is quite obvious too that Mervyn left John Robinson with time to follow his own studies, for while working at Moorfields Robinson published two substantial articles in *Theology*.

Notes

1 Bishop John Bickersteth in conversation with the author.
2 Letter to the author from Roy Avery, 21 March 1995.
3 Lambeth Palace archives.
4 Letter from William Temple to MS, 11 June 1943.
5 Letter from Arthur Valle to the author, 12 April 1995.
6 Ibid.
7 Ibid.
8 Letter to the author from Miss U. R. Walker, 8 March 1995.
9 Bishop Bickersteth, as above.

10 They are now in the possession of the Rev. Charles Lansdale.

11 Equal adherence to catholicism and evangelicalism was not unique to MS. Cuthbert Bardsley, appointed Bishop of Coventry in 1956, was just as easily labelled an Anglo-Catholic Evangelical.

12 Letter from Arthur Valle, as above.

13 Diana Collins, *Partners in Protest: Life with Canon Collins* (Gollancz, 1992).

14 Ibid.

15 Private information.

16 Signed but undated letter to the author.

17 Joseph McCulloch, *My Affair with the Church* (Hodder & Stoughton, 1976).

18 'I hope you gathered from Stafford Cripps that he was really pleased with the Albert Hall meeting. I think it was a really important event': William Temple to MS, Lambeth Palace archives.

19 John A. T. Robinson, *Honest to God* (SCM, 1963).

20 Eric James, *A Life of Bishop John A. T. Robinson* (Collins, 1987).

21 Ruth Robinson, in conversation with the author.

Chapter 5

The great love
of his life

It was in 1945, the year John Robinson joined the team at Moorfields, that Mervyn Stockwood began substantially to broaden his horizons. Archbishop Fisher appointed him to the British Council of Churches, he joined the Central Religious Advisory Committee of the BBC and he was elected a Proctor in the Convocation of Canterbury. He was now so often in London on business that Stafford Cripps, once he had become Chancellor of the Exchequer, supplied him with a *pied-à-terre* at 11 Downing Street, where he seized many golden opportunities to rub shoulders with the great and the good. It was this immediate post-war experience of centralized Church and political pomp that prompted Robinson in later years to comment that he always thought Mervyn had walked the corridors of power too young.

It was in 1945 too that Mervyn published his first book (not in 1946 as he mistakenly recorded in his entry in *Who's Who*), the first of a number of slim volumes. This was called *There Is a Tide* (the title was of course taken from an Act IV speech by Brutus in *Julius Caesar*). It consists of sermons preached at St Matthew and was dedicated to his bishop, Clifford Woodward. In an Introduction, Mervyn asserts that the Labour Party 'would be a little more robust if it would study Christian theology and its implications'. He never had much truck with the idea that some people might be compelled, from honest intellectual argument, to assume the mantle of atheism. 'I detest capitalism and all its manifold ramifications', he went on to proclaim; this was just the kind of sweeping statement that was inevitably destined to be played back when he took to a thorough enjoyment of the fruits of capitalism. Three years later he published another slim volume, *Whom They Pierced*, a meditation for the Three Hours Devotion, and managed to extract a brief Foreword from William Wand, a former Archbishop of Brisbane and since 1945 Bishop of London. Like the previous book of sermons, it was not an original production, but was based on addresses delivered in 1946, when he had been invited to take the Good Friday Three Hours at Holy Trinity, Brompton, and in 1947, when he spent Good Friday at St Martin-in-the-Fields, engagements indicative of the importance prestigious London churches now attached to having him in their pulpit.

It was also during John Robinson's time at Moorfields that Mervyn became active in local government, standing in 1946 as a socialist for his local St George West Ward of Bristol City Council. There was at that time, thanks to a Nonconformist revival in Bristol in the early years of the twentieth century, a strong Christian representation on the City Council anyway, and in 1946 there was an all-party group of councillors. But Mervyn never made any secret of his own party allegiance. He pledged to build the city's first health centre with the rather catchy slogan 'Go into labour with Labour', and served on both the Health and Cemetery Committees. At council meetings, Kitty Pople, then a young local government officer, remembers Mervyn sporting a red tie. 'If he thought a thing was right for the city he went for it totally, with no concern for what his opponents thought about his words or actions. He was responsible for starting all our ante-natal clinics, which won the admiration and gratitude of hundreds of women like myself after the war.'[1] In 1967 a Bristol Health Centre was named after him.

Mrs Pople saw a good deal of Mervyn Stockwood the priest as well as Mervyn Stockwood the Councillor. 'His stipend was meagre by today's standards, but he was known to leave a florin or half-crown on the table after a home visit.'[2] When Harry and Kitty Pople's second child, Michael, became terminally ill at the age of four, 'Mervyn was a tower of strength'. He often took Kitty to hospital in his own car,

well outside the parish area. Nothing was too much trouble for him, and as a confirmed bachelor he had a wonderful understanding of and empathy with mothers and children. I cannot speak too deeply of his spiritual and practical help over those difficult months, during which I was expecting our third child. Mervyn was to perform a funeral and a christening in quick succession and with great grace.

Harry Pople confirms how Mervyn was able to 'move from tragedy to triumph with apparent ease, and never allowed his personal feelings to take precedence over his care for others'.

Mervyn's empathy with women, however, was largely restricted to those who were safely married or who in some other way posed no threat. His heart he only ever gave to men, and two out of the three people with whom he was most emotionally involved were schoolboys when he first met them. One was Dick Chapman, in 1948 a 17-year-old pupil at Bristol Grammar School. The headmaster, John Garrett, had previously been the first headmaster of Raynes Park County School (his portrait is drawn in *Something in Linoleum* by Paul Vaughan[3]). Garrett was homosexual, knew Mervyn and introduced him to Dick, a lively, intelligent and extremely attractive lad, who ended up spending most of his spare time with Mervyn. Mervyn used to visit Bristol Grammar School every Wednesday lunch-time to take confirmation classes for boys unable to be instructed in their parish church. Roy Avery, then an assistant master and later headmaster, 'observed him regularly as a sort of school chaplain', and remembers him especially attending the school's annual Shakespeare production.[4] Dick's father was a maths don at Oxford, and while at school in Bristol Dick had lodgings in Mervyn's parish. Before long he found himself spending most evenings doing his prep in Mervyn's flat. There developed what Dick has described as 'a very close and intense relationship'.[5] Dick had no interest in the Church, yet because of his fondness for Mervyn he attended St Matthew, which he describes as 'absolutely marvellous. It was quite simply the centre of the community. On Sundays it was standing room only.'

It was at about this time that Mervyn began to supplement his 'meagre stipend' by journalism, and Dick remembers that every time Mervyn wrote a newspaper article the pair of them would go to 'a posh hotel' for dinner. Soon Mervyn left Dick in no doubt that he was in love with him. Although extremely fond of Mervyn, Dick did not reciprocate the intensity of Mervyn's feelings, although he believes that Mervyn thought he did. Dick was in fact sexually attracted to boys of his own age, and Mervyn's behaviour towards Dick was beyond reproach – which was just as well if only because at that time all homosexual conduct was illegal. On the occasion when Mervyn appears to have left Dick in no doubt about his feelings he gave him 'a very chaste embrace' and they then repaired to the church, where 'Mervyn said some prayers. I think he wanted somehow to dedicate our relationship to God.'

The love affair with Dick was never consummated. 'I think', Dick Chapman says now, 'that Mervyn had an aversion to sex. Absolutely nothing happened, and I am sure this was not a strain for Mervyn. I don't believe he felt in the least frustrated.' Neither was Mervyn shy about showing off his dazzling young friend. Dick was introduced to, and photographed with, Stafford Cripps, and when Clement Attlee and his wife arrived for tea, Dick too was invited. Mervyn remained in touch with Dick spasmodically after Dick left school, and on occasions when he was invited to preach at the University Church in Oxford he would lunch with Dick's parents. Part of the attraction for Mervyn had been the academic background from which Dick had come – a far cry from the prosaic life of his parishioners. Asked whether in later life Mervyn appeared embarrassed by recollections of his love for him as a boy, Dick Chapman replied 'I never saw Mervyn embarrassed by anything! He was just wonderful company, and very warm and nice. He would return to the flat in the evening and immediately tell me five funny things that had happened to him that day.

'There was one very romantic evening when he took me to dinner at a riverside hotel, and after dinner, walking by the bank, we both discovered we could recite Keats's "Ode to a Nightingale".' When Dick's older brother got engaged at the age of 22, Mervyn was horrified, not because of the heterosexual nature of the relationship, but because he thought the couple far too young. But he was definitely 'put off' one day when he and Dick encountered a courting couple – although it may have been the public display of a private matter that the fastidious Mervyn found unpalatable. There were visits to the theatre in Bath, and on one occasion Mervyn collected Dick after he had been performing in a school production of *Macbeth*. Dick was taking the part of Lady Macduff, and Mervyn said to Dick 'Don't bother to change'. The boy had the presence of mind at least to scramble out of his dress and wig, but Mervyn insisted there was no need to remove his make up, and whisked him off to some sort of café which, looking back, Dick Chapman now believes was a gay resort. 'Mervyn suddenly panicked and we left.'

Mervyn was later to tell Dick of another boy he had fallen in love with, this time an Etonian. 'I was quite good-looking', Dick recalls with becoming modesty, 'but David was a scorcher. Mervyn told me *he* had been the great love of his life.' This was David Tankard, 'a Greek god of a boy' in the opinion of a contemporary at Eton, the MP Tam Dalyell. Mervyn casually drops David's name into his autobiography without any explanation as to who David Tankard is nor how it came about that on the occasion of Clement Attlee's seventieth birthday he 'went with a schoolboy to dinner', the 'schoolboy' in question being David. Mervyn leaves with the reader the vague implication that Attlee's seventieth birthday dinner took place at 10 Downing Street, but as Attlee lost the October 1951 General Election and celebrated his seventieth birthday on 3 January 1953 he was by then out of office. Neither, at the time of Attlee's seventieth birthday, was David Tankard a schoolboy. He was born on 10 July 1932, left Eton in 1951, and at the time of the birthday party he would have been 20. David's recollection is that he and Mervyn had tea with Attlee – 'perhaps high tea?'[6] It is therefore perfectly possible that David was taken to Downing Street to meet the Prime Minister, but it would have been within a few months of October 1950, when he first met Mervyn, for David was chairman of the Eton College Political Society and capitalized on his good fortune by inviting Attlee to speak at Eton, an engagement which must have been extended while David was still at the College. It seems unlikely that David Tankard would have forgotten attending a seventieth birthday party for Attlee, and it looks as though, perhaps for romantic reasons, Mervyn decided to switch the scene of his introduction of David to the Prime Minister from high tea to a swish dinner.

David and Mervyn had met in October 1950 because David attended a weekend in Moorfields for public schoolboys to acquaint themselves with the working class. Mervyn was 37, David 18. 'I remember', David Tankard has written, 'that he was enthusiastic about the presumed benefits to be derived from the mingling of diverse socio-economic backgrounds.'[7] He goes on: 'We stayed overnight in the homes of some of the parishioners. As it happened, I was assigned to stay at the vicarage. If I had been assigned to stay with a parishioner on that occasion, I would presumably never have come to know Mervyn.' By this time, an ugly modern vicarage had been constructed next door to the church, replacing the pre-war vicarage in which Mervyn never lived, and he had vacated the flat at 94 Church Road. Perhaps one might surmise that Mervyn arranged to have an Etonian billeted on him because he would have thought that more glamorous than having a boy from Blundell's or Kelly, and he would not have been averse to a good report on him being taken back to the headmaster, Robert Birley; Mervyn was hoping to become a chaplain at Eton.

As with Dick Chapman, Mervyn was careful to cultivate David Tankard's parents, and managed to persuade his father, the pianist

Geoffrey Tankard, to give a recital at St Matthew. During the summer holidays Mervyn took David off to Devon and the Channel Islands. And this was far more than a brief flirtation on Mervyn's part. David married – twice – and remained in touch with Mervyn for the rest of his life. He and his wife (to whom Mervyn would send his love) were entertained at Bishop's House, and David was a guest at Bath during Mervyn's retirement. 'Clearly our friendship was most vital during the first two or three years', he writes.

At that time I believe it was important to both of us. I was an idealistic adolescent and I was impressed and filled with admiration for Mervyn's public presence and powerful preaching, and I was also delighted by his personal warmth, charm and humour, and his ability to relate to me, a mere boy.

It is harder for me to know how Mervyn perceived me, especially as he never directly disclosed his feelings for me. However, I suspect that his public life was so demanding that he yearned for a private relationship with someone who admired and respected him, a relationship where he could let down his guard and relax and share confidences and enjoy private jokes.[8]

Subsequently, David Tankard elaborated as follows:

I believe that Mervyn loved me . . . My relationship with Mervyn was entirely platonic . . . Nevertheless, his voice, his smile, his manner and his words conveyed affection . . . I have no reason to believe that Mervyn was other than celibate in his relationships with myself or others, but he and I never talked about such intimate matters . . . He was discreet and correct towards me . . . However, while I commend his reserve, in recent years I have come to believe that, in the later years of our friendship, there was a degree of idealization and unreality in our relationship . . . as time passed, there was a certain degree of fantasy about the relationship on his part. To be more specific, I suspect that he preferred to imagine me as a charming youth than as a mature adult passing through middle age and beyond.[9]

David Tankard has perceptively hit upon two strands in Mervyn's personality; his need to play the role of a father figure without the stamina to see it through, and his overpowering nostalgia. 'You are much in my thoughts to-day for two reasons', Mervyn wrote to 'Dearest David' on House of Lords notepaper on 28 February 1977.

1. All Christmas cards that I receive are put in a box in my chapel and I take out a few each day to pray for the senders. Yours was the first.
2. Yesterday I discovered a large box of papers and documents that had been lost in the loft of my house for years and years ... Among them were letters from you and a photograph of yourself when you left Eton – and another photograph when you stayed with me at St Matthew's Vicarage in 1950 (27 years ago). And other photographs when we had such a happy holiday in Jersey. What memories have been recalled.

Also, having an unusual memory for dates, I remember you were born, I think, on July 10, 1932 when I preached a sermon in a little village in Shropshire, called Yockleton, on the text 'Take this child away and nurse it for me and I will give thee thy wages'! Enough of nostalgia. How are you? When shall I see you again?

He told David he was still very active, would love to retire but could not afford to do so.

Although obviously capable of intense emotional involvement, it is the view of practically everyone who knew Mervyn Stockwood for any length of time, and was in a position to make any kind of meaningful assessment, that Mervyn was a lifelong celibate. This is the unequivocal opinion of Bishop Bickersteth.[10] Canon Michael Hocking has written 'I knew [Mervyn] for 53 years and never heard of any lovers, nor was there any whisper in Cambridge or Bristol of anything of this sort'. Canon Hocking once asked Mervyn 'if he ever meant to marry. His reply was: "I don't think so. I am far too selfish."'[11] This of course was a justifiably veiled response, and there was every reason why Mervyn should have declined to advertise his homosexuality. He had good cause to distrust clerical gossip; he told several people he had ceased to make his confession because on one occasion the seal of the confessional had been broken. He may also have felt better able to deal dispassionately with homosexual issues if he was seen to do so from a neutral position rather than as a priest or bishop whose own sexual orientation could be considered by others prejudicial.

A boy from Repton, one of about 30 public schoolboys who joined a weekend at St Matthew in 1952, was Philip Crowe, later to become editor of The Church of England Newspaper and Principal of Salisbury and Wells Theological College. He can still remember Mervyn looking at the clock while giving a talk, directing the boys' eyes to the clock too, and ending, as planned, dead on twelve o'clock. Canon Crowe stayed with a family with two teenage girls, one of whom thought Mervyn marvellous while the other could not stand him. He attended the evening People's Service and found it 'very exhilarating. That weekend certainly shaped my own ministry, as I think it was intended to do.' Five years earlier the chaplain at Clifton College had alerted the boys in his charge to a public schoolboy weekend at Moorfields, and one of those who attended, and heard Mervyn speak on the job of a parson, was Tony Crowe, who became a parish priest in Mervyn's diocese and a pioneer of services of blessing for gay couples – an enthusiasm of Tony Crowe's that was to prove a mixed blessing where his friendship with Mervyn was concerned. He, like Philip Crowe, recalls that Mervyn was good at encouraging vocations, and remembers vividly the Midnight Mass at Christmas 1950, with balloons in the church and punch afterwards in the parish hall. He was sufficiently impressed to record visits to St Matthew in his teenage diary, Mervyn's sermons being noted as 'witty and sensible'. He remembers, too, being warned, just as Mervyn had been on his visits from Kelly College to slum areas, that if he was not careful he would pick up a bug in Moorfields.

When John Robinson left Moorfields it was to become chaplain at Wells Theological College, and it was there that he came to tutor a friend from childhood, John Bickersteth. Like Robinson, Bickersteth came from a deeply ingrained ecclesiastical background, and had played with John Robinson when visiting his maternal grandfather who, like Robinson's father, was a canon at Canterbury. Now that he was training for ordination he heard from Robinson about Mervyn's dynamic training methods. 'I had heard he was a great showman', Bishop Bickersteth recalls, 'that he was a jolly good preacher, that he was an ardent socialist.' Bickersteth's father had been a middle-of-the-road country parson, and Bickersteth's own churchmanship was Central to High, certainly not Anglo-Catholic. John Robinson told him he thought he needed a bit of 'de-Bickerstething', by which he meant he should forget about his rather cosy rural background, not to mention his episcopal connections (his paternal grandfather had been Bishop of Exeter and a distant cousin Bishop of Ripon), and get his hands dirty in a downtown parish. He remembers on their first meeting 'Mervyn gave me half an hour of his time, was quite brusque, but perfectly friendly and nice. But there was no indication he wanted to have me.' One of Mervyn's many gifts, however, was as a talent-spotter, and John Bickersteth was to be consecrated suffragan Bishop of Warrington and preferred, in 1975, to Bath and Wells, ending up Clerk of the Closet to the Queen. So a letter arrived inviting Bickersteth to become the junior assistant curate at Moorfields in September 1950. There were at this time two other curates, a contingent kept fully employed because by now Mervyn was in constant demand at conferences and as a visiting preacher.

The parish John Bickersteth joined five years after the war still bore signs of bombing. On visits into Bristol for post-ordination training he remembers cycling along roads roped off on either side and with wasteland where once houses had stood. 'Come on, John', was the first thing Mervyn said to his newly ordained deacon, 'I must teach you the catholic faith.' Bickersteth had never before entered a church where incense was burnt; Mervyn invariably wore a biretta when he was in a cassock, and of course wore a biretta at Benediction on Saturday evening – but wearing a biretta at Benediction was where young Bickersteth drew the line. 'As a trainer of curates, Mervyn took immense trouble. He was a tremendous parish visitor, and insisted that his curates covered a certain number of houses each week. And we had to submit a list of the houses we had been to.' John Bickersteth says that the curates were slightly frightened of Mervyn's secretary, 'because she could erect a barrier between us and Mervyn', and he soon spotted 'that he loved rich people. Most of his friends were Tory and rich, and he made the acquaintance of the richest men in Bristol.'

Yet alongside the quest for wealthy and influential friends, whose affluence may well have provided Mervyn with comfortable weekend accommodation but whose goodwill was also tapped for the benefit of the Church (when Mervyn arrived in Southwark there was not even a bishop's discretionary fund, and the coffers were filled as a result of his contacts in Cambridge and Bristol), there always remained the genuine pastor. For example, he taught John Bickersteth how to administer the Sacrament to the sick. 'I should think each month we must have taken the Sacrament to thirty parishioners, and I can remember doing so on my bike, with the pyx bouncing round my neck. Mervyn always used to say, "Talk beforehand, but when you've given the blessing, smile at the recipient and walk out, so that you leave the Almighty with them and not your own natterings". Mervyn believed that God was to be glorified in everything. He liked the limelight, but it is bunkum to think it was always the glorification of Mervyn. It wasn't. He had a passionate concern for the Kingdom. If ever there was a man who wanted to promote the Kingdom it was Mervyn Stockwood.'

When John Bickersteth married in 1955 his wife was to find Mervyn difficult to deal with. Bishop Bickersteth is quite clear that 'Mervyn wasn't good with women. He could be awfully naughty at the dinner table, turning his back for ages on a woman neighbour if he found someone else more interesting.' One reason Mervyn warmed to Bickersteth was because he was a genuine countryman, and Mervyn had a kind of emotional hankering for the outdoor life – about which he really knew nothing at all. Bickersteth says 'Mervyn went into the country to cope with his solitude, he was such a lonely man. But he knew nothing about the country at all. He didn't know a cowslip from a primrose.' By the time John Bickersteth became a member of the House of Bishops Mervyn had been at Southwark 15 years, and was regarded by the other bishops as a kind of elder statesman. 'He didn't utter all that often but when he did he expected what he said to come as a bombshell for everyone! Or to be the definitive word. You know – Mervyn has uttered!' In retirement, when Mervyn became an honorary assistant bishop to his former junior curate, Bickersteth says 'He was totally and wonderfully loyal. And he gave me some sound advice for my own retirement. He used to say, "When you retire, never say Yes to anything until they've said they will cover your expenses. It's very difficult to ask afterwards!"'

Within a very short time of being elected to Bristol City Council Mervyn had become an influential member of the general management committee of the local Labour Party. On 1 November 1950 Tony Benn – or Anthony Wedgwood Benn as he was known in those less egalitarian days – was selected to succeed Sir Stafford Cripps as the parliamentary candidate for Bristol East, and the following day Hugh Dalton noted in his diary: 'Tony Crosland told me, in confidence, that he had worked this by introducing Anthony Wedgwood Benn to Rev. Mervyn Stockwood, close friend of Stafford, and key man in the Bristol South-East Party.'[12] In October the following year Dalton met Mervyn for the first time 'with Tony [Crosland] in the street, just outside the Grand Hotel. I rather liked him at first impact. Tony says he is a cynical Christian, but Clem [Attlee] should have made him a bishop.'[13] The idea that a 'cynical Christian' was fit to be a bishop was a cynical remark in itself, and while Mervyn Stockwood may have had his faults, cynicism towards his faith was not one of them; bored with religion he may sometimes have been, but never cynical. In any event, in October 1951 Mervyn was still only 38, he had been a priest only 14 years, and his entire ecclesiastical experience had been confined to just one parish. What either Anthony Crosland or Hugh Dalton knew about the workings of the Established Church seems to have been remarkably little. Attlee certainly hoped for Mervyn's preferment, but not as early in Mervyn's career as this, and after 1951 he was never in a position to do anything about it.

Nevertheless, Mervyn's frequent preaching engagements outside the diocese would by this time have ensured he captured the attention of that nebulous network of spies whose task it was to keep tabs on potential episcopal material and report to the prime minister's office. Having previously declined the see of Southwark, in 1946 Frederick Cockin succeeded Clifford Woodward as Bishop of Bristol, and he used to say 'Whenever I go to Mervyn Stockwood's parish I think I must tell him he really has gone too far this time, but I always come away thinking he is the only good parish priest in my diocese!' He nearly lost Mervyn's services in 1947 when he was seriously considered for the University Church of St Mary the Virgin, Oxford, but his well-publicized left-wing sympathies put a stop to the appointment; the Bishop of Oxford, Kenneth Kirk, did not fancy a maverick socialist preaching to undergraduates. St Mary the Virgin, scene of Cranmer's last day on earth, and the site of the founding of the Oxford Movement, would have provided an inspiring setting for the kind of pastoral work Mervyn was later to undertake in Cambridge, but his failure to obtain the incumbency was probably a blessing in disguise; he never really felt at home in Oxford, whereas Cambridge he had already learned to love.

Nevertheless the undergraduates of Oxford were not entirely denied the benefit of Mervyn's views. He was invited to deliver three lectures at the University Church on the subject of Christianity and Marxism, and these were published in 1949.[14] The copy Mervyn signed for his mother was later (after her death in 1967 presumably) extensively annotated by Mervyn, and it may have been that he hoped at some time to have it reissued. He states that the Communist Party 'is, and presumably always will be, wedded to atheism', and as it is impossible to think of Mervyn as an atheist it is difficult, despite Bishop Bickersteth's honest assertion, to imagine him actually joining the Party, attracted though he was by its social and economic ideals. Something of his own Christian credo comes through in these Oxford talks. A good Churchman, he told the undergraduates, 'is to be judged not by his adherence to rules and order, still less by the method whereby he carries out his ecclesiastical duties, but by the honest endeavour to devote his life to the transformation of society'. Again:

Churchmen must realise that it is not their particular privilege to sit on every political fence; instead they must step into the arena and take sides. It is useless to complain of the lack of spiritual values in the life of the nation if the exponents of these values hold themselves aloof, and leave it to others to exercise control. I am not suggesting that the Church should start a party of its own, or identify itself with any existing party, but I am convinced that Churchmen, as individuals, should place themselves at those strategic points at which the day to day decisions are made, and the minds of people influenced; in national and municipal politics, in industrial and trade unions, in education and journalism, in welfare and social organisations. It is only thus that the political and economic conditions of society can be made to meet the deepest needs of man, whose nature is fundamentally spiritual.

Meanwhile, Mervyn's relations with Tony Benn got off on the wrong foot. Mervyn invited Benn to stay at the vicarage, and when Benn explained he would have his wife with him, Mervyn airily suggested she could stay somewhere else.[15] Much later – on 20 January 1966 – Mervyn invited Tony and Caroline Benn to lunch at the House of Lords, when Benn conceded that 'although he was rude to Caroline – by ignoring her as he does all women – it was nice to gossip'.[16] Benn says he got on quite well with Mervyn but always felt a slight hesitation about him. 'You felt he would always end up on the winning side, but I was very pleased when he became a bishop. Although he was what I would call a café society bishop. He had broadly liberal instincts. Politically he was a Roy Jenkins figure.'[17]

It would have been surprising had Mervyn Stockwood and Tony Benn enjoyed particularly cordial relations. Gay rights have never been at the top of Benn's political or social agenda, his Church allegiance was always considerably more puritanical than Mervyn's, and his passionate and patently sincere advocacy of unadulterated socialism, even to the extent of disclaiming his hereditary peerage, could not be in greater contrast to Mervyn's happy embrace of all things material. At the same time it is worth recording that in 1955 it was Mervyn who proposed that Bristol City Council should present a petition to both Houses of Parliament praying for legislation to enable Tony Benn to disclaim his father's viscountancy. It seems that Mervyn blotted his copybook when he attended a party at Tony Benn's house 'and insisted on going upstairs and blessing my oldest son, who was about six months old, and woke him up. I didn't care for that very much.'[18] Benn was one of those who seems to have over-reacted to Mervyn's personality, for when he attended his 50th birthday party at Bishop's House he noted that Mervyn was wearing 'a huge purple cassock'. All bishops wear a purple cassock, and Mervyn's could not have been either huge or small. A cassock is a cassock. He objected, too, to Mervyn's chaplain (Michael Mayne) calling him 'My Lord', 'which was slightly overdone'.[19] Tony Benn may have been pleased when Mervyn became a bishop, but his pleasure appears to have waned with the passing years. On 4 November 1964 Harold Wilson suggested a midday service in the Crypt of the Palace of Westminster for members of the Government. Mervyn and Donald Soper, who was to be ennobled the following year, conducted the service, which Tony Benn thought 'an imaginative idea and except for Mervyn's egocentric sermon, everything went well'.[20] The display of egocentricity was apparently repeated on 20 April 1966, when Mervyn and Lord Soper again conducted a service in the Crypt, which Benn thought 'a pleasant ceremony though Mervyn was as egocentric as ever and his sermon was largely about his own political and spiritual experience'.[21]

Following the failure to move from Bristol to Oxford in 1947 a more disappointing setback occurred in 1951, when Robert Birley, Headmaster of Eton College since 1949, offered Mervyn the chaplaincy at Eton, and then reneged, because he feared the Provost would object to his politics. Next Mervyn received a pressing invitation from one of the Church's least appealing bishops, Ernest Barnes, to become Provost of Birmingham. Mervyn had once addressed the Birmingham Diocesan Conference on 'The Future of the Church of England', but one wonders why on this occasion he even troubled to take the train to Birmingham to discuss the matter. Barnes was a cantankerous controversialist, who did not believe in the Virgin Birth, harassed clergy who reserved the Sacrament and wanted to have the Host analysed in a laboratory. At a confirmation service, Barnes once preached on the sterilization of the unfit, and a girl he had confirmed went home and asked her parents if she could be confirmed again. Mervyn had no hesitation in declining a preferment many would have regarded as a sure sign of enhanced status. In 1952 he received some small compensation for not going to Oxford, Eton or Birmingham; he was appointed an honorary canon of Bristol.

This was also the year of the Redfield Revue, a production of a 'Charade in Three Acts'. 'We act it, you guess it', the audience was told. Mervyn played the part of Miss Screwy and John Bickersteth was billed as a Methodist 'mummy opener' by the name of Club Footed Cuthbert. At one point the scene seems to have shifted to a staff meeting of the Redfield United Front, held in the year 1980, when Mervyn, somewhat unfortunately, was listed as 'the late' Vicar of St Matthew. John Bickersteth is now Miss Hilda Hairpin, and a programme note explains that 'the late vicar of St Matthew resigned two years ago . . . because he objected to a woman becoming Bishop of Bristol. So he lost his stipend. He stood in a recent General Election as a Tory Candidate, but was defeated by the Socialist, Comrade Bickersteth. He is therefore unemployed and living in reduced circumstances at the Earl Russell. He has applied for a pension.' Much else took place of a nature inevitably incomprehensible to those not present on the night (of 26 February 1952), two female roles, those of the Rev. Charlotte Haggy and Miss Piston, being undertaken by a friend and colleague of Mervyn's who was, to put it mildly, an eccentric: the Rev. Richard Blake-Brown.

Blake-Brown and Mervyn had met at Cambridge, where Blake-Brown studied at Magdalene. He later served as a chaplain in the navy, and arrived at St Matthew as a curate shortly after John Bickersteth. Bishop Bickersteth writes:

His background Mervyn perfectly justifiably kept from us. We knew that Mervyn was befriending him. He was hilarious most of the time, full of risqué stories, adored by the ladies of the congregation, who revelled in his naughtiness. On the stage he was a laugh a minute – off it too, come to that. I remember only one sermon that he preached, one Michaelmas Day, when he got up and said, 'We know very little about angels, apart from the fact that they were none of them women.'

Bishop Bickersteth says that Blake-Brown 'would sink into black depressions when no doubt his failures weighed heavily', and thinks he was 'nearly unfrocked for something. Rumours flew around most of the time, but because everybody loved him no one minded, and liked Mervyn Stockwood all the more for putting him into the St Matthew's family.'[22] The fact that Blake-Brown sailed as close to the wind at St Matthew as elsewhere is not surprising. Since 1934 he had corresponded with Marcus Oliver, a close friend of the writer and painter Denton Welch. Blake-Brown, who wrote long-forgotten novels of a sub-Firbankian character, also enjoyed corresponding with grand people like Lady Oxford, and was friendly with Norman Hartnell, whom he introduced to Mervyn. In 1942 he had started to write *outré* letters to Welch, but his truly fanatical devotion was reserved for Queen Mary; his lavatory even contained a pop-up portrait of Her Majesty. Alas, on the one occasion when he was invited to preach at Queen Mary's wartime residence, Badminton, his sermon was considered so outrageous he was not invited to take a glass of sherry with her after the service. His unlikely marriage, to a lady he occasionally condescended to take to dinner at the Ritz, proved equally disastrous; the honeymoon lasted ten days, starting at the Savoy and ending at Claridges, and to Marcus Oliver Blake-Brown described his wife as the one person who 'ever since I married her has bored me more than any other human being I've ever known'.

This would hardly have been likely to shock Oliver, to whom Blake-Brown intimated that a steady supply of German boys was more to his liking, and herein lies a clue perhaps to Bishop Bickersteth's suspicion that at one time he was nearly unfrocked. In early life he certainly resigned holy orders, and presumably found a bishop willing to re-ordain him. During the year he served as a curate at St Matthew he made the acquaintance of David Tankard, to whom he sent a number of his famously exotic letters, 'composed with verve and flair and penned in inks of more than one colour and sealed with a wax seal'.[23] Dick Chapman likewise received 'several letters from him (in the late '40s) in envelopes absolutely covered in Edward VIII stamps'.[24] A further 20 years were spent in the diocese, as chaplain to Bristol Prison, with which address he frequently inscribed the visitors' book at Bishop's House in Southwark. He suffered from Ménière's disease, which may, aided and abetted by drink, have contributed to his sad but somehow appropriately dramatic end. He was discovered burnt to death in his room in the prison, having apparently stumbled over an electric fire. By this time Mervyn was Bishop of Southwark, but he did not hesitate to travel to St Mary Redcliffe in Bristol to preach at Blake-Brown's funeral. It was the day of commemoration of Saints, Doctors and Martyrs of the Church of England, and Mervyn fastened on to the fact that Blake-Brown had hated saints and had only once recognized a martyr – himself; he felt he had been martyred if he had attended a dreary church service. As for doctors, Mervyn recalled that when Blake-Brown became bored with his sombre Cambridge MA hood he often draped over his surplice a hood of scarlet or purple, to which he had no entitlement whatsoever. 'Merry and kind' was how Mervyn summed up the character of this most quixotic of Anglican clergymen. Who but someone as basically merry and kind as Mervyn would ever have taken the risk of letting him loose in Moorfields?

Notes

1 Mrs Kitty Pople, letter to the author, 10 March 1995.
2 A florin was the equivalent of 10p in today's currency, a half-crown 12.5p, but the gift would have been worth at least £1 when the average industrial wage was only £8 a week.
3 Paul Vaughan, *Something in Linoleum* (Sinclair-Stevenson, 1994).
4 Letter to the author from Roy Avery, 21 March 1995.
5 Dick Chapman, in conversation with the author.
6 David Tankard, letter to the author, 18 July 1995.
7 David Tankard, letter to the author, 29 June 1995.
8 Ibid.
9 David Tankard, letter of 18 July 1995.
10 Bishop Bickersteth, in conversation with the author.
11 Canon Michael Hocking, letter to the author, 10 March 1995.
12 Ben Pimlott (ed.), *The Political Diary of Hugh Dalton* (Cape, 1986).
13 Ibid.
14 Mervyn Stockwood, *Christianity and Marxism* (SPCK, 1949).
15 Tony Benn, in conversation with the author.
16 Tony Benn, *Out of the Wilderness* (Hutchinson, 1987).
17 Tony Benn, in conversation with the author.
18 Ibid.
19 Benn, *Out of the Wilderness*.
20 Ibid.
21 Ibid.
22 Bishop Bickersteth, letter to the author, 6 April 1995.
23 David Tankard to the author, 18 July 1995.
24 Dick Chapman to the author, 18 July 1995.

Chapter 6

Free to be unorthodox

By 1953 Mervyn Stockwood had such itchy feet that he left St Matthew, Moorfields in the capable hands of his curates and set out on a visit to Russia – because, he says, he had been commissioned to write a book. But that commission, and hence the journey, came about surely because he was still uncertain in his mind about the truths of the Communist system and the relationship between Christianity and Marxism. *I Went to Moscow* was the less than riveting title of the book he wrote, published in 1955 and dedicated to the memory of Stafford Cripps, who had served as ambassador to Moscow for two years during the war. In his autobiography Mervyn says the country he found was 'a servile state ruled by terror and corruption', a 'prostitution of socialism; an affront to human dignity'. But there was not much of that sort of language in the book he wrote on his return. On the contrary, he often found himself in a fix, 'but the people invariably helped me out of my difficulties with infinite patience and kindliness'. He had nothing but praise for his dealings with them; he had never found so much graciousness in any country; he returned 'with not a single disagreeable memory'. The book contains some amusing and unconscious self-parody. 'Of course', he tells us on one occasion, 'I broke my fast with caviare.' 'I am not a teetotaller . . .' 'I have no objection to ritual.' He greatly admired the apparent lack of prosti-tution (in the literal sense), and equally admired the efforts of the police to suppress it. 'It's a pity we do not learn from the Soviets', he moralized. 'London is a disgrace and I often wonder what foreigners think of us. It's about time the Government took a tougher line. Instead of a nominal fine, prostitutes should be placed in homes and given the chance to win their way back into useful employment and citizenship. And sentences of life imprisonment should be passed on pimps who treat prostitution as a commercial racket.' Mervyn was now in full spate.

Furthermore, the police would be doing a greater service to the state if they spent less time searching for minor motoring offences and more time cleaning up the streets. I have often argued the point with policemen and I am invariably told that nothing can be done. Since going to Moscow I refuse to believe it. My one regret is that an atheistic Government has been successful where a Christian Government has failed.

The idea that the government of Winston Churchill was inherently 'Christian' was to assume that because the nation possessed an Established Church, Christian morality would automatically flow as from some sort of holy well in Downing Street. As for the idea of locking up pimps for life, this was a blimpish concept worthy of the most reactionary Tory politicians of the time. Mervyn was not a natural writer nor a sparkling observer of the passing scene; and when the proletariat did not come up to scratch his contempt scarcely knew any bounds. He discovered on his travels that Russians were more polite than Englishmen ('not that that would be difficult'), and gave as an instance the fact that on his last day in London he had taken a taxi 'from Paddington to my club in Pall Mall [the Athenaeum, to which he had been elected in 1949]. Although the driver gave me no help with my cases, I gave him a ninepenny tip. He neither thanked me nor wished me good-day; instead he looked at the coins with contempt and scowled. And that', Mervyn went on, now thoroughly hot under the collar again, 'is not the first time I have suffered from the boorishness of ill-mannered clods.' No wonder he found the humble degraded Russian peasant a pleasant change from his own brutish countrymen. It is a pity that the only substantial book, apart from his autobiography, Mervyn ever attempted tells us so little about its ostensible subject and depicts Mervyn himself in the least attractive garb of the many he was to wear, the mantle of the pompous prelate.

Twenty years after his visit to Russia, Mervyn was still flirting with, or at any rate entertaining, Communist luminaries. In December 1975 Tony Benn recorded in his diary that he and his wife had been invited to dinner 'at the Bishop's Palace' [sic], to meet Gordon McLennan, General Secretary of the Communist Party. 'I'd like to meet Gordon McLennan', Benn wrote, 'but Mervyn Stockwood is such an old gossip that he'd tell everybody that he's had a dinner party for the Secretary of the Communist Party and myself so I don't really think I can accept.'[1]

*

On Mervyn's return from Russia he was considered in a vague sort of way for the job of head of religious broadcasting, but the BBC in those days was rigidly conservative, and there was never any serious chance of his being appointed. He would surely have hated it if he had been, for the BBC was also a hidebound bureaucracy, and he would have spent most of his time writing memos and having his ideas stamped on by the Director-General. Yet it was equally obvious he could not stay in Bristol for the rest of his life, and a move of some sort was becoming essential. He was not an academic, and a university appointment as such would not have been appropriate. However, it dawned on Lord Adrian, the Master of Trinity College, Cambridge, that a blend of parish, university and civic life (St Mary's served as civic church to the city, which meant visits from the mayor and corporation) might give Mervyn new impetus if he were to take over Great St Mary's, the sadly moribund University Church whose incumbent, George Whitworth, appointed in 1947 and now 77 years of age, had indicated his desire to leave.

Adrian's opinion of Mervyn was crucial, for Trinity were the patrons of Great St Mary's with St Michael, but of almost equal importance were the views of college deans and chaplains, who would be expected in some measure to co-operate with Mervyn, and might not be too thrilled if he started to poach their undergraduates. Roland Walls of Corpus Christi, where Mervyn had stayed during the Lent term of 1954 to help with a teaching mission conducted by Michael Ramsey, recently appointed Bishop of Durham, could be depended on; Walls was an eccentric to whom Mervyn was devoted, despite his enjoyment of meals taken at the British Restaurant. Someone else whose good opinion of Mervyn could be taken for granted, and in whose chapel he had twice preached, was the Dean of Clare, for he was John Robinson, who had moved to Cambridge from Wells. Another affirmative response came from the Dean of Gonville and Caius, Hugh Montefiore, who was asked by the Dean of Trinity, Professor John Burnaby, if his college chapel 'could stand someone like Mervyn at the University Church'.[2] Montefiore had been a student at Westcott House when in 1949 Mervyn had been invited to lecture. He himself had preached at the University Church when he found the congregation not much larger than the choir, and knew from personal experience how run down this ancient foundation had become. (George

Reindorp recalled being glad to have the mayor and councillors present to bring the congregation up to two dozen when he was invited to preach prior to Mervyn's appointment.[3]) Montefiore's efforts in the pulpit were not however entirely in vain. The subject of his sermon one Trinity Sunday was, as tradition at the time dictated, ordination, and sparse though the congregation may have been, his sermon was heard by a young undergraduate, Jeremy Walsh, who went forward for ordination, in 1957 became one of Mervyn's Cambridge assistants, paid by SCM, and eventually Bishop of Tewkesbury. Although Montefiore's acquaintance with Mervyn was slight, he did not hesitate to speak up for him, and a further advantage was the fact that the diocesan bishop was Edward Wynn, the former Dean of Pembroke with whom Mervyn had been so friendly as an undergraduate. (He was succeeded as Bishop of Ely a year after Mervyn's arrival in Cambridge by the Bishop of Newcastle, Noel Hudson.) Unlike Kenneth Kirk, who had felt so uneasy at the thought of Mervyn taking over the University Church in Oxford, Wynn was happy to institute Mervyn, and so after 19 years he said goodbye to St Matthew, and on 26 May 1955 he left for Cambridge. 'The actual parting', he was to write, 'seemed like a divorce because I felt I was deserting the family I loved. In spite of all the problems, there are few jobs more rewarding than that of a parish priest.' Asked whether Mervyn had thought of himself as a success at St Matthew, Bishop Bickersteth said 'I should have thought so. With huge justification.'[4]

Mervyn was instituted on 1 June. There was no vicarage for Mervyn and his mother (or for Winkie, Mrs Stockwood's cat) to move into, for in the past Trinity had depended on appointing a vicar who was a don and would live in college or who was wealthy enough to afford to buy his own house, and one of Mervyn's stipulations about taking on the job was that sufficient endowments should be sold to purchase a vicarage. He alighted on 39 Madingley Road, not exactly next door to the church, Great St Mary's being situated in the centre of the city, facing King's and almost adjacent to the Guildhall. The vicarage is way out to the north-west. It is odd that Mervyn was later to regard 39 Madingley Road as adequate for himself, as a bachelor, but potentially in-adequate for any married successor; it remains the vicarage today, and has been described by the current incumbent, John Binns, as 'a spacious five bedroomed house with a large garden . . . more suited to a family than a single person'.[5] One consequence of the distance of the vicarage from the church was a number of offers of hospitality from college chaplains, who realized Mervyn could not keep popping home between engagements, and who placed rooms and decanters of sherry at his disposal. If the list of those who have claimed the privilege of easing Mervyn's domestic life in this way is anything like accurate, they may not have realized their kindness was being replicated. Mervyn in any case enjoyed an element of subterfuge in all his activities, often keeping his relationships in separate compartments. Eric James, newly arrived as one of the chaplains at Trinity, recalls that from his own rooms he had a good view of rooms occupied by two undergraduates, Andrew Henderson and James Mitchell, and on one occasion, after Mervyn had been to visit them, he came on to Eric's rooms and said 'Do you know someone called Andrew Henderson? I must meet him some time.' 'It was', says Eric James, 'a curious mixture of guilt and secrecy.'[6] There was another trait of Mervyn's that Eric was quick to spot. Eric had served his title under George Reindorp at St Stephen's, Rochester Row, was missing parish life, and had hastened round to Great St Mary's as soon a Mervyn was inducted; Mervyn immediately asked him if he would like to act as unpaid curate. 'By his second Sunday he had had a mace carved, and he said he wanted me to walk a yard in front of the mace bearer, and he would walk a yard behind. I realised that here was a man with a reputation for being a socialist for whom this kind of hierarchical ordering of processions was of infinite importance. Especially if he was the chief person in the procession! Little things like this quickly taught me the complex nature of Mervyn.' Someone who noticed, from Cambridge days together, that there was 'always a strange mixture of the Tory and Socialist' about Mervyn was Jeremy Walsh.[7]

There had been a church on the site of Great St Mary's since at least the reign of King John, and the building Mervyn had known as an undergraduate, and of which he was now the pastor, dated from 1478. Those who had subscribed to the cost included Richard III, Henry VII and Francis Bacon. The custom of a University sermon dated back to 1303, and for centuries the church had been a centre of disputation. One major rumpus had to do with tobacco. In 1607 undergraduates were forbidden to smoke during the sermon, and as a result, eight years later James I declined to attend a service at St Mary's, so addicted was he to tobacco. The pulpit now entrusted to Mervyn had been occupied by Erasmus,

Cranmer, Ridley and Latimer, so it would be a mistake to imagine that Mervyn was the first to stir up controversy at Great St Mary's, and he never went so far as those whose conduct, Archbishop Laud complained, amounted to 'profane, scurrilous and coarse jests'. On the contrary, his stated aim when he arrived was – 'without usurping the functions of the college chapels' – for the church to 'bear lively witness to the Christian tradition of our University'. Because of its geographical position between the Senate House and the Guildhall he also hoped it might be 'of service to town and gown'. And he wanted it 'sufficiently maintained and restored' so that Cambridge might be proud of its University Church.[8]

Francis Longworth-Dames thinks the first year nearly killed Mervyn.[9] Every Sunday evening the Bishop of Ely would telephone to see how he was getting on. The first tussle he had to deal with was a request from the Cambridge Inter-Collegiate Christian Union to lend them his church for a mission to be conducted by Billy Graham, the American evangelist supported at that time by only a handful of Anglican bishops. Dr Graham has always been a courteous and undogmatic propounder of the Gospel, easy to get along with and far less 'enthusiastic' than some of his more ardent followers; CICCU actually demanded that for the week of the mission they should take possession of Great St Mary's, excluding Mervyn, and even his bishop, from any of the activities. To this impertinent suggestion the vice-chancellor returned a dusty answer. When the mission did take place, one of those who attended was John Burnaby. He thought Graham's biblical analysis in-adequate, the Eucharist in particular not coming in for sufficient mention. Eric James was asked to give a lunch for Billy Graham; the other guests included Professor Burnaby and Mervyn. Eric, new to his job and somewhat overawed by the ethos of Cambridge (this was the first lunch he had ever given for anyone), was dreading the encounter between Burnaby and Graham. But Dr Graham walked straight up to Burnaby, shook hands with him, and said he was so glad the Professor had been to his mission every night, he was well aware there was much amiss with what he had said, he would shortly be going on study leave and he would be extremely grateful if the Professor would furnish him with a reading list. This, of course, completely took the wind out of Burnaby's sails. After the lunch, Mervyn told Eric it was he who had told Billy Graham to behave as he did.

Someone else who attended the Billy Graham mission was an

undergraduate at King's, the future Labour Member of Parliament Tam Dalyell. King's, despite the ravishing liturgical tradition of its chapel, was, says Dalyell, 'a centre of religious scepticism', and he had crossed the street to Great St Mary's with the express purpose of heckling.[10] 'I dared to interrupt Billy Graham, and all hell was let loose on my unsuspecting head. I don't think this had happened to Billy Graham before, and the vicar of All Souls', Langham Place, who also happened to be there, said there was evil – me, presumably! – in the house.' The result was that Mervyn got in touch with Dalyell. 'It was', he recalls, 'the beginning of a very moving relationship. He took an enormous amount of trouble. I was Church of Scotland, my outlook then was nothing approaching what it is now, and Mervyn had a considerable effect on my social outlook. I would say that at Cambridge he exercised a great moral influence. He was a very eloquent portrayer of obligations, and of the whole tradition of Crippsian Christian socialism.'

The numbers of undergraduates now famous whose paths crossed Mervyn's during his four years at Cambridge are legion, among them Lord Owen, one of three people to whom *Cambridge Sermons* is dedicated, and Jonathan Miller and Peter Cook, whose revue *Beyond the Fringe* Mervyn much enjoyed in 1961. 'Mervyn was a breath of fresh air', according to Tam Dalyell. 'He was extremely hospitable and generous late into the night. He had many of the attributes of the really good teacher. He was strong on the obligations of public schoolboys. It would be wrong to say he was a snob but he did have a soft spot for upper-class schoolboys, of whom I was one.' Tam Dalyell having been at Eton with David Tankard would have been recommendation enough, but Mervyn may also have realized he was in line for a baronetcy.[11] Dalyell was not blind to Mervyn's faults. He says 'He made a great song and dance about liking to hear other people's point of view, but when you stood up to him he didn't really like it'.

There was virtually no parish at Great St Mary's, and no one seemed quite to know how it should utilize its connections with the University, who claimed to own it. Hence when Mervyn arrived the place was scarcely alive, and he had little difficulty in stirring up expectations when for his first sermon he chose as his text 'If you must bore men, well and good; but must you bore your God also?' This was a snide reference to his obligation, at his induction, to assent to the Thirty-Nine Articles. Before long he realized that if he was careful not to tread on the toes of the college chaplains by enticing away their undergraduate communicants it should be possible for the University Church to minister to both the town and the university. He instituted a Sunday parish communion for the town, which attracted, to begin with, a congregation of no more than two dozen, partly because Mervyn was determined to impose some recognizable signs of catholic worship on a parish which in the past hardly seems to have known where it stood. P. N. Waggett, Vicar from 1927 to 1929, had been a Cowley Father; E. C. Essex, who succeeded him in 1930 and held the living for 17 years, had been the Evangelical vice-principal of Ridley Hall; while Mervyn's immediate predecessor, George Whitworth, had been vaguely Central Church. Mervyn wore vestments, said Mass daily, and had the Sacrament reserved in a side chapel. He also heard confessions – very well, in the opinion of Mary Howard, whose husband became Mervyn's curate in September 1956. She also recalls that 'to be part of the social scene' by the end of Mervyn's first year 'you had to go to Great St Mary's'.[12] Until Robin Howard's arrival there was a part-time curate, Norman Hill, who unfortunately enjoyed poor health 'and rather a chaotic personality', which did not suit the methodical Mervyn.

As at Bristol, Mervyn balanced the sacramental aspect of worship with Matins, with a sermon restricted to 20 minutes. A sung Matins was unlikely to clash with college worship, and was the service most public-school undergraduates (and most undergraduates still were from the public schools) had been brought up on, and before long town and gown were beginning to mingle. Soon Mervyn had hit upon another method of satisfying two disparate congregations; he held Evensong for parish worshippers, closely followed by a half-past eight popular service for undergraduates, run on the lines of the Moorfields People's Service. Preachers invited to the late evening service included Stephen Spender, Nye Bevan and Malcolm Muggeridge. It was the cleverly timed proximity of the two evening services as much as the entertaining nature of the guest preachers that ensured an impressive queue of young men and women in King's Parade, the undergraduates waiting to file in as the parish left. All this was being built upon an inheritance that included, for example, a choir of 'three men between the ages of seventy and eighty' who walked out anyway when the parish communion was introduced. For the first of the undergraduate evening services a temporary choir was recruited by Paul Rose, who was to become precentor at Canterbury; most of them were veterinary and medical students who sang in the morning at St Andrew the Great, and most of them liked Great St Mary's so much that they stayed.

The programme every Sunday was an 8 a.m. Holy Communion, a Parish Communion and address at 9.45 a.m., followed by Matins at 11 a.m. Evensong was at 6.30 p.m. and the 'Short Evening Service' at 8.30 p.m. The parish could not afford a verger, and when Mervyn was on his own he had to do everything himself. There have been a number of places of worship in which it is claimed that Mervyn said 'Show me where to kiss the relics, or are they already sitting in the pews?' Great St Mary's remains the most likely candidate, but doubtless Mervyn was so pleased with the line that he trotted it out on future occasions, on visits to down-and-out parishes in Southwark. Andrew Henderson was sometimes deputed to chauffeur the visiting preachers, and he and James Mitchell (who later became a successful publisher) were two of Mervyn's earliest undergraduate adherents. When, in 1959, Mervyn published eight of his Cambridge sermons in what Lord Runcie believes was the best book he wrote,[13] *The Faith To-Day*, Andrew and James were chosen as two of the dedicatees. (It was in the same year, his last at Great St Mary's, that Mervyn published *Cambridge Sermons*, and edited *Religion and the Scientists*, another direct outcome of his Cambridge ministry.) It was small wonder that the church became packed out when Mervyn was able to induce people like Fred Hoyle, at that time a Fellow of St John's College, Cambridge, the Mistress of Girton, the Professor of Biochemistry and the Cavendish Professor of Experimental Physics to lecture, as they did in the Lent Term of 1957. Mervyn saw it as a major part of his task to influence, through the services at Great St Mary's, a generation of undergraduates destined to become future leaders. He was fortunate to be operating in a university town at a time when college chapels were pretty full anyway. Hugh Montefiore thinks the influence of the war was still at work. 'People bereft of their usual props often find God', he says, and certainly active service had resulted in a good many members of an earlier generation seeking ordination, perhaps the most notable being Robert Runcie, who won a Military Cross and became Archbishop of Canterbury. The future Bishop of Lincoln, Simon Phipps, serving as Eric James's fellow chaplain at Trinity, had also won a Military Cross.

When Mervyn arrived in Cambridge, Clare College had on its staff, in addition to John Robinson, the most heavily decorated priest in the Church of England, although he denies the war had any particular influence on his decision to be ordained (he trained originally to be a chartered accountant) – the chaplain Bill Skelton. Flying with fellow heroes like the man who wanted to marry Princess Margaret, Group Captain Peter Townsend, Skelton had been awarded the DSO and bar and the DFC and bar. He was one of the clergy Mervyn was to sweep off with him to Southwark when he became bishop, and it is amusing to note that when he and Mervyn met up in Cambridge, Bill had no recollection of ever having seen him before, whereas Mervyn said he remembered Bill perfectly as a boy at Blundell's during his first year there as Missioner. The reason Mervyn was so acutely aware of the youthful Bill may just possibly have been because his uncle was chairman of the School Governors – and also Duke of Somerset.

It was at Cambridge, though his friendship with Simon Phipps and Fr Harry Williams, a Fellow of Trinity, that Mervyn met Lady Elizabeth Cavendish, daughter of the tenth Duke of Devonshire and a lady-in-waiting to Princess Margaret. But however hotly he may have been in pursuit of dukes and their daughters, Mervyn was never less than an inspired and inspiring cleric. Within a year he had recruited 40 servers and an astonishing 120 readers. John Collins, at one time general secretary of the Christian Socialist Movement, wrote after Mervyn's death that he was 'quite simply the most electrifying preacher I have ever heard',[14] a sentiment echoed by Andrew Henderson. He has said 'We were all electrified by Mervyn's driving purpose and trenchant eloquence, not to mention his presentational panache. But he was much more than a successful impresario. He enabled many of us to illuminate and to integrate our most traditional understandings of religious faith with contemporary interpretations that have lasted a lifetime. The politics were important but it was the magnetism that seemed to flow from a luminous core of faith that made him someone to follow. Repeatedly he came back to the Christian call to replace self with God at the centre of our lives. To know Mervyn was to witness his moving and often hilarious struggle to practise what he preached.'[15] Henderson, whose father was consecrated Bishop of Tewkesbury and in 1960 was preferred to Bath and Wells, himself went on to be ordained, and was one of the concelebrants at Mervyn's Requiem Mass. He owed Mervyn a particular debt of gratitude. His father was quite unable to accept that Andrew was homosexual and wished to live with another man, and it was

Mervyn who interceded with Bishop Henderson on Andrew's behalf. After Bishop Henderson's death, Andrew's mother told him Mervyn had said 'Do you honestly want Andrew to be alone and lonely, like me?'

John Collins has recalled that Mervyn filled Great St Mary's 'to overflowing – the side aisles and the galleries were packed each Sunday with undergraduates and townspeople who came to hear Christianity made more relevant (and often, therefore, more disturbing) than ever before . . . Most of his congregation came from conventional Christian backgrounds but Mervyn Stockwood gave us a whole new way of looking at our faith – taking for example the Lord's Prayer and asking what we meant by "thy Kingdom come, thy will be done, on earth as it is in heaven". From there it was but a short step to the issues of the day – Suez, *Look Back in Anger*, Harold Macmillan's "You've never had it so good".'[16] John Collins added in a letter 'I shall always be grateful to Mervyn for showing me the Christian road to socialism'.[17]

As with every aspect of Mervyn's life and personality, contradictary opinions about his preaching flourish. One of his godsons, Michael Miller, has written 'I am intrigued that my son, now an undergraduate, has read [Mervyn's] Cambridge sermons some forty years after they were written and finds them as fresh and relevant as they clearly were at the time (even if the wording is somewhat archaic)'.[18] Lord Soper, on the other hand, has frankly expressed contempt for Mervyn's efforts in the pulpit, just as he has expressed deep suspicion about his sexual orientation because he sported a bow tie.[19] Ronnie Smartt, a member of the University Labour Club, recalls that 'MS's usual dress when he was walking about Cambridge included a splendid large bow tie, giving him a kind of stage incognito'. Mr Smartt recalls also that the congregation 'were told quite firmly that sixpence on the plate was not enough, and I parted with a precious half-crown; the price of two bottles of Guinness'.[20] Murray Irvine, chaplain at Sidney Sussex College and later Provost of Southwell, writes:

I don't think I was alone in being apprehensive when I heard that Mervyn had been appointed to Great St Mary's. I had heard him preach once or twice and not liked it much. He was too egocentric in the pulpit for me.

I think I felt that there was not room for another lively church in Cambridge if our chapels were not to collapse. I was of course wrong.

It was a *brilliant* appointment. Mervyn was extremely tactful from the first in his relations with the college chaplains. He went out of his way to make friends with us and soon won our respect and affection.[21]

Having made that handsome admission after his poor initial impression of Mervyn, the Provost Emeritus went on to explain an important part of Mervyn's delicate but tactfully handled ministry in Cambridge.

To attend one's college chapel in one of the smaller and more intimate colleges showed a kind of commitment that many undergraduates were not ready for. It was possible to enquire about Christian faith more anonymously at Great St Mary's and this suited many. For example, I don't remember David Owen, at that time a charming young medical student, ever appearing in his college chapel, but he became a keen Christian and a socialist under Mervyn's influence.[22]

Mervyn was given to wearing very unclerical suits and startling ties in those days. One Monday I met him in the market place wearing a dark suit and dog collar, and (I think) a respectable hat.

'Mervyn,' I said, 'what has happened?'

'Happened?' he said.

'Why are you dressed like that?'

'Oh,' he said, 'I have to work on Mondays in this place. I have done sick communions, I have had a confirmation class, I have said prayers with the City Council – so I said to God, "If you treat me like that, I'll wear one of your collars!"'

Mervyn still occasionally wore a bow tie after his consecration, and firmly refused to wear gaiters (for one thing, they were extremely expensive). But so that he could dress correctly on formal occasions he did purchase apron, stockings and knee breeches. Thus attired, he was accosted at a Buckingham Palace garden party by the greatest clerical wit of his day, Henry Montgomery-Campbell, since 1956 Bishop of London. 'Incognito, I see, Mervyn', said the bishop.

Despite being discovered by Provost Irvine agonizing over how to sack an incompetent gardener at the church, Mervyn told him at the end of his life 'the Cambridge years were the happiest years of his ministry'.[23] When Murray Irvine retired as Provost of Southwell Mervyn discovered his new address in Devon and 'wrote me a charming letter. He wrote again when he heard of my wife's death shortly afterwards and pressed me to go and pay him a visit. I went to Bath and had forty-eight hours of almost non-stop reminiscence about Cambridge in the fifties and our many mutual friends. He only stopped talking to drop peas we were about to eat on the floor and scoop them up again.'

Although his parish was sparsely populated (there were less than 20 permanent residents, Mervyn told the college deans and chaplains in a talk on 27 April 1956), Mervyn claims in his autobiography that he made three pastoral visits to parishioners every day, and Hugh Montefiore says 'He was a great vicar of St Mary's. I was deeply impressed by the way he would visit humble people in the town when they were in trouble. He never spared himself.'[24] Montefiore was also 'deeply impressed' on his returning home one day to discover Mervyn involved in a spitting competition with his youngest daughter. But things do not seem always to have been so harmonious at Great St Mervyn's, as the undergraduates came to re-christen the University Church. Mervyn had appointed a one-armed organist, Dr Douglas Fox, a very remarkable man he had previously known in Clifton, who had lost his right arm in the First World War. Mervyn could be said to have enjoyed a lively tune, but Fox was a serious musician, not the sort of man who could tolerate the vicar shouting 'Right, last verse' when he had become bored with a particular hymn. Tony Crowe, the Clifton schoolboy who had kept an adolescent diary while attending St Matthew, Moorfields, now caught up with Mervyn again, having entered Westcott House to train for the ministry, and he remembers many a blazing row in the organ loft. Things were more creative in the nave, however. Mervyn had always encouraged lay participation in worship at St Matthew, and at Great St Mary's he allowed a woman – Pamela Hill – to read the Epistle at the Eucharist for the first time in the church's history. By the end of his first term he had started an Advent Carol Service, and certainly no one in the congregation thought it second best to the famous service of nine lessons and carols held every year at King's.

In 1956 Mervyn was elected as a Labour member of the Romsey Ward of Cambridge City Council. For the benefit of those who doubted his whole-hearted allegiance to the sons of toil he was perfectly capable of making fun of himself. At a Labour Party conference he once preached on the text: 'The heart of a wise man inclines to the right. The heart of a fool to the left.' 1956 was the year that his real breakthrough in Cambridge came – was handed to him on a plate, really, with Anthony Eden's invasion of Egypt. Ronnie Smartt remembers a march and rally, which was 'subject to some quite nasty assaults from right-wingers, mainly from the University's Pitt Club class, whom I found quite vicious and frightening. MS kept on making the sign of the cross as if to exorcise the proceedings from the platform: it cannot have been a pleasant experience.'[25] It must have been fairly obvious where Mervyn's sentiments lay with regard to the invasion, but in preaching on Suez, as he did at Matins on 4 November 1956, he took as his text the words of John: 'If we say that we have no sin we deceive ourselves . . .', and in a carefully reasoned address, taking his tone from the measured utterances of the Archbishop of Canterbury, Dr Fisher, he presented both sides of the argument, including the Government's case, making a clear distinction between the Church's duty not to identify with party politics (although he said the individual was free to do so) and its obligation to criticize particular aspects of Government or Opposition policy if it believed they were contrary to Christian principles.

Mervyn's charity was never better displayed than in his sermon on Suez. He said: 'Anybody who listened to the Prime Minister last night must, I should have thought, have realised that they were listening to a man who honestly believed he was acting in the best interests of his country. A man does not easily court unpopularity, risk political suicide, divide the nation as it has not been divided for years, estrange our allies and hurt our friends unless he is absolutely convinced in his conscience that he must do what he is doing, and that ultimately the world will believe that he is right.'

Only a matter of weeks before the parish was caught up in the great Suez debate Robin Howard arrived as curate; he was to remain until Mervyn left, and saw Great St Mary's through the interregnum. He had trained at Westcott House, and it was the Principal since 1947, Kenneth Carey, appointed Bishop of Edinburgh in 1961, who suggested him. In a letter to Howard dated 3 March 1956, Carey wrote,

I think on the 'pro' side that it would be a most fascinating job. Mervyn is doing a tremendous lot to make the University Church what it ought to be. He has got literally hundreds of undergraduates interested in various courses that he has been running there, and he has also worked it up remarkably as a Parish Church. It is really in this latter connection that he so badly needs help . . .

Mervyn is a most unusual and altogether intriguing person. He is on fire with the Kingdom of God, and he does not mind how unusual his methods may be in commending the Faith to other people. In churchmanship he is what I suppose used to be called 'a liberal catholic'; but you will find he is very strict indeed about saying the offices and having a daily Celebration, and all that sort of thing. It is in fact inside a 'catholic' framework that he feels free to be unorthodox.

But 'on the "con" side', Carey went on to warn Robin Howard,

it is no use blinking the fact that he is not everyone's 'cup of tea'. But personally I like him enormously, and the more I see of him the more I realize what a tremendous pastoral concern he has for other people. But no one could hold the views that he holds, and hold them so strongly, without occasionally coming up against other people and sometimes being most unfairly criticized. One of the remarkable things about him, however, is the way in which he can differ hopelessly with someone and yet retain the other person's respect and affection.

By 20 March Mervyn was writing to Howard to say he was so glad he wanted to come to Great St Mary's (he had been serving his first curacy in Sunderland), but mentioned 'a number of financial hurdles' that had to be overcome. But there was no need to worry, he said, 'because if I cannot get the money from the church I will write round to various friends to guarantee your salary'. Joining St Mary's was evidently something of an act of faith. Six days later Mervyn was writing to Howard to say he could not make any promises about his stipend 'because St Mary's is more or less bank-rupt, but I shall hope to get you up to the £400 when you start here'. As the accommodation eventually found for Robin Howard with two spinster ladies in Russell Street was going to cost £4 a week, that would leave the curate with £4 a week to cover every other necessity.

In his letter of 20 March, Mervyn had written,

As I told you, my method is to leave my curates to pursue their own course, providing I am satisfied they are working hard, and not wasting time. I don't know what your gifts are in the context of Cambridge – you must find that out for yourself and go where the spirit leads you.

I think I stressed the importance of preaching. Great St Mary's is more of a preaching shop than I really like, but it cannot be helped. I try to

take infinite pains over my own sermons and we usually have courses
which I work out six months or a year ahead. I expect my curates to
send me their sermons in full at least a week before they are scheduled
to preach.

As you probably realise, all vicars have their idiosyncrasies, and it is
wise for curates to be tolerant and put up with them! My idiosyncrasy is
that I expect all church services to go with the precision of the BBC
time-table. The one sin I find quite unforgivable is for a parson to be late
in the morning. Anything else I can forgive, but not that. An electric
clock is kept in the vestry and I expect the clock to determine the priests'
movements in the morning!

Mervyn's conduct during the two years Robin Howard worked
for him was to stretch Howard's tolerance to the limit. Indeed,
looking back over that often stressful time, Canon Howard
wonders how he ever survived, and without the support of a new
young wife he probably would not have done so. 'I am bound
to say your hint at possible matrimony fills me with alarm and
dismay!!' Mervyn informed Howard on 27 March. But he hastened
to add

My fears are merely practical and domestic, they have nothing whatever
to do with principles! In fact, I much prefer my assistant clergy to be
married, because I find that they work harder, and they are only too
anxious to get out into the parish away from their homes!! Whereas if
they are unmarried they are invariably looking around for a partner, and
waste a lot of time as a result, either upon what I would consider
unnecessary calling, or writing unnecessary letters.

In fact, Canon Howard recalls that his engagement 'caused great
consternation. Mervyn couldn't cope with the marriage at all,
he was so embarrassed about the whole thing. Mary and I were
married at Great St Mary's, and beforehand Mervyn gave us a most
embarrassing marriage interview. He had no idea what to say.'[26]
Robin Howard had evidently expressed alarm on receiving
Mervyn's letter of 20 March, for on 27 March, under 'Paragraph No
2', Mervyn wrote:

Sermons: I fully appreciate what you say, but for the time being I shall
be happier if I can see your sermons in advance . . . I think it may help if,
when you have written a sermon, during the previous week you take it

into church with you when you say your prayers, turn it over in your mind, and make it a subject of prayer. That is what I try to do, and it is usually helpful. And when the time comes, I feel I am preaching a sermon and not delivering an essay.

3. I appreciate what you say about the difficulties of getting up in the morning . . . in most jobs, men who clock in late lose part of their pay. I often think that would be an admirable practice to introduce into the Church, especially if the perques were distributed to the clergy who were punctual!

Since arriving in Cambridge, Mervyn's attitude towards choir-boys seems to have mellowed. On 17 August he told Robin Howard that on 8 September they would be taking the choirboys 'to the sea by car, and it would be a good opportunity for you to get to know them. The choirboys are an important part of our set-up, because, as we have no young people in the parish, they are the only youngsters we get for Confirmation and I look to them for our future servers.' On 10 September the parish was due to hold a party at Westcott House to welcome their new curate, and Mervyn went on to tell him 'Especially I want you to keep a look-out for people who ought to be coming forward for Confirmation. Confirmation classes begin in October, so we should be rounding up people in September.' He explained also there were 'lots of people who live in Cambridge who come to Evensong, but I haven't a clue as to their identity. It means that after the service we have to try to establish contact with them as they leave the church – but that's not easy; I hope you're good at that sort of thing.'

Mervyn had regretted being unable to accommodate Robin at the vicarage, and explained on 27 August, 'as we have no help I have nearly all my meals at the milk bar in town', which does not say a lot for the culinary skills of his mother – always taken out by Mervyn, according to Canon Howard, on Ascension Day, for some reason. It was in this letter that Mervyn told Howard he did not encourage the use of Christian names. His churchwarden always called him 'Sir', 'and it's a bit difficult if a youngster comes into the vestry and addresses me by my Christian name. It's quite impossible to prevent that kind of thing, but I try to minimise it as much as I can. If only both sides would call me "vicar" the problem would be solved.' The problem might have been solved even more neatly, and appropriately, if at a church where all the trappings of catholic worship were observed the clergy had been

addressed as Father. But even in Moorfields Mervyn was universally called Mr Stockwood – probably the only Anglican parish
priest who wore a biretta and said Benediction ever to be so styled.
Even on a return visit when he was a bishop the congregation
welcomed him as 'Mister' Stockwood!

Once Robin Howard was installed in the parish, Mervyn
displayed one of the most disturbing aspects of his personality, his
inability to confront certain issues on a personal basis. Day after
day Robin would find memoranda 'To Mr Howard; From the Vicar'
awaiting him in the vestry. There were minute instructions about
celebrating Holy Communion. There were further instructions
about when to arrive in church, and eight pages of pep-talk about
lay involvement, ceremonial and what the servers were to do. As
for the subject of preaching, that was sometimes deemed worthy of
a dated and signed letter. On 14 September 1956 Mervyn told
Howard, 'I may have given you a wrong impression yesterday
about preaching at Matins. I do *not* expect "Third Programme"
sermons, ultra-intellectual and academic . . .' A four-page undated
memorandum offered helpful advice on preaching to public
schoolboys, eleven itemized tips in all. Howard was strongly
advised to avoid references to 'sport, motor-cars, esprit de corps,
the Empire, Purity (or its alternative name "Temptation") and
slang', and if ever he preached in his own school chapel, to avoid
any reference to his own time at school.

'This sermon is alright [sic] as far as it goes', he was informed one
morning, 'but for a sermon being preached between 2–3pm on
Good Friday there seems to me to be too little emphasis on Christ's
atoning work . . .' 'I think there will be people in the congregation,
particularly older professional people, who will think you are
unrealistic . . .' 'You must *press home* the argument . . .' 'This has
the makings of an interesting and helpful sermon, and it will be
worth your while to develop it.' And so on, and so on, and so on.
Paragraph 9 of one criticism informed Robin Howard that his
sermon 'peters out in an indecisive way'. Pages and pages of
another of Mervyn's screeds began hopefully enough: 'I think the
general scheme will do very well.' Why did he not just stop him
in the street and tell him so? (He would have been unable to do so
on the telephone as his curate was not connected!) 'This has the
makings of an interesting and helpful sermon' was how Mervyn
opened one of his notes, and no doubt he thought he was being
kind and helpful. As far as Canon Howard was concerned, he

says 'To work for, Mervyn was hell. After six weeks I very nearly left.'[27]

'I hope you will not think me super-critical, but I was distressed at the appearance of the server this morning', Mervyn told Robin Howard on 6 June 1957. Then appeared a memorandum 'To Mr Howard; From the Vicar' on the subject of the Vestry Prayer, this time written in red ink. 'The matter of choirboys' discipline is a difficult one', Mervyn noted in a memo marked Private. Even the matter of the curate's day off was one Mervyn apparently could not bring himself to discuss face to face but had to consign to a typed memo. 'Of course I accept your apology for lateness this morning', Mervyn told a penitent Robin on 18 December 1956. But it took him eight pages of a handwritten letter to do so. Six pages were devoted three days before Christmas to telling Robin that Mervyn was glad he felt it right to remain at Great St Mary's. It does seem that Robin's ability to appear in church on time left something to be desired. On 31 January 1957 Mervyn wrote to say 'Thank you for your letter. I shall celebrate this morning, after that the incident is closed', but it took Mervyn three pages to close it. On 17 February it required a two-page letter to tell Robin that Mervyn could not 'help feeling that there are times when you take the Communion Service a little too quickly'.

'I'm afraid my curates must often feel that their vicar is the sort of hard man who boils his potatoes in a widow's tears!' Mervyn wrote to Robin Howard on 18 December 1958. 'However, I always hope they realise that behind the apparently hard exterior is a loving heart that only wants them to reach the heights.' This letter was signed 'Yours affectionately'. And clearly, despite the endless nagging and attention to detail, that affection was returned. Howard's wife nursed Mervyn when he had influenza, and both she and Robin noted the extreme austerity of Mervyn's private life, the lack of heating or any proper bed linen. It is interesting that even after Mervyn's death, both Robin and Mary Howard were wondering why he never married. They had no idea that he was homosexual.

Towards the end of 1957 Mervyn had been presented with the subject for a sermon quite as controversial as Suez – the Wolfenden Report on Prostitution and Homosexuality. On 3 November that year, at the 8.30 p.m. service, he duly delivered himself, concentrating almost entirely on the report's recommendations for legalizing homosexual conduct in private between two consenting men over 21. (Legislation to this effect was eventually enacted after a decade of heated debate.) Reasoned discussion, at any rate in public, on the subject of homosexuality was rare at the time, both in secular and ecclesiastical circles, and Mervyn certainly came down on the side of common sense, not to mention theological liberalism, when he said 'To assume that homosexuality is a deliberate perversion, and that by an act of will a homosexual can change himself into a heterosexual is to ignore the evidence. Hence both the law and the Church should deal with man's nature as it is and not as they think it ought to be.' This was a far cry from the stunted opinions of the man due in 18 months' time to consecrate him to the episcopate, Geoffrey Fisher, who had thundered that homosexual indulgence was a shameful vice and a grievous sin from which deliverance was to be sought by every means – but whether he meant by means of sexual repression aided by cold showers or by aversion therapy was never clear. Mervyn also quite bravely jettisoned the concept of 'natural' and 'unnatural', saying 'What is "natural" for one man is not necessarily "natural" for another'.

It has to be borne in mind that at a time when every single homosexual act between men was punishable by imprisonment, few practising homosexuals in a stable and happy relationship sought publicity for their life-style, and Mervyn's experience of 'happy homosexuals' was naturally limited, although by this time he would have known that Dick Chapman had fallen in love at Oxford with an American undergraduate, with whom, as it happens, he was to live for the rest of their lives. The only sort of homosexual Mervyn was likely to have met in the course of his pastoral work was one in some sort of legal trouble or spiritual or emotional turmoil. Hence his implication that all homosexuality tended to be promiscuous, with unhappy consequences. 'From the cases that have come my way', he told his predominantly student congregation, many of whom were no doubt still uncertain of their own sexual orientation, 'licence seems to lead to more unhappiness than does restraint. In a marriage, home, family economics and children help to keep the partners together, even when the infatuation was passed.' We now know, of course, that this is often not the case; at least 50 per cent of marriages fail. 'Those factors', Mervyn continued, 'are absent from a homosexual relationship. Partners rarely keep together. They pass from one infatuation to another in rapid succession, and the results are exhausted nervous systems, disillusionment and a smudging of sensitivity.'

In addition to knowing nothing of stable homosexual relationships, of which thousands of instances abound, Mervyn was of
course labouring on this subject under the disadvantage of himself
being homosexual without being able to say so. And in any case,
many of his personal reactions to being homosexual would have
been conditioned by the prevailing social climate of the day. It is
inconceivable that he ever 'came out' to his family, and few fellow
clergy could have been relied upon not to gossip had he chosen to
confide in them. The concept of a bachelor priest or schoolmaster
still retained respectability, so it was fairly easy for a homosexual
priest, of whom there were as many then as there are today, to
shelter behind the garb of celibacy, whether he was celibate or not.
Mervyn surely had his own case in the forefront of his mind when
he issued the following advice: 'Because of the prevailing state
of public opinion, which affects all of us, a great many practising
homosexuals cannot escape from a deep sense of guilt. No matter
how unreasonable that sense of guilt may be, a man should
think twice before he burdens his conscience with it.' He ended by
advocating platonic love. 'Whatever your views may or may not be
on the practice of homosexuality, do not be afraid of the friendships
that come naturally to you.' And he cited the classic and rather
over-worked examples of David and Jonathan, Jesus and John.
'Happy is the man', he said, recalling, perhaps, his passion back in
Bristol for Dick Chapman and David Tankard, 'who has experienced a friendship of such a sort. So far from being sordid and
beastly, it can be one of the most ennobling and gracious factors
in his life.' It was only a pity that he felt it necessary to suggest
that the converse, a consummated love affair, had necessarily to be
'sordid and beastly', and these are the sentiments, surely, of a man
who, if only subconsciously, finds his own sexuality a cause of
considerable distress.

Mervyn's membership of Cambridge City Council, on which
Labour was in a minority, never measured up to the opportunities
provided in Bristol. It was rather a frustrating business, and he felt
unable to muster much respect for his Tory opponents who 'tended
to be small businessmen who could not make up their minds
whether the major evil was socialism or the university. They
disliked both.' He found it far more congenial to make trips to
London, where he and Tom Driberg, Donald Soper, Canon John
Collins, Stanley Evans, later to become Principal of the Southwark
Ordination Course, and other disciples of Christian socialism met

from time to time in a private room at a pub called The Lamb, in Bloomsbury. Here they thrashed out their differences over such issues as pacifism (Mervyn was not himself a pacifist). Minutes were taken by Driberg, and the result was a pamphlet, entitled *Papers From The Lamb*,[28] published, appropriately enough, on May Day 1959, which happened also to coincide with the day of Mervyn's consecration. His was one of 23 names appended to the pamphlet, which dealt with Common Ownership, Human and Racial Equality, International Peace, Unity Among Christians and Christians and the Soviet Union. The outcome was the creation in 1960 of the Christian Socialist Movement.

Mervyn's relations with Tom Driberg never seem to have been particularly close (Driberg declined to join the Common Wealth Party, for instance, and Mervyn may well have felt nervous about Driberg's flagrant and dangerous pursuit of young working-class men), and relations were drawn no closer in the last year of Driberg's life when Mervyn expressed serious reservations about Driberg's proposal to publish an autobiography, aptly entitled *Ruling Passions*.[29] This was in 1975, shortly after Driberg had been made a life peer (he took the title Lord Bradwell), and shortly also, as it happened, before his death. That part of the manuscript already completed and shown to Mervyn detailed Driberg's indiscreet and promiscuous life, but elicited from Mervyn a generous if cautious response. 'I enjoyed not only the book', he wrote to Driberg on 19 March, 'but it's [sic] style, and, above all, it's [sic] use of words . . . It is a joy to rediscover the loveliness of English.' But Mervyn went so far as to say he doubted whether it would be possible for Driberg 'to remain happily in the country if the manuscript was published in its present form'. He thought 'the general reaction would lead to ostracism. And there would be much hurt all round.'

Mervyn's advice was both objective and well meant, but Driberg was by this time under threat of a second heart attack, and seems to have misinterpreted Mervyn's words of caution. 'Do *you* think people would abandon me?' he apparently asked Christopher Hitchens. 'A furious Hitchens shopped the bishop to *Private Eye*.'[30] Mervyn could have been in no doubt about Driberg's reckless nature even before he read *Ruling Passions*. On his seventieth birthday Driberg was given a 'hard-core gay porn magazine'. It had been left under his pillow, along with a magnifying glass. When telephoning to thank his thoughtful benefactress Driberg told her he had passed on the magazine to a bishop of his acquaintance.[31]

Driberg's biographer, Francis Wheen, has confirmed that the bishop in question was Mervyn Stockwood.[32] On 19 August 1976 Mervyn preached at Driberg's somewhat chaotically organized funeral, held at St Matthew's, Westminster, describing him as 'a gadfly, a searcher for truth' who 'liked to sting, to annoy, especially the pompous'. He was, said Mervyn, a nonconformist, but 'of his loyalty to the socialist cause there was no question'. When *Ruling Passions* was published posthumously the following year Mervyn did not hesitate to review it for *Books and Bookmen*. 'This book is a feast of good things for those with long memories', he wrote. 'His activities in the days of appeasement, his career as a journalist – as gossip writer and war correspondent – his dealings with the high and mighty and the down and out constitute a splendid kaleidoscope. And what is more he describes events with a verbal delicacy which in these jargon-shrouded days is all too rare.'

There was an amusing postscript to Mervyn's friendship with Tom Driberg. When he was researching Driberg's life, Francis Wheen went to Bath to interview Mervyn, who said 'I would never have preached at his funeral if I'd known then what I know now, that he betrayed his country and sent people to their deaths'. Asked by Wheen 'What people? What deaths?' Mervyn slipped into his cloak and dagger persona. '"You mustn't press me," he growled mysteriously.'[33]

It is an extraordinary fact that Mervyn's ministry in Cambridge lasted a mere four years. He established Great St Mary's as perhaps the most famous ecclesiastical forum of its time, and established it so firmly that after his departure enormous care was taken to appoint incumbents of equally outstanding talent in order that the tradition Mervyn had established might be maintained – and yet within only three and a half years moves were afoot to have him join the bench of bishops.[34] Even more extraordinary, looking back with hindsight, is the fact that the foremost advocate of Mervyn's consecration was Geoffrey Fisher, a Freemason with a reputation (a good deal of it, as we can now see, undeserved) as an authoritarian schoolmaster, and that the final decision as to whether Mervyn's name should be sent to the Queen was taken by a Conservative prime minister. But when in 1958 the incumbent Bishop of Southwark, Bertram Simpson, a little known bishop who had presided since 1941 over a little known diocese, decided to retire, Fisher strode into action, suggesting in April 1958 to Sir David Stephens, the Prime Minister's appointments secretary, that Mervyn was 'really the best person'. And it certainly seems as if Fisher never envisaged Mervyn, who was still not quite 45, remaining in one diocese for the rest of his career. If he makes mistakes, the pragmatic Fisher told Sir David, Southwark would be 'a very good place for him to make them in, while he will really bring great strength and vigour'.[35] A short-list of candidates for the vacant see was prepared, six names eventually going forward for Harold Macmillan's consideration, but there was no doubt which candidate was Fisher's preferred choice. He assured Macmillan, who took a keen personal interest in church appointments during his six and a half years as Prime Minister, liked springing surprises and had a soft spot for well-bred socialists, that Mervyn was a man 'of undoubted strength of personality, strength of conviction and proved powers of leadership'. And he thought it sensible not to pretend that Macmillan would have been unaware of Mervyn's political sympathies, explaining that he was not required to say that Mervyn had never said anything unwise. 'What I *can* say', the Primate told the Prime Minister, 'is that he has never been a propagandist for any political or ecclesiastical view, but merely a propagandist for religious realism.' He added 'I hope that I have shown that any supposed tinge of political partisanship can be completely ignored'. He stamped his seal of approval (it was he, after all, who would be going to consecrate Macmillan's ultimate nominee) with the assurance that Mervyn Stockwood's was the name that 'could be recommended with the most conviction'.

From Macmillan's point of view, the fact remained that if in due course Mervyn acquired, by seniority of consecration or by translation to Canterbury, York, London, Durham or Winchester, a seat in the House of Lords (he did so quite quickly, as it turned out, in 1963) he could very easily vote against the government, so by nominating to the Crown a known socialist Macmillan was taking a minor political gamble.[36] At the end of the day, however, Macmillan believed the Church, in the persons of the Archbishops of Canterbury and York, had an almost overriding right to nominate the successors to the Apostles, and in consequence he wrote, in November 1958, inviting Mervyn to accept the bishopric of Southwark. Mervyn was obviously so bored with the details of his elevation when he came to write his autobiography that he misdated the year of Macmillan's letter 1959!

It is usually cynically assumed that when someone is asked to be a bishop he retires to pray while his wife goes upstairs to pack.

Mervyn of course had no wife, and he put the customary process of consultation among friends on an absurdly formal footing, summoning John Robinson, Kenneth Carey and Eric James to a meeting in Hugh Montefiore's rooms at Caius. Someone else Mervyn tried to entice to the meeting was Michael Ramsey, who in 1956, on the long-delayed resignation of Cyril Garbett, had been swiftly translated to York. He happened to be in Cambridge at the time, but the attendance of so august a person would hardly have been appropriate, and Ramsey stayed away. But it seems on the face of it that Mervyn nevertheless managed to ask Ramsey's opinion privately as to whether he should agree to his name being sent to Buckingham Palace, although he ought to have realized that by this time Fisher, as a matter of courtesy, would have been in communication with Ramsey about the appointment, and conversely, that at such a late stage the Archbishop of the Northern Province would hardly be likely to advise against acceptance. Apparently Ramsey contented himself by merely telling Mervyn 'If you decide to become a bishop I shall be glad to welcome to the bench a man who, when all of us, like sheep, are saying "Yes, yes, yes" will have the courage to say, "No, no, no, no no"'. This is, however, as far as one can judge, an unattributed verbal quotation, recorded in *Chanctonbury Ring*. We only have Mervyn's word for it that these are Ramsey's words, they hardly amount to advice, and to quote them contains an element of boasting. It may be that Mervyn invented them in order, retrospectively, to appear well with Ramsey, whose good opinion he constantly sought but did not always gain.

Both Eric James and Hugh Montefiore believe that by the time of the meeting at Caius, Mervyn had already made up his mind to accept, and that what he really wanted was confirmation that he had made the right decision. A not inconsiderable inducement even for a reluctant parson to accept a diocese was that his stipend would jump from £400 or £500 a year to £1,250, soon to be substantially increased. Mervyn had not been at Great St Mary's long, yet he had probably achieved as much there as he ever would. He was now 45, a suitable age to take on a diocese, and another might not be offered after the age of 50. What little he knew at first hand of Southwark would have indicated that here lay another challenge; he was not being asked to minister to the tranquil farms of Hereford or Gloucestershire. By the time he was due to preach at Matins on 30 November he seems to have been pretty clear about what did lie ahead: 'Hundreds and hundreds of drab streets housing a working class to whom the Church of England means next to nothing, to whom a bishop is as relevant as an Ethiopian ambassador, to whom our liturgy and our gospel are meaningless mumbo-jumbo.' (The 'Ethiopian ambassador' enjoyed a prominent role in Mervyn's lexicon. Indeed, Mervyn made constant reference to His Excellency, without necessarily ever having met him. 'So-and-so', he would say, 'knows rather less about that subject than the Ethiopian ambassador', a remark which not infrequently led people to imagine that the ambassador and Mervyn were accustomed to meet at least once a week.)

As long ago as 1943 Mervyn had been in correspondence with William Temple on the subject of worker-priests, and plans that had been formulating in his mind on this subject were ones he could never hope to implement without using his own episcopal initiative. Not very many people decline the offer of a bishopric, although a good many accept reluctantly, and all we know of Mervyn's character and subsequent prelatical conduct would lead one to imagine it took him only a short time to agree to don the purple. There is no harm in ambition if it means having a pretty good knowledge of your abilities and wishing to gain an opportunity to exercise them. A born showman like Mervyn will naturally yearn for the largest platform available, and the opportunities at the time for a bishop to make a splash, to influence events and to play a creative role in the life of both the Church and the nation remained considerable. Whatever it was that Mervyn had against the Ethiopian ambassador, it was not true in 1958 to say that bishops were irrelevant. They were listened to with respect, and if anything, given too much credence, not too little.

Mervyn seems, however, to have gone through the rigmarole of consulting Fisher at Lambeth Palace, who apparently said to him 'Now, Stockwood, sit down and tell me your reasons for not going to Southwark. There is no hurry. Take as long as you like. Then I'll tell you why you're wrong.' No snatch of conversation attributed to Fisher could have a greater ring of authenticity; anyone who ever met Fisher could hear him saying it. Eric James had no doubt that Mervyn should accept. 'I thought he was a brilliant administrator of a certain sort, and one of the shrewdest judges of human beings I had ever known. He could be wildly wrong, often because he was attached to people, and I never knew him to say he was wrong. Yet I thought he would make a brilliant bishop.'[37] Only Kenneth Carey advised Mervyn not to go to Southwark, and that was because he had looked up Mervyn's student records at Westcott House, noted constant references to ill-health, and told Mervyn that Southwark would kill him within a year. In the event, Mervyn easily outlived Carey. Once the offer had been accepted, Mervyn gathered up two or three of his favourite undergraduates and embarked on a quasi-pilgrimage, which took in Sandringham, the Shrine of Our Lady of Walsingham,[38] and a good dinner – a fairly typical Mervyn mix of the sacred and profane.

Notes

1 Tony Benn, *Against the Tide* (Hutchinson, 1989).
2 Bishop Montefiore in conversation with the author.
3 Bishop George Reindorp, quoted in *Church Illustrated*, May 1959.
4 Bishop John Bickersteth, in conversation with the author.
5 Rev. John Binns, letter to the author, 4 July 1995.
6 Canon Eric James, in conversation with the author.
7 Bishop Jeremy Walsh, preaching at a Requiem for MS at St Matthew, Moorfields on 25 February 1995.
8 Mervyn Stockwood, in *The Cambridge Review*, 12 May 1956.
9 Canon Francis Longworth-Dames, in conversation with the author.
10 Tam Dalyell, in conversation with the author.
11 Tam Dalyell is in reality Sir Thomas Dalyell of the Binns. But having in 1973 established his claim to the baronetcy, one of the earliest, and remaindered through the female line, he decided not to use it.
12 Mrs Mary Howard, speaking to the author.
13 Lord Runcie, preaching at MS's memorial service in Southwark Cathedral.
14 John Collins, in Belsize Park Parish Magazine, February 1995.
15 Rev. Andrew Henderson, in conversation with the author.
16 John Collins, as above.
17 John Collins, letter to the author, 3 March 1995.
18 Michael Miller, letter to the author, August 1995.
19 Lord Soper, in conversation with the author.
20 Ronnie Smartt, letter to the author, 21 March 1995.
21 Very Rev. Murray Irvine, letter to the author, 21 March 1995.
22 '[Mervyn Stockwood] certainly had a profound influence on my life': David Owen, writing in his autobiography *Time to Declare* (Michael

Joseph, 1991). Lord Owen turned to MS for advice over an emotional crisis shortly after MS had gone to Southwark, and quotes a letter from MS. 'It is at times like this we find our true bearing and find the worth of our convictions . . . I wish so much that I could help you but I know that in the affairs of the heart we have to settle our problems for ourselves. But you have my thoughts, my prayers and my love.'

23 Very Rev. Murray Irvine, as above.

24 Bishop Hugh Montefiore, in conversation with the author.

25 Ronnie Smartt, letter to the author, 21 March 1995.

26 Canon Robin Howard, in conversation with the author.

27 Ibid.

28 *Papers From The Lamb* (Malvern Press, 1959).

29 Tom Driberg, *Ruling Passions* (Jonathan Cape, 1977).

30 Francis Wheen, *Tom Driberg: His Life and Indiscretions* (Chatto and Windus, 1990).

31 Ibid.

32 Francis Wheen, in conversation with the author.

33 Wheen, *Tom Driberg*.

34 In 1959 MS was succeeded as incumbent by Joseph Fison, who became Bishop of Salisbury. He was succeeded in 1963 by Hugh Montefiore, eventually Bishop of Birmingham. His successor in 1970 was Stanley Booth-Clibborn, who became Bishop of Manchester. And in 1979 Michael Mayne was appointed; he became Dean of Westminster.

35 Fisher Papers at Lambeth Palace.

36 Including the five most senior bishops, who enter *ex officio*, 26 diocesan bishops of the Church of England have seats in the House of Lords.

37 Canon Eric James, in conversation with the author.

38 He was the first English diocesan bishop to preach at the restored Shrine at Walsingham (in 1965), and he became an Honorary Guardian, dedicating the Jubilee Cloister in 1972.

Chapter 7

'The house where I want to live'

In his autobiography, Mervyn Stockwood says he wrote to Archbishop Fisher to inform him of his acceptance of the see of Southwark, a letter presumably written as a matter of courtesy and in addition to one he would have sent to the Prime Minister from whom the request to propose his name to the Queen had come. Fisher hastened to assure him that both he and Michael Ramsey, Macmillan 'and many others' had earnestly desired this appointment and Mervyn could therefore conclude 'that to the utmost of your ability you are following a call of the Holy Spirit'. He told him he did not know what fortunes awaited him as a bishop (which was perhaps just as well; to say that Mervyn Stockwood's episcopate was to prove a controversial one would be putting it mildly), and added, not too grammatically, 'No doubt there will be plenty of things of which I shall want to give you advice, and on which, arising out of the experience and practice of the Church, you will want violently to think otherwise'.

However much of a soft spot Macmillan may have had for 'well-bred socialists', and however much Fisher himself may have courted controversy, it was a brave appointment. Realizing perhaps that Fisher inevitably only had a short time left to serve as his metropolitan, Mervyn lost no time in rewarding him for his favours by lambasting him for behaving at bishops' meetings as though he was still a headmaster addressing a group of sixth-formers (for 17 years, Fisher had been headmaster of Repton, where one of his pupils had been Michael Ramsey, now Archbishop of York). He hated, too, Fisher's adherence to Freemasonry, a subject on which Mervyn was quite unable to contain himself. Although Mervyn was shortly to cross swords with Michael Ramsey, 'the person he couldn't abide was Geoffrey Fisher', according to his first chaplain, Michael Mayne. 'Some of the angriest letters Mervyn ever wrote were to Fisher.'[1]

Two sisters who attended Great St Mary's, Gladys and Kathleen Cannons, set about making chasubles and a purple cope, as a gift to Mervyn from the congregation. The curates provided a mitre, as did the Bristol Methodists, and the undergraduates clubbed together to buy a crozier. Uncertain about all the episcopal garments he might need, and even about much of the ritual, such as administering ordination, that is peculiar to a bishop, Mervyn turned for advice to a former colleague on the Liturgical Commission, Arthur Couratin, formerly Principal of St Stephen's House, the catholic theological college in Oxford, and now vicar of an Anglo-Catholic church in Southwark, St Peter's, Streatham. Mervyn mentioned that he had difficulty reading the small print in the ordination and communion books in normal use, and Fr Couratin told him that one of his ordinands at St Stephen's House, now his curate at St Peter's, David Brecknell, had written service books for use at St Stephen's House; he would ask him to put his skills at calligraphy to use in producing an Ordinal for the new bishop. This was followed by a complete Communion Book, again painstakingly written out by David Brecknell, presented to Mervyn as a gift from St Peter's, a church close to Bishop's House where, on St Peter's Day, Mervyn would repair to sing Pontifical High Mass; here, too, he sometimes observed the Maundy custom of washing the feet of certain selected parishioners. Fr Brecknell had been ordained deacon by Bertram Simpson; on 24 May 1959, at Mervyn's first ordination, he was one of 15 candidates priested by Mervyn. Ten deacons were also ordained, and Fr Brecknell, now retired in the Chichester diocese, recollects that the service was 'very swift', Mervyn having managed to reduce proceedings to one hour and ten minutes. With his 'gratitude and appreciation', Mervyn bequeathed to David Bracknell 'all the Service Books Ordinals and Missals' it had taken Fr Bracknell an hour a page to produce.

It was on 8 March 1959, when he referred to 'a thrilling four years', that Mervyn preached his farewell sermon at Great St Mary's. He said he thought a debate held in the church during his incumbency, on the rights and wrongs of nuclear warfare, had been perhaps the best discussion he had ever heard in Cambridge. On leaving the city, the first thing he did was take himself off to Rome for Easter, where unexpectedly he found himself being granted a private audience with the Pope, John XXIII, apparently because the Pontiff knew of Mervyn's 'passionate concern for Christian unity', and because the Holy Father shared Mervyn's 'hopes and prayers'.[2] Pope John gave Mervyn a verbal message of greeting to Archbishop Fisher, which Mervyn wrote down on a scrap of paper and duly delivered to Lambeth Palace on his return to England to prepare himself for consecration.[3] This he did not by going into retreat, nor even, as Michael Ramsey had done, by reading Pope Gregory the Great's *Regula Pastoralis*, but by tagging along for a week behind Roger Mortimer, since 1949 the somewhat forbidding Bishop of Exeter. His choice of mentor may possibly be considered a little unfortunate; Dr Mortimer was nothing if not prelatical and far from averse to a tipple. In 1955 he had failed to be translated, because Fisher told Anthony Eden there was 'a real lack of something in him which would be still more evident in London'.[4] In order to pick up some tips on administration, Mervyn is also said to have consulted Marks & Spencer – and when, in 1978, he wrote *The Cross and the Sickle* he seriously considered as an alternative title *Marx and Sparks*.

Mervyn was going to require all the tact he could muster in his dealings with William Gilpin, an ardent train-spotter he had inherited as suffragan Bishop of Kingston upon Thames. The other Southwark suffragan, Robert Stanard, the Bishop of Woolwich, had been appointed Dean of Rochester, and during the interregnum Gilpin was in charge of the diocese. Mervyn asked to see him and was rebuffed, being told that he would be far too busy for the next three months to meet, even for a meal. Relentlessly, over the next seven years Mervyn invited the Bishop of Kingston to lunch; equally relentlessly, the Bishop of Kingston declined to accept Mervyn's hospitality. It is just possible that Gilpin, who was 57 in 1959, thought he should have been chosen to succeed Simpson as diocesan bishop, although it is extremely rare, if not in fact unheard of, for a bishop to become diocesan of a see in which he has served as a suffragan. At all events, until he retired in 1970, William Gilpin remained a thorn in Mervyn's side. Eric James says 'Mervyn's discipline is revealed in the way he played that relationship. He made a rule that he would never speak negatively about him outside Bishop's House, and he treated him publicly as if he was someone he trusted.'[5] What Mervyn trusted him with in particular was the education portfolio, a subject to which Mervyn attached enormous importance but which he realized would keep his uncooperative suffragan's hands full.

Even before his consecration, Mervyn had two important appointments to set in train. First of all he needed a domestic chaplain, so he wrote to Garth Moore, Chancellor of the Southwark Diocese, who also happened to be a don at Corpus Christi, Cambridge, to ask if he could suggest some names. Moore sent two or three, including that of an undergraduate he had known at Corpus, Michael Mayne, 30 years of age and assistant curate at St John the Baptist, Harpenden. Mayne had only been ordained two and a half years, and although it was fairly common practice at that time for a young priest to become chaplain to a bishop in order, in effect, to serve a second curacy, it must have seemed a bit like the blind leading the blind, with neither Mayne nor Mervyn having had any experience of episcopal life. In 1954 Mervyn had been a missioner at Corpus Christi while Michael Mayne was still an undergraduate, and although they could hardly be said to have met, Mayne at least had seen something of Mervyn Stockwood in action. Mervyn clearly took the appointment of his first chaplain seriously, driving him to Long Melford on the Norfolk coast, where they stayed a night in a hotel. Mayne accepted the job, the first and the longest serving of seven loyal and often long-suffering chaplains to do so.[6] Michael Mayne was just one of a truly astonishing string of men whose talents Mervyn spotted early on in their careers; in 1979 he became Vicar of Great St Mary's, Cambridge, and seven years later he was appointed Dean of Westminster.

In planning to place Southwark on the map Mervyn was assisted by the fact that there could not have been a greater contrast between himself and Bertram Simpson, a kindly widower who lived a simple life, and had no interest in ceremonial whatsoever. He always looked somewhat bemused if, in the cathedral, members of the congregation knelt for his blessing while he processed up the nave. Someone who spent almost all his ministry in the Southwark diocese, Douglas Rhymes, remembered that Simpson, 'a charming person and a very good bishop in his way', could 'get his mitre skew-whiff and sit any old how on his throne, showing his suspenders'.[7] The see itself, Canon Rhymes has recalled, was 'a perfectly ordinary, normal diocese'. It was not to remain so for long, partly because of the second urgent appointment waiting to be filled, the suffragan bishopric of Woolwich. Mervyn lost no time in offering it to John Robinson. In some ways it was the most momentous thing he ever did, for had Robinson still been a don at Clare when he wrote *Honest to God* it might well have sold a respectable 3,000 copies.

It was fairly tough on Fisher that within weeks of pushing,

successfully, for a potentially dangerous, at any rate unorthodox, appointment to Southwark, he should have been asked by that very same appointee to approve an adventurous theologian under 40 as his suffragan. The arrangement has always been that a diocesan bishop is at liberty to choose a suffragan without consulting anyone, and to send two names in order of preference direct to the Prime Minister. But the archbishop of the province could refuse to consecrate a candidate of whom he disapproved, and as a matter of courtesy and common sense a diocesan bishop almost invariably consults with his archbishop. If the sovereign approved an appointment and an archbishop refused to consecrate there would be a constitutional crisis. So from the start Mervyn went out of his way to explain to Fisher what he had in mind. He told him he wanted as Bishop of Woolwich someone who understood what he was trying to do (almost certainly a reference to his desire to set up as soon as possible a new form of training for the ministry), who had 'the intellectual competence and theological knowledge' to advise him, who was accustomed to the teaching of ordinands (as John Robinson had been at Wells), and who would, at the same time, 'diligently carry out the normal pastoral and routine duties of a suffragan bishop'. He had already had a look round Southwark, was appalled at the unchurched areas like Rotherhithe and Bermondsey, and felt less than overjoyed at the prospect of working with those 'essentially conventional Churchmen' already in important diocesan posts. Above all, he emphasized to Fisher that he must have somebody with whom he could talk. 'Being made as I am', he explained, 'I can always work best when I can put my mind against another man's mind.'

Mervyn must have been seriously alarmed in the third week of February 1959 when he received from Fisher a long, detailed and carefully worded letter asking him to think again 'before choosing your two names'. In essence, Fisher, who had consulted Michael Ramsey and Sir Henry Thirkill, the Master of Clare, thought it would be a mistake for Mervyn to import into the diocese another bishop with views so similar to his own, one, moreover, lacking in *gravitas*. Thirkill had told Fisher that although while at Clare John Robinson had grown, he was still immature, was not always tactful, indeed that occasionally he was 'unconsciously harsh and brusque'. Fisher was by no means blind to Robinson's 'courage and far-sightedness' but he was quite sure the time was not yet ripe for him to become a bishop.

To add to Mervyn's anxieties, Robinson was considering the offer of a chair in biblical studies at Manchester University. On 7 March Mervyn asked Fisher to talk to Robinson, and he outlined the pros and cons of appointing him to Woolwich, the most serious argument against the plan being a possible misuse of his abilities. 'Theologians like Robinson are much too thin on the ground as it is', Mervyn wrote. 'It would be a serious blow to the Church if he were removed from theological work.' On the other hand, what was wanted in the new Bishop of Woolwich was a man who, 'while capable of doing his routine duties in his stride, will have the mind and theological grip to tackle experimentally a situation which is probably the major problem that confronts the Church in Europe'. He meant the problem of the deprived inner-city area, to most of whose inhabitants the Church had long ceased to have any relevance at all.

Mervyn told Fisher he could think of no one else who had the particular qualifications for which he was looking. He said that the Prime Minister's Appointments Secretary 'and others' had put forward the name of Ernie Southcott, Vicar of Halton in Leeds, who had pioneered house communions and whom Mervyn said he admired, but he doubted Ernie's 'theological competence for this particular work'. He added (and nothing Mervyn ever wrote was sadder or truer) 'Moreover he is, by nature, so intense I should, for temperamental reasons, find it difficult to work with him. And I think he might overwhelm the clergy.' As Provost of the Cathedral, Mervyn had found installed his old friend from Westcott House, George Reindorp, and when, in 1961, Reindorp was appointed (by the Crown) to the bishopric of Guildford, the Crown reserved the right to appoint the new Provost. On the repeated urging of Sir David Stephens at Downing Street, the nominee was Ernie Southcott.

Mervyn thought it wise to conclude this letter by flattering the Archbishop. 'You, with your vastly greater experience and insight, will see things that I do not see', he told Fisher. 'And you are in a position, which I am not, to see the overall picture.' He assured Fisher that if, after he had talked to John Robinson, he and Robinson felt he should stay in academic work, he would be satisfied. Fisher duly saw John Robinson, and wrote to Mervyn the same day, 19 March, to say he thought John ought to remain in Cambridge. Yet retaining respect for the convention whereby at the end of the day a diocesan has the right to choose his own suffragans, he said it was up to Mervyn and John to 'judge as best you can. Having given him my own advice I have done all that is proper for me to do.'

Mervyn followed up a meeting in Cambridge with Robinson by a letter in which he spoke of a church he had already discovered in Southwark with a congregation of two. 'This is probably an extreme illustration', he wrote, 'but it will help you to understand what is in my mind when I say that in some parts of the diocese we must work out a new pattern if the Church is to come to life.' Then, as he was bound to do, he placed responsibility for a final decision on the shoulders of his former curate. 'I am particularly anxious', he wrote, 'that [the Archbishop] shall not think that I have been bringing unfair pressures upon you. I can only repeat that if you think you should stay in Cambridge I shall accept your decision without question – and with respect.' He was of course desperately anxious that John should accept the vacant bishopric of Woolwich, and having made 'one of the most difficult decisions' of his life, he did so. 'My dear John', Mervyn wrote in acknowledgement of the good news, 'I need hardly say how delighted I am to have your letter. I always look back to your curacy at St Matthew's as the most constructive period in my ministry there; and I am quite sure that with you at my side in Southwark I shall be able to do things which if left to myself I could never do.'

For all his occasional posturing, throwing about of his weight and almost congenital inability to say sorry or admit to ever having been wrong, there was a genuinely humble side to Mervyn's complex character, and he would have been the first to admit he was no theologian in the academic or technical sense. He had prophetic gifts (as all bishops are supposed to have), he was an innovator and an enabler, but he knew from the start that without people around him to put his visions into practice they would remain mere pipe dreams. Although there are still people today who would argue that John Robinson should never have been made a bishop (and as they rather like to have it both ways they go on to say that having become a bishop he should have given up developing his theological ideas), it is difficult to see what job Mervyn had to offer Robinson save a suffragan bishopric. The Provost's stall was occupied. There was no university within the diocese with a professorial chair. In time the Southwark Ordination Course would need a Principal, but the Course had not yet been established. In the event, John Robinson proved himself to be a wise and sympathetic pastor to the clergy in those parts of the diocese for which he had particular responsibility. The Master of Clare had got his manner somewhat out of focus. Robinson was shy and diffident, with a disconcerting, nervous laugh, but he was to fulfil all the expectations of Fisher and Thirkill in the way in which he matured into the episcopate, in many ways complementing Mervyn's overtly extrovert, but in reality clamped-up, personality. Douglas Rhymes thought that 'Robinson was in some ways much more open than Mervyn. He would talk about himself in a very open fashion, and most of the clergy who were gay trusted Robinson more than Mervyn. Mervyn was hampered by his inability to cope with his own sexuality.'[8]

Mervyn was not in the least emotionally involved with John Robinson, and was free, in their relationship as colleagues and brother bishops, to explore in full a mutually sustaining friendship, in terms of his ministry the most important friendship he ever had. Robinson's widow, Ruth, has said 'Their incompatibilities didn't matter. There was tremendous give and take. John having become an established university figure, their original roles, as mentor and curate, became reversed, but I never detected any sense of envy between them. They trusted one another and had tremendous respect for one another, although they didn't always trust each other's judgements – and with justification on either side! Both were generous people, and as John was no sort of prima donna he posed no threat to Mervyn. Their collaboration was a gift to the Church.'[9] She has described Mervyn as 'a benevolent autocrat, very conscious of status, of being the Father in God and having ultimate responsibility. I got on well with him because I wasn't scared of him.' Indeed, with John safely out of the way (for he might have been rather shocked) Ruth had endeared herself to Mervyn one day in Cambridge by getting out the Ouija board.[10]

Even after John Robinson had written to Fisher confirming his acceptance of the bishopric if it was offered, there looked as if, at the last minute, there might be a hitch. Mervyn was informed that the Prime Minister wished to discuss the appointment with Fisher. 'I think I am running into some difficulty with Downing Street', Mervyn told Robinson on 12 May, 'but I intend to put up a fight.' Fight he did, but the battle lasted a month, the announcement of Robinson's appointment to Woolwich being made on 2 June 1959, by which time Mervyn himself had been a bishop a month.

All these exhausting negotiations had been taking place while Mervyn had no permanent address from which to run his diocese. Bishop Simpson had resided in Wimbledon and had diocesan offices at 5 Kennington Park Place, a property that had been leased to the London County Council on 25 December 1950 for 21 years, the Council leasing back to the Church Commissioners certain rooms purely for the business use of the Bishop, including a chapel. Writing from Cambridge on 12 December 1958, Mervyn had told the Commissioners 'The house at Kennington, even if we could get possession of it, is too large'. He dismissed the property in Wimbledon as too small and 'geographically unsuitable' and asked the Commissioners to consider 'buying a suitable house in Black-heath, Dulwich, Greenwich or on the river'. He hoped any house eventually purchased would be large enough to contain 'a private residence for the bishop, an office for the bishop, secretary's quarters, housekeeper's quarters, chaplain's flat and a small chapel'. He particularly asked 'that the house be in quiet surroundings'.

Mervyn was told there were 'still some attractive properties at the top of Croom's Hill and Maze Hill' with 'good gardens and views over the river', but in a dilapidated condition, and on receipt of this information he wrote to say that because of his many com-mitments in Cambridge over Christmas it might be difficult for him to look at any likely homes, and 'If, therefore, you cannot get hold of me I suggest you get into touch with the Viscountess Monkton [sic] of Brenchley who is helping me in these matters. She knows exactly what I am looking for and is advising me on my domestic arrangements.' Mervyn was in good company with his spelling; King George VI consistently misspelt Monckton 'Monkton'. But the idea of consulting Lady Monckton did not find favour with the Church Commissioners, who told Mervyn on 17 December they thought it unlikely they would find anything suitable before Christmas, but if they did they would of course promptly let him know. 'It will then be for you to seek any assistance you wish from Lady Monckton . . . or anyone else you like. But we would not wish ourselves to consult anybody other than yourself.'

Mervyn explained that Lady Monckton knew 'how to watch for domestic points' better than he did, and he intended asking her to vet potential property for him. He certainly had odd ideas about accommodation. He said the Commissioners would 'presumably want a house which is large enough, not merely for a bachelor bishop but for my successors who may very well be like the present bishop of Exeter, married with four children. When I came to Cambridge', he explained, 'the patrons of the diocese [he must have meant the parish; the diocese does not have patrons] had to buy a vicarage because there had never been one at Great St Mary's. The vicarage is perfectly adequate for my needs but if my successor is a married man with children it will be quite useless.' As we have seen, the vicarage in Cambridge turned out to be 'a spacious five-bedroomed house'.

With good cause, Mervyn explained in the new year to Sir Malcolm Trustram Eve,[11] the First Church Estates Commissioner, that as he was 'a helpless bachelor', Lady Monckton was very kindly helping him tackle his domestic problems (clearly Mrs Stockwood, now aged 79, was regarded as past it), and he went on to reiterate that his present home in Cambridge 'would be no good for a married man with children'. By the same token, his new episcopal residence 'should be of sufficient size for my married successors'. And he repeated his desire that the house should be in a quiet area.

My experience as a parish priest for nineteen years in the east end of Bristol convinced me that many tragedies might have been averted if only the bishop had been able to invite to his house tired and broken down clergymen for rest and quiet. I regard this as one of the most important parts of the job especially in a diocese like Southwark where so many of the clergy are single handed and over worked.

He said there had been a suggestion he should live in Croydon (at that time an isolated island in the Canterbury diocese) but he was not particularly keen about this. 'It is my habit', he explained, 'to go to Communion every morning and I think I ought to do this in my own diocese and not in somebody else's.'

By 13 January 1959 the Church Commissioners had prepared a report on 38 Tooting Bec Gardens, a substantial but not enormous property built in 1906. 'It is quite clear that no expense was spared', they concluded, having inspected the 'rich and rather over decorated cornices and ceiling mouldings'. They found three reception rooms, three double bedrooms, two single, a billiard room and two maids' bedrooms but only one bathroom. Apart from the 'two servants' bedrooms' and the billiard room the Commissioners found the decorations to be in 'firstclass order, though the downstairs rooms have been papered and painted in accordance with the rather individual taste of the present owner', a gentleman who in any case appeared to be 'in some doubt' as to whether he really wanted to sell the property.

It was certainly a house with both advantages and disadvantages, somewhat overlooked from the opposite side of Tooting Bec Gardens, 'especially in winter when the leaves are off the trees'. As for Mervyn's stipulation about 'quiet surroundings', 38 Tooting Bec Gardens, now Bishop's House, was 'the last house on the North side at the corner where Tooting Bec Gardens meets Tooting Bec Common', and traffic today hurtles past. Despite nine-foot brick walls on two sides of the garden the pollution from noise and petrol fumes is pretty grim, and even the walls have been known to fail to keep out intruders. While enjoying a late luncheon on the lawn one afternoon, Mervyn was astonished to see two young men leap over the wall from an adjoining and empty house. Majestic in magenta cassock, Mervyn rose to accost them.

'What do you think you're doing?' he bellowed.

'Just passing through', one of them called over his shoulder, as with considerable panache he sped on his way.

Having weighed the pros and cons, the Commissioners pronounced: 'Our considered opinion is that this is not the right house', and they said they intended to continue the search. The site was 'on one corner of a busy cross roads and traffic noises are fairly considerable'. And this was in 1959. They thought the accommodation insufficient, there would be difficulty extending, and the owner did not seem to be in any hurry to sell. Neither was he likely to sell 'at a price favourable to the Commissioners'. On 13 January Mervyn had been writing to 'Dear Sir Malcolm'. A fortnight later he was sufficiently confident of his forthcoming episcopal status to change to 'My dear Trustram Eve' when he wrote to reject a suggestion that he might take up temporary accommodation in Bishop Simpson's house, which he was about to vacate. 'The point is', Mervyn explained,

I don't want to have the expense of two moves. If I go to Dr Simpson's house in Wimbledon I shall have to face the cost of curtains and stair carpets etc. As I hope I should not be in the house for more than a few months this would inevitably be a waste of money. As I have no private means and as the next few months are going to be very expensive for me I am anxious to avoid all unnecessary expenditure. It might be better to try and find a furnished house somewhere. So far as I'm concerned I am prepared to live in a furnished room anywhere but I have to take into consideration my aged mother.

Apart from expense, another reason Mervyn was unenthusiastic about Wimbledon was because he had found that 'Dr Simpson spent between eight and nine hours a week travelling from his house to his office – in fact, an entire working day. This', he said, 'strikes me as an appalling and unjustifiable waste of time.' By the end of January Mervyn had been to Tooting Bec Gardens to see the house there for himself, and on 6 February he told the Commissioners 'I am sorry there are snags with regard to the Tooting Bec house as I rather liked it. I imagine the Commissioners will now think that the quickest solution to the problem is to build a new house.' He wanted temporary accommodation fixed by Easter, when he was due to go abroad for three weeks' holiday, and 'I do not want to concern myself with housing problems at the time of my consecration'.

By 23 February the Estates and Finance Committee had decided 'to bid £10,000 (and no more) for vacant possession [of 38 Tooting Bec Gardens] and completion by 30th April; otherwise not to buy'. Three days later it was reported that the owner was 'indisposed with pleurisy'. By 2 March his wife had been told her husband had not very long to live 'and therefore he cannot be moved from the house'. So Mervyn was informed that 'a small suite of furnished rooms (lounge, dining room, two bedrooms, bathroom and w.c.)' had been reserved for him at Artillery Mansions in Victoria Street – suite 5W, in fact. The Commissioners would pay the rent, while Mervyn was to be responsible for 'any *private* telephone calls (of which a note should be kept), electrical heating, and laundry (for towels and bed linen)'. The Commissioners offered to pay for the storage of Mervyn's furniture and his removal, and said they would help with the cost of meals served in his room. It all sounded rather unsatisfactory and makeshift, and when Mervyn wrote on 20 March to say he had been to see the rooms he was so disenchanted he even got the address wrong, referring to Artillery Buildings.

I realise that in the circumstances it's probably the best that can be done. I hope however that I shall not have to stay there long because they are gloomy to say the least. Moreover there is not enough accommodation there for me to have my mother with me because obviously I must have a room where I can see people and a room where my secretary can work. Have you any further news about the house in Tooting Bec?

They had. The owner had been moved to hospital and was 'said to be dying. This means that it is not possible to ask him to sign a contract for the sale of the house. All we can do is wait on events . . .' As far as Artillery Mansions was concerned, Mervyn was sharply told it was intended to house his mother as well as himself and that he should make use of the diocesan offices in Kennington. Bowing to the inevitable, Mervyn asked if it would be possible for the Church Commissioners to 'negotiate with Bishop Simpson about the use of the office furniture. I understand that it belongs to him. I am in no position to buy it because I haven't the resources.' He said he would prefer the Commissioners to deal with Bishop Simpson about it because he did not want to be put in the position of having to ask for personal favours.

As there was clearly no chance of proceeding with the purchase of 38 Tooting Bec Gardens while the owner hovered between this world and the next, other property came under consideration, and Mervyn was writing in the middle of February to the Archdeacon of Lewisham, secretary of the Southwark Diocesan Board of Finance, to say 'I am so very grateful to you for making enquiries about the house at Dulwich. This makes me keener than ever to have the house at Tooting. The more I think about it the more it attracts me. Moreover as soon as I got to the house this morning with you and Lady Monckton I said to myself – this is the house where I want to live.'

By April the owner of Mervyn's dream house had died, and his widow agreed to sell the property for £10,000 by 24 June. Plans were being drawn up for an extension to be built, at a probable cost of £8,000, to include office accommodation and two additional bedrooms, and this was where eventually Mrs Stockwood lived. After her death the flat was taken over by the current domestic chaplain. Having already negotiated a salary of £683 a year for Michael Mayne, Mervyn now turned his attention to his own financial affairs. He was due to meet the Commissioners at Tooting Bec Gardens on 28 April to talk about alterations to the house, and on 24 April he wrote to say 'As I told you on the 'phone I also want to discuss with you my income and my allowances etc. It would be a great help if you could let me have some notes about this when I arrive.' His letter was minuted 'stipend at rate of £2,500 pa'.[12]

Was Geoffrey Fisher playing games when he decreed that Mervyn should be consecrated on May Day? Possibly, but 1 May 1959 was also the 54th anniversary of the founding of the diocese, the Bishoprics of Southwark and Birmingham Bill having received the Royal Assent on 15 August 1904. Consecrated at the same service, but taking a back seat, was a new suffragan Bishop of Barking, William Chadwick, Vicar of Barking since 1947 and Bishop of Barking, in the diocese of Chelmsford, until he retired in 1975. Both stayed the night before their consecration, as is customary, at Lambeth Palace, and Fisher covered, for Mervyn, what Michael Ramsey would have called 'his academic nakedness', by conferring on him a Lambeth Doctorate of Divinity. (In 1963 Sussex University made Mervyn an honorary Doctor of Literature, and in 1977 he received an honorary DD from Bucharest.) The Fishers were next-door to teetotal, but Mrs Fisher rummaged around for some brandy for Mervyn, in case he should feel faint during the protracted service, pouring it, unfortunately, into an old TCP bottle.

By tradition, the cleric being consecrated invites his own preacher, and presumably, as he was going to become a diocesan, Mervyn claimed the right, and chose a notable Cambridge eccentric, Frederick Simpson. Knowing all he did of Simpson, Mervyn was taking a large and deliberate risk, especially as the patron of the Friends of Southwark Cathedral, Princess Margaret, would be present. He was sending out a signal, perhaps, that risk-taking would be the hallmark of his episcopate. Simpson was an idle Fellow of Trinity, the author of a half-finished life of Louis Napoleon, and one of his unattractive habits was to wander into someone else's church during the sermon, switch all the lights off and wander out again. He had a dry sense of humour to compensate, however – of a distinctly donnish variety. In the Suggestions Book kept in the Parlour at Trinity College he noted in November 1958 'There was a cockroach floating in the tea served to me in the Parlour this afternoon. The head Combination Room waiter tells me – whether truly or not I cannot say – that both the kitchens and his pantry are alive with them. If so, more care should be taken to strain them off; for it is not a pleasant discovery to make half way through one's meal.'

'Simpson was a lonely man', Mervyn was to write of him in 1990. 'He had acquaintances and admirers but few friends. He longed to love and to be loved, but his idiosyncrasies damaged personal relationships.'[13] He could have been writing about himself. After much feigned hesitation, Simpson, by then 75 and a stranger to London for the past quarter of a century, condescended to accept the invitation to preach. It meant preparing an entirely original sermon; he seems only to have had one previous sermon, on the subject of the Good Samaritan, and there were few in Cambridge who had not already heard it – several times. But before going to all the trouble of concocting a sermon worthy of the consecration of Mervyn Stockwood, Simpson desired to know the height of the pulpit desk. He pronounced it too low. So he ordered a new one. The evening before the service of consecration he joined the two bishops-elect at Lambeth Palace for dinner, and on departing was heard to exclaim to the Fishers 'And may I just say, had you offered me alcohol I would have refused it'.

Next morning he became obsessed with the fear that he might need to leave his allotted seat during the service in order to relieve himself, so tense with nervous expectation had he become. And although under strict instructions not to move to the pulpit before the consecrating bishops had repositioned themselves by the pulpit, he began his sermon (a sermon later described by Fisher as 'deplorable') while the bishops were still moving from the sanctuary. Fisher became so incensed during the delivery of Simpson's address, which contained not one mention of the new Bishop of Barking (Simpson constantly addressed his remarks to 'his dear Mervyn'), that at one stage he opened a box of cough lozenges, and his hands were trembling so much with rage that he spilt the entire contents on the floor. After enjoining Mervyn to maintain 'such little as is left of the parson's freehold', to remember his prayers and to cling to courage, he ended on a truly camp if authentically catholic note: 'And so, my brother, whom in age I might call my son, whom, this service ended, I shall salute as father, as I kneel to kiss your ring and ask your blessing, I doubt not I shall receive it from a prophet new inspired.' Simpson was rewarded for his laudatory efforts by being made an honorary canon of Southwark, and when he died in 1974, at the age of 90, Mervyn and John Robinson buried his ashes in the Fellows' Garden at Trinity.

Mervyn claims that when he went to Buckingham Palace to pay homage on his appointment to Southwark the Queen offered him a cup of chocolate. Perhaps she had been forewarned that he intended arriving for his audience in Convocation robes rather than gaiters and gave orders to have the gin locked up. The night before his enthronement he spent in prayer in the cathedral, accompanied by Michael Mayne, who slept on a camp bed in the vestry. Nye Bevan and Walter Monckton were among old friends from Bristol who attended. Mervyn had been back to Cambridge to stay with the Master of Christ's College, and it was there that he wrote his enthronement sermon, which opened with the words 'The Church exists to further the Kingdom of God'. This may seem an unsurprising statement, but it typified his attitude to his ministry. He cared little for the Establishment, and a great deal of church activity bored him to death; not only ecclesiastical administration, but services too. In retirement he attended an Alternative Service Communion and became extremely irritated by repetition of 'The Lord be with you'. 'After the fifth "The Lord be with you"', he recounted afterwards, 'I turned round and said, "Of course he is, he was here five minutes ago."' On meeting Douglas Rhymes after a diocesan synod he asked Rhymes if he was all right, because, he said, he noticed he had arrived before the synod began and didn't leave before it ended. On the eve of a meeting of the General Synod in York, he asked his chaplain at the time, Giles Harcourt, to gather up all the relevant documents. They amounted to 501 pieces of paper.

'Now', said Mervyn, 'I am going to do something that will shock you.'

'I doubt it', said Giles, whereupon Mervyn dumped the whole lot in the wastepaper basket.

'Now then, who are you looking at?' Mervyn asked.

'I know you are longing to tell me', the dutiful Giles replied.

'You are looking', said Mervyn, 'at the freest man in the Church of England.'

When it came to the conduct of his quarterly bishops' meetings he devised a very simple method of overcoming any possible danger of ennui: he accepted the generous hospitality of a Roman Catholic Tory, Lady Robson-Brown, who supplied, at her home in Cheam, a swimming pool, a sauna and virtually unlimited drink and food. Hugh Montefiore, who attended these exhausting sessions when he was Bishop of Kingston, has written:

They were extraordinary affairs. We used to start at 11 a.m. with champagne and a swim. It was essential to get any business done before lunch because it was gargantuan (with caviare flown in on one occasion from Iran), with copious drink to match. After that there was a tendency, shall I say, to ramble on the part of M, until tea at 4 followed by a sauna, and so back to base after a hard day's work . . .[14]

Notes

1 Michael Mayne, in conversation with the author.

2 Mervyn Stockwood, *Bishop's Journal* (Mowbray, 1964).

3 MS was again received in private audience by Pope John XXIII, on 7 April 1962, when he presented the Pontiff with a chocolate Easter egg.

4 Fisher to Eden, quoted in Bernard Palmer, *High & Mitred: Prime Ministers as Bishop-Makers 1837–1977* (SPCK, 1992).

5 Canon Eric James, in conversation with the author.

6 Not one of MS's chaplains is referred to in his autobiography, and only two were remembered in his will.

7 Canon Douglas Rhymes, in conversation with the author.

8 Ibid.

9 Mrs Ruth Robinson, in conversation with the author.

10 Ibid.

11 In 1963 created Lord Silsoe.

12 By the late 1960s MS's stipend, along with most other diocesan bishops, would have gone up to £3,000 p.a. at a time when the Archbishop of Canterbury was paid £7,500 p.a.

13 Eric James (ed.), *A Last Eccentric* (Christian Action, 1991).

14 Letter from Bishop Montefiore to the author, 9 May 1995.

Chapter 8

A column in the
Evening Standard

Mervyn Stockwood's ministry in Southwark, destined to last 21 years, occurred at a crossroads in the history of the Church of England. While thousands of people remained unchurched – as they always had been – there existed, when he became a bishop, a ground swell of optimism and enthusiasm among educated Christians, an enthusiasm recognized by the formation of radical organizations like the Keble Conference Group and Parish and People. In 1963 these two organizations merged, many of their ideas for reform having by then been absorbed by Southwark, whose publicity-conscious Bishop and clergy rode high while the tide was in but tended to be blamed for failure when it went out again. Provost Irvine remembers that the 1950s were

boom years for Christianity in Cambridge. Undergraduates were more interested in religion than in politics. Most college chapels flourished and several central parish churches offering different brands of Anglicanism were also thriving. I used to reckon that about half the undergraduates at Sidney Sussex College, a very average and unglamorous college, were doing something about religious observance.[1]

The *Church of England Newspaper* announced in 1960 that a new Church of England was being born, 'a Church efficient, sophisticated and progressive, a Church with money enough and to spare', and at his first confirmation, John Robinson told the candidates 'You're coming into active membership of the Church at a time when great things are afoot. I believe, in England, that we may be at the turning of the tide. Indeed, in Cambridge University, where I have recently come from, I am convinced the tide has already turned.' Certainly many of the undergraduates who had come under the influence of deans and chaplains like John Robinson were going on to offer themselves for ordination, and Mervyn started his episcopate with 25 theological colleges in full swing. Within a decade, some 20 per cent of residential accommodation was empty, and closures and amalgamations began to take place. His own college, Westcott House, was to merge with a Methodist foundation. The Church of England, since the Second Act of Supremacy of 1559 'by law established', still held sway in the public domain. In the direct aftermath of the Second World War the BBC actually saw it as part of its God-given mission to lead non-churchgoers 'to see Christian commitment as involving active membership of a congregation'. The BBC acted as a propaganda machine, with prayers even being incorporated into *Children's Hour*. But in the first ten years of Mervyn's episcopate there was a 19 per cent decline in church attendance; almost inevitably, the numbers of men offering themselves for ordination began to slip as well. In 1963, 636 men were ordained to the priesthood. Ten years later the figure was 373.

The diocese of Southwark had itself been born on a wave of Victorian expansionism. Between the years 1866 and 1870 no fewer than 427 new churches were built in England, and new dioceses were quick to follow: Manchester had been created in 1847, Truro came into existence in 1877, Liverpool in 1880, Newcastle two years later, Wakefield in 1888 and Birmingham in 1905. Southwark, largely carved out of Greater London south of the Thames and incorporating parts of the dioceses of Rochester and Winchester, was created in the same year, retaining the remains of a former palace used by bishops of Winchester, a diocese dating back to 604.

In 1959 Mervyn was taking charge of a population of 2.5 million, 400 churches and 600 clergymen. (Today there are still some 390 churches in Southwark and about 400 clergy.) He inherited nearly 100 listed churches, including medieval buildings in the Surrey commuter belt, examples of the work of Wren's pupil Nicholas Hawksmoor, and porticoed memorials to the Battle of Waterloo. St Nicholas, Charlwood was 900 years old; St Matthias at Richmond was the mid-nineteenth-century work of George Gilbert Scott. The diocese incorporated wharves, new housing estates, slums and leafy countryside, with Guildford to the west, Chichester to the south and the squalor of Brixton contrasting with the architectural splendours of Greenwich. One of the first inspections Mervyn made of his diocese, its northern boundary being marked by the Thames, was in a boat with Beverley Nichols and John Betjeman, after which Mervyn pronounced himself disgusted by 'the sheer hideous slumdom of the south bank of the Thames'.

Mervyn was hoping to build up Southwark in the way that he had created from nothing two thriving parishes, and he realized that in addition to a suffragan bishop with the prophetic insights of John Robinson he would need a nucleus of radical clergy to push through reforms and initiate enthusiasm. In 1959 there was no particular glamour attached to working in Southwark. That would change before long, and it was entirely Mervyn's own electric personality that induced friends he had made in Bristol and Cambridge to follow him to some of the most depressed areas of south London. Eric James left Trinity and was inducted by Mervyn to St George's, Camberwell in succession to an alcoholic parish priest who became a Mirfield monk. Likewise Bill Skelton, who had by now been chaplain at Clare for seven years, eagerly left Cambridge, and feeling 'captivated by Mervyn's personality' was inducted as Vicar of Bermondsey at Michaelmas 1959. Skelton had never had a previous living and had only ever served in a parish for two years as a curate. Now he had three curates training under him and was chairman of the board of three schools. The wharves and docks were closing down; manufacturing industry was moving out. He says: 'Mervyn wanted me in Southwark, and Bermondsey happened to be vacant. He had no idea of my capabilities!'[2] At least Mervyn had matched the parish to the parish priest in terms of churchmanship; both were low, and Bill Skelton remained there ten years, in 1969 taking up a non-parochial job. Being a parish priest at heart, this was something Mervyn could never comprehend, but the relationship between Bill Skelton and Mervyn Stockwood was not seriously tested until, in 1985, when Skelton became Master of a City livery company, he invited Mervyn to emerge from retirement to be his guest speaker at the Mansion House. 'By the end of the dinner', Skelton recalls, 'he was absolutely pissed. At the time I was very angry. I felt he had really let me down.'[3]

Mervyn endured the cramped and 'gloomy' accommodation in Artillery Mansions until the end of July 1959, when he was loaned a larger and airy flat in Lennox Gardens, and it was here, in September 1959, in the heart of fashionable south-west London, that Michael Mayne (who had signed the visitors' book at Artillery Mansions on 26 June) joined Mervyn to start his six-year stint as chaplain. And it was in Lennox Gardens, on 20 October 1959, that a hilarious contretemps occurred with Princess Margaret. Simon Phipps had been assigned as an escort to Princess Margaret before her marriage in 1960, and through both Phipps and Elizabeth Cavendish Mervyn had received the entrée to Kensington Palace before he became Bishop of Southwark. Now, with Princess Margaret's link with the cathedral, he was to see a good deal of her, and on 20 October she had been to Deptford to open a new youth club. Mervyn by this time had hired the first of a series of less than satisfactory housekeepers; they tended to be kind but not much good at cooking, and this one was deaf. Princess Margaret, who had been invited to lunch, for some reason left her Deptford engagement ahead of Mervyn, who should have departed first in order to be in Lennox Gardens to receive her. To make matters worse, all the traffic lights, as is usually the case when royalty wish to speed across London, had been held at green, so that the princess arrived well ahead of her host. Nothing daunted, she rang the doorbell. 'We've come to lunch with the Bishop', she announced when eventually the hard-of-hearing housekeeper answered the intercom.

'He's not here. Who are you, anyway?'

'Princess Margaret.'

'Well, you're early.'

With a royal car parked and a princess shouting into an intercom, it was not surprising that by the time Mervyn arrived every window in Lennox Gardens was open wide, jammed with curious faces. Mervyn did not seem particularly displeased.

While waiting to move into his official episcopal residence, Mervyn, without consulting the College of Arms, invented a spurious coat of arms for himself, a conceit that only came to light when Chester Herald was asked by Mervyn to have his seal mounted as a paperweight. Apparently the proper procedure is for a bishop to impale his family arms with those of the diocese, and if he has no arms of his own, to apply for a Grant of Arms 'under the hands and seals of the Kings of Arms (to whom the function of granting arms has been delegated by the Sovereign since the Middle Ages)'.[4] Mervyn may perhaps be forgiven for not being *au fait* with all this rigmarole. When building work had been completed at 38 Tooting Bec Gardens and Mervyn was able to move in, in the late summer of 1960, he found himself in possession of a comfortable house, more palatial in appearance from the outside than it turns out to be within, with a paved garden veranda and an iron balcony over the garden door. It was centrally situated within the northern area of the diocese, but it could never have been very handy for the cathedral, and today it takes the bishop at least an hour to drive to a cathedral service.

Mervyn established his private chapel at the top of the house. It is now a bedroom, and the bishop's chapel has been transferred to the new extension, where a paten and chalice bequeathed by Mervyn are in frequent use. Some criticism has been levelled at Mervyn for the extent of the hospitality he extended at Bishop's House, and for the prelatical way in which he conducted himself there. It has to be remembered that even though he had not been transplanted to a palace such as he would have inhabited had he been appointed to Peterborough or Chichester or Bath and Wells, his new surroundings were an intoxicating contrast to anything he had ever experienced before, as a child or an adult. By middle-class standards, his domestic background in the past had always been dowdy, and for many years his accommodation in Bristol had been little more than primitive. Speaking in the House of Lords in 1977 he recalled that he had begun his ministry 'in one room in a foul slum'. Now, on 25 March 1961, he was to have his private chapel consecrated and his home blessed by the Archbishop of Canterbury, who earlier that morning, in the cathedral, had consecrated the Provost, George Reindorp, on his appointment as Bishop of Guildford. The Fishers were due to stay to lunch, and although Mervyn detested puddings, he thoughtfully had his chaplain telephone Lambeth Palace to enquire what the Archbishop's favourite pudding was. Back came the reply: bread and butter pudding. Told about this while enjoying a glass of sherry before lunch, Fisher said 'Absolute nonsense! My favourite pudding is prunes and custard.'

Mervyn had not waited for any formal blessing of Bishop's House before he was entertaining Queen Elizabeth the Queen Mother. She paid her first visit on 5 November 1960, returning on 26 March 1976 when Mervyn gave an 80th birthday party for Mary, Duchess of Devonshire. On that occasion the guests included the Cardinal Archbishop of Westminster and Dame Cicely Saunders, a pioneer of the hospice movement. This was the aristocratic milieu into which Mervyn as a bishop moved as to the manner born; he now had a house in which he could entertain royalty and to the house royalty were duly invited, most frequently Princess Alexandra and her husband, who lived in the diocese, nearly as often, Princess Margaret and her husband. Princess Margaret and Lord Snowdon were there on 19 July 1962, and again on 2 February 1963. The parties, and the guests invited to them, were often exotic. The notorious Richard Blake-Brown was there for an 'Oscar Wilde Birthday' celebration on 16 October 1961 (Oscar Wilde was born on 16 October 1854), and somewhat daringly, Blake-Brown was invited again, on 19 July 1962, to meet Princess Margaret. The attitude seems to have been 'any excuse for a party'. During Mervyn's 20 years at Bishop's House there were parties for mayors and town clerks, for rural deans, for servers from Bristol; there were Michaelmas ordination lunches, lunches for ambassadors and lunches for old boys from Kingsland Grange; for boys too from Highgate School and for curates. There were parties for senior incumbents and parties for junior clergy, tea parties for nuns, and a party to welcome the new Bishop of London. Lunches for the diocesan clergy were a frequent occurrence; every year there was a mid-Lent party. Elizabeth Cavendish and John Betjeman, who had met Mervyn at Clifton at the start of the war, became regular visitors; on 21 May 1962 they were invited to meet Michael Ramsey, who had succeeded Geoffrey Fisher as Archbishop of Canterbury, when Hugh Gaitskell was there as well. From the other side of the political divide, Lord Hailsham and Lord Boothby were invited. A future Archbishop of Canterbury, Robert Runcie, came over from Cuddesdon, where he was Principal, in November 1961. Mervyn celebrated his own birthday with parties; on 21 December 1961 he gave a dinner to celebrate the silver jubilee of his ordination. Jo Grimond and his wife were guests; so was the novelist Pamela Hansford Johnson. Two gay clergy and their partners were invited to dinner on 3 February 1963 with Princess Margaret and Lord Snowdon. The Archbishop of Canterbury's chaplain and his lay secretary were entertained. So was the Apostolic Delegate. Cyril Cowderoy, the Roman Catholic Archbishop of Southwark, and Mervyn exchanged hospitality annually. There were parties for new incumbents and there were ecumenical parties; there were buffet lunches for the Liturgical Commission and, in 1966, an Election party, when presumably Mervyn was in jovial mood, for Labour won.

Now that Mervyn was London-based and a bishop he was in demand to grace the tables of society hostesses. On 14 July 1966, for instance, he found himself in the company of Tony Benn at a very grand lunch party given by Lady Pamela Berry, who rather cultivated socialists, at which, according to Tony Benn, the guests ate with gold knives and forks 'and the food was superb'. One of Mervyn's problems when acting as host was the lack of a hostess to accompany female guests to the drawing-room after dinner while the men drank port, an archaic custom upon which Mervyn insisted, even if there was only one unfortunate female present – a custom to which one evening Jennie Lee took strong exception. 'Leave the table!' she exclaimed. 'I intend to leave the house!' So saying she strode to her car, and had to be retrieved in the drive by the chaplain.

Diana Mosley and her husband, whose brains if not his politics Mervyn greatly admired, were entertained at Bishop's House. Caryl Brahms, Bernard Levin, MPs, stockbrokers, Cambridge philosophers and trade union leaders all made their way to Tooting Bec Gardens. During the four weeks of the 1968 Lambeth Conference Mervyn extended hospitality to 104 bishops and their wives. Ned Sherrin, the film, theatre and TV producer, was perhaps a more than usually sophisticated guest and thought the food 'awful, usually charcoaled chicken'. He remembers that sometimes at dinner, when Mervyn was feeling let down by the Labour Government, he would lambast 'hopeless Harold'. On one occasion Sherrin telephoned Mervyn to ask him to supply a literary grace for a Foyles lunch. Within minutes Mervyn had rung back to suggest 'For the food we eat and the books we read we give thanks to God, the author of life'.[5]

The expense incurred was considerable, and it soon became commonplace for Mervyn to submit to the Church Commissioners a larger expense account than any other bishop. For his birthday party on 24 May 1963 a guest list of 57 was headed by the Archbishop of Canterbury and Mrs Ramsey – and that gathering was followed by a second birthday party three days later. It was estimated when Mervyn retired that in 20 years 9,000 people had passed through the house, and at one time the Church Commissioners suggested he might consider making economies. So he instructed his chaplain to find out how much the other bishops spent on entertaining, and was overjoyed when it was reported back to him that one bishop had not spent anything that year at all. 'There you are', he said. 'You see, I'm spending his share as well.' Mervyn believed it was his Christian duty to offer hospitality. He also enjoyed his role as host, and loved to spring surprises. After a staff meeting one day he told his chaplain to fetch champagne and glasses on to the lawn. No one knew why. When the glasses had been filled he raised his own and proposed a toast 'To our ascended Lord'. It was Ascension Day. On another occasion he organized a dinner party for eight bishops, to celebrate notable milestones in his life, producing an appropriate bottle and quotation for each course. His arrival at Great St Mary's, for example, was commemorated by a 1955 wine, and a quotation from Christopher Anstey: 'Granta, sweet Granta, where studious of ease, four years did I slumber for a Lambeth D.D.' The year of his appointment to Southwark was marked by a 1959 Château Maison Blanche, and Laurence Sterne was called to mind: 'Shower down thy mitres upon those heads which are aching for them, and shall ache from them.' As he was unable to find a bottle to coincide with the year of his birth he fell back upon a 1912 Taylor's port – to commemorate the year of his conception.

Mervyn was a great one for celebrating anniversaries, constantly looking over his shoulder. In February 1961 he had had nine former Bristol parishioners to Bishop's House for a party, followed by dinner at the George Inn in Southwark. The same month he was back at Great St Mary's to preach, and he was back again for the Harvest Festival, when the new vicar, Joseph Fison, secreted a gift for Mervyn in the pulpit. Confidently expecting to discover a fine claret, Mervyn only managed to locate a large bottle of Lucozade. That Easter he had teamed up with his former bishop, Dr Claxton of Bristol, to climb Mount Snowdon; on 24 March 1961 he was actually in Bristol, to present a testimonial to the headmaster of the secondary modern school in his old parish.

A peculiarity of Bishop's House was that the telephone number was ex-directory. It was not that Mervyn was afraid of the clergy ringing him up, although on the whole they were encouraged to make contact through their rural dean; it was the press he feared. He was invited very early on by Charles Wintour, editor of the *Evening Standard*, to contribute regular articles, and this he did partly because he enjoyed publicity and partly to earn money to help subsidize the needs of his clergy.[6] Unlike John Robinson, who could have become a millionaire through earnings from royalties had he not set up a charitable trust fund, Mervyn never earned huge sums by his pen, but what he did earn went into a fund lodged at Coutts. On his death the fund was liquidated and bequeathed to the Church Missionary Society. And one result of his journalism, taken in tandem with his newsworthy exploits as bishop, was that before long he was in almost constant demand by journalists to comment on his and other people's activities. Not only was Stockwood a pillar of the Church, Matthew Coady wrote in a profile of Mervyn in the *Daily Mirror* in May 1969, 'but a column in the *Evening Standard* as well'. At the start, Mervyn had no press officer; the resident household at Bishop's House consisted only of his mother, in a separate flat, a chaplain, and – by day – a housekeeper, a secretary and a chauffeur. Once Mervyn's secretary had gone home and the telephone rang there was only Mervyn or a chaplain to answer it.

While Mervyn enjoyed publicity, like many who court the press he rather dreaded being pursued by them, and being egocentric he was extremely vulnerable to criticism. 'Publicity kept him going' in the opinion of one perhaps rather jaundiced colleague, but it is hard to credit that when informed of a disastrous train crash in Lewisham he said to his chaplain 'Take me to where the cameras are'. The fact that such a story is believed does, however, indicate the impression he gave to many that he thoroughly enjoyed the limelight. Whether in principle Mervyn should have gone, as he did, to the scene of the crash is a matter for debate; probably the only justification any priest can have for tripping up the emergency services can be to administer the last rites to the dead or dying, but in fairness to Mervyn it can be assumed he thought his presence would identify the local Church with the suffering. On the other hand, assuming there would be other clergy available on the spot it is also fair to suggest that the wisest course for a bishop to take is to stay away from the scene of an accident and to visit the injured and bereaved in the morning.

At the beginning of his episcopacy there is no question that Mervyn dived head first into controversy, learning some painful lessons as a result. When a magistrate sent a West Indian woman to prison for what Mervyn considered a petty offence he lashed out at the magistrate. A few days later the stipendiary had a heart attack and died. It was never seriously suggested that Mervyn's criticism was the cause of the heart attack but it was an unfortunate incident, to put it mildly. Within four months of taking office he felt he had to deal in a heavy-handed way with what was technically a breach of church discipline. The elderly curate of St Andrew's at Carshalton was insisting on using the Roman Rite when celebrating Holy Communion, even though his newly installed rector had told him to desist. The curate resigned, but then unfortunately withdrew his resignation. Believing he was dealing with 'an inflexible bigot', Mervyn refused to accept the withdrawal, and in fact, if he seriously intended stamping on illegal liturgical practices, he had no alternative. But the thought of a bishop shutting a cleric out of a church in which he was licensed to officiate was meat and drink to the press.

'You are doing a great job', Archbishop Fisher told him, 'though very often doing things in the wrong way.' He must be more careful to consult, 'even in small things'. Even if it was true that Mervyn was 'doing things in the wrong way', he had been encouraged to act vigorously by Fisher himself. In addition to unexceptional instructions to 'bridge the gap between the Church and the vast untouched masses of people' in the diocese, the Archbishop's mandate had been 'to introduce liturgical order'.[7] And it is interesting to note, in view of the later stormy relationship between Mervyn and Fisher, that initially all was milk and honey. In the autumn of 1959 Mervyn was writing to the Archbishop to say 'I do want you to know how much I treasure your wonderful friendship since my consecration. As you know better than anybody, life has not been easy during the past six months but it has made all the difference to know that you have been at my side to advise and encourage and to be a friend. For that and much more I am deeply grateful.'[8] One opportunity Fisher had taken to support Mervyn during the very early months of his episcopate had been occasioned by an article Mervyn wrote in the *Daily Express* on the subject of birth control and family planning, a subject on which Mervyn had felt strongly ever since his formative days in Bristol. The article provoked a stern rebuke from the Apostolic Delegate, who in the opinion of Fisher was 'if not anti-Church of England ... so ignorant of it as to be in effect hostile'. At the 1958 Lambeth Conference the Anglican bishops had decided that the practice of birth control could be a positive Christian duty, and Fisher informed the Apostolic Delegate that his rebuke to Mervyn was uncalled for, indeed, that in writing to one of his diocesan bishops in the way he had, he had violated the rules of diplomatic courtesy.

Michael Mayne says: 'Mervyn had a very Laudian view, that because of the comprehensiveness of the Church of England you can be diffuse in matters of belief but the authorized Book of Common Prayer provided the uniformity people had a right to expect. The *Daily Telegraph*, as you might expect, had their knife into him, and after a few months he became hypersensitive about the press.'[9] In fact, so hypersensitive had he suddenly become that he went off to Florence to recover his composure. There he looked after the American Episcopal church, and enjoyed the company of Simon Phipps and Julian Grenfell, who in 1976 was to succeed as the third Lord Grenfell.

At his first diocesan conference, held in June 1959 at Church House in Westminster, for the diocese of Southwark had no premises of its own convenient for the purpose, Mervyn again referred, as he had at his enthronement, to his plans to establish a new form of training for the ministry. He told the delegates of his appointment of Eric James to St George's, Camberwell, and to Eric's surprise Mervyn went on to announce that he hoped Eric would bring with him to the parish half a dozen graduates who would earn their living by day in industry and at night would study for the priesthood. 'And in this connection', he said, 'the new Bishop of Woolwich will be of great assistance.' The new Bishop of Woolwich was due to be consecrated in Canterbury Cathedral on 29 September, without, unfortunately, his wife Ruth in the congregation, for she was to suffer a severe brain haemorrhage only twelve days before the service. Mervyn went on to explain that when those graduates were fit for ordination some might become 'curates in the ordinary way, or they may feel they can be of greater use if they remain where they are and discover their way to a new pattern of priesthood'. He said he was fully alive to the dangers of the scheme, but he was prepared to take risks 'in order that we shall do something to get alongside that large section of our society which has little or nothing to do with the Church'.

In other words, Mervyn was planning to import into Southwark from France the concept of worker-priests. For many years the Church of England had employed clergy in non-parochial jobs, as prison, hospital, school and army chaplains, and the clergy had worked as schoolmasters, often as headmasters; William Temple, like Geoffrey Fisher, had been headmaster of Repton. But the idea that a priest should work in industry not as an industrial chaplain, as Simon Phipps was to do for example, in Coventry, but on the shop floor, actually earning his living at a lathe, was a Catholic and continental idea about to be given a much higher profile in Southwark than it had previously enjoyed.

In anticipation of his consecration, on 30 November 1958 Mervyn had said from the pulpit of Great St Mary's

I think it's likely that in addition to the parochial system we need a more flexible type of Church organisation and that in addition to the parochial priesthood we need an order of worker-priests – men who will stay on the ground floor, earning their livings as factory hands, bus drivers, railwaymen, trade union officials, shopkeepers and schoolmasters. And as they go about their daily jobs it will be their duty to act as Christian propagandists and to build up the Church.

As early as 1943 he had been in correspondence with Temple about worker-priests, Temple telling him on 3 July that year:

I think it might be a very good thing that some clergy should be working in ordinary jobs, still carrying on spiritual ministrations as they have opportunity; but economically dependent on their secular job, and if there were a strong demand for a number of clergy to be allowed to do this, as far as I can tell at present I should support the proposal that it should be permitted as an experiment.[10]

What came as a surprise to Eric James, with whom Mervyn had often talked over his plans for the future while they were both in Cambridge, was Mervyn's inference that Eric was to run what became known as the Southwark Ordination Course. Eric says that on this matter Mervyn had never consulted him.[11] 'He made several mistakes by wanting to do things too fast and too publicly. I knew my hands would be full for the first year in Camberwell pulling the parish together.' While Eric took a keen interest in the setting up of the course, and frequently discussed its progress with John Robinson and Mervyn, he says that 'John Robinson was the brains behind it'.

Not only was Robinson the brains behind the Southwark Ordination Course (and in his autobiography, Mervyn gives Robinson full credit 'as the driving force'), he moved with incredible speed. It was decided that evening classes would be held in the cathedral chapter house in St Thomas's Street, and that candidates should serve in the Southwark diocese for at least five years after ordination, a restriction lifted in March 1962 because by that time the course, which was already in place by September 1960, was subject to supervision by the Central Advisory Council for the Ministry. Mervyn was determined that the curriculum should bear comparison to any training undergone in the traditional residential theological colleges, and he had a good deal of initial opposition to overcome from fellow bishops who could not see how such an ambition could be achieved. (Similar initial scepticism was to be expressed about degree courses run by the Open University.) The lectures, held on two evenings a week, were arranged in association with the University of London, and lasted two hours. Candidates went into retreat once a year, paid three visits to parishes and attended a series of residential weekends. After 1962 these eventually took place at a house called Wychcroft near Bletchingley in Surrey, made available to the diocese at a peppercorn rent by one of Mervyn's wealthy friends, a Guardian of the Shrine of Our Lady of Walsingham, Uvedale Lambert. Lambert, who was High Sheriff of Surrey and died in 1983, also owned South Park at Bletchingley, where before long he was distributing generous hospitality. Wychcroft provided accommodation for 30, and the age range of the ordinands was between 30 and 55.

Mervyn's visits to Wychcroft were conducted on the lines of a royal tour. His arrival was timed for 3 p.m. Into the hall his chaplain was instructed to bring 'all bags, coats etc. from Bishop's car'. In a memorandum that ran to eight pages, the chaplain was reminded to say 'hallo' to the staff, and to ask 'if the booze situation' was 'all right for after Chapel and during dinner', when usually '2 red per table' were deemed to suffice, 'depending on course'.

After announcements, the chaplain was instructed to

1 Unpack Bishop's bags.
2 Take *Blue* suitcase to chapel, together with crozier. (Unpack and assemble.)
3 Place books open at appropriate places . . .
4 ASSEMBLE BOOK REST for Bishop on Altar, square on centre.
5 15 minutes beforehand switch on Chapel lights: 5 minutes beforehand ring Chapel bell 10 times, and light candles (keep matches in R.H.S. cassock pocket).

Before 'Ist Evensong' the chaplain was to 'double-check that Alec [the warden] will have the drinks ready for when you all come out'. The chaplain was warned to take 'the CASH-BOX' with him into Chapel, for 'the contents have been known to disappear'. Clearly writing from great experience, Mervyn drew his chaplain's attention in Paragraph 11 to the fact that sherry was popular in cool weather, soft drinks and beer in hot weather, 'spirits in all weathers'.

Paragraph 16 dealt in some detail with the vital matter of 'Bishop's Bedroom'.

(i) Draw curtains.
(ii) Put on bed-side light.
(iii) Fill the ecclesiastical hot-water bottle if necessary, and collect at same time from kitchen jug of cool water (and glass) to be placed next to bed-side light.
(iv) If cold wrap pajamas round hot-water bottle.

As if that were not enough, the chaplain was to make sure Mervyn's electric razor was out and that 'all surfaces are tidy with clothes and cases put away'. When preparing the chapel for communion in the morning he was reminded the wine should be 'Resurrection WHITE (not calvary red)'. At 7.20 a.m. he was to 'Take TEA TO BISHOP (almost black Tea, with only a dash of milk)'. And so it went on, reams of minute and precise instructions – although it is charitable to assume that some of this baloney devised by Mervyn was a form of self-parody. At lunch the chaplain was quite seriously, however, instructed to 'get Bishop to tell of walks in Countryside, etc.' At 4.15 p.m. he was to 'Check hot water is on in pantry, for Tea. 4.25pm, Check tea is ready. Start pouring hot water into Teapots.' It was actually not so much a royal tour as a military operation, planned by a general who had no doubt his staff were incompetent idiots. It is small wonder that Canon Paul Oestreicher, now on the staff of Coventry Cathedral, once remarked that every chaplain who ever worked for Mervyn Stockwood should have been given a medal.

It almost immediately became apparent that the Southwark Ordination Course – 'to train men from a wide experience and background with no age limit and open to men wishing to serve a full-time parochial ministry and to men who want to engage in some form of supplementary ministry' – could not take up all John Robinson's time, so he was appointed Chairman of the College Council and undertook to lecture in Christian Doctrine. What was needed was a full-time Principal, and Mervyn, true to form, chose 'an unusual man with an unusual history'. Stanley Evans, vicar of Holy Trinity, Dalston, whom Mervyn had known since 1955, was a former Communist who had once denounced Mervyn as a fascist because of his criticism of the Soviet Union. But Mervyn believed he had 'a first-class mind', that his eyes had been opened by the

Russian invasion of Hungary, and that his invitation to Evans to join him in Southwark 'gave him a new lease of life'. Stanley Evans was duly appointed Chancellor to the cathedral and a canon, and in addition to his duties as Principal of the Ordination Course he taught Practical Theology. He was to prove yet another of Mervyn's inspired appointments. Eric James has written 'Without Stanley Evans the ordination course would never have got off the ground'.[12] When Evans was killed in a car crash in 1965 John Robinson described him as 'a man of metal they seldom make nowadays, and of whom the Church and the country have only a few'. He recalled that because of Evans's adherence to Communism, no patron was prepared to offer him a benefice for 20 years after his ordination, 'yet he had gifts possessed by few of his contemporaries'.

Paul Oestreicher thinks that 'one of the brave things Mervyn did' was to allow John Robinson to appoint Stanley Evans.[13] 'He was a cuss of a man and a disaster at the cathedral but a really great man. That appointment could have gone woefully wrong but in fact students who totally disagreed with his politics came to respect him enormously.' Another rising star whom Mervyn appointed vice-principal of the Southwark Ordination Course in 1970 was Peter Selby, a man far more radical than Mervyn himself, who in 1984 was consecrated Bishop of Kingston and in 1993 became William Leech Professorial Fellow in Applied Christian Theology at Durham University.

The first crop of students trained for the ministry at the Southwark Ordination Course were ordained by Mervyn at Michael-mas 1963. Meanwhile the maverick Chapter at Southwark was supplemented by another new canon, Douglas Rhymes, who had been in the diocese since 1950. Originally he was a minor canon and sacrist, but when in 1962 it was decided to make further use of the facilities at Wychcroft by initiating a course in lay training, Rhymes was made a residentiary canon and director of lay training. He was also invited to teach Ethics to the Ordination Course, another interesting idea because, although he had not at that time made public his own sexual orientation, Mervyn would have been in no doubt, and neither would John Robinson, that Douglas Rhymes was homosexual. He later described Stanley Evans, with whom he had to work, as 'a martinet who never thought himself wrong, who ruled the ordination course with a rod of iron'.[14] (Mervyn used to say he had no fear after death of meeting his Maker, only of meeting Stanley Evans.) In 1964 Douglas Rhymes was to contribute to a decade of almost unprecedented theological and sexual exploration with a book called *No New Morality*.[15] 'Our cathedral chapter', he recalled, shortly before his death in 1996, 'was the most difficult you could ever have. It was a bit like the Ministry of all the Talents. Evans found it difficult to work with anybody. Eric James [who became precentor in 1964] was a star in his own right.' Rhymes was joined in his lay training work by a formidable theologian, Cecilia Goodenough, holder of a Lambeth Doctorate of Divinity and daughter of an admiral, who 'was very anti-clerical. She thought it disgraceful that women should want to demean themselves by being ordained!'

Mervyn's first Provost, George Reindorp, had 'been regarded in the past as a bit of a "showman"', Archbishop Fisher told Harold Macmillan when recommending him for the bishopric of Guildford. But with links going back to Cambridge student days, Reindorp and Mervyn had got on in Southwark pretty well. Now the man who had to cope with Mervyn's sometimes eccentric if inspired appointments to the cathedral staff was Ernie Southcott, foisted upon Mervyn by the Crown. In his autobiography, Denis Healey remembers Southcott as 'a tall, gaunt Canadian with black hair, a dark-brown face, hooked nose, and an enchanting smile'. Healey regarded Southcott's Christianity as 'numinous' and says he inspired him more than any priest he had ever met.[16] Eric James thinks that Ernie Southcott, who taught Pastoral Theology to the Ordination Course, was 'in a way one of the most brilliant provosts that Southwark ever had, or could have', while Roger Royle, who became succentor and a minor canon in 1968, thought Ernie Southcott 'an incredible character, sort of wild. He wanted to get close to Mervyn. One Christmas night we had "Hark the Herald Angels Sing" and Ernie was belting this out while Mervyn was actually cringing. Ernie would go up to Mervyn to be close to him, and Mervyn would physically pull away.'[17]

It was in May 1963 that Mervyn's successor at Great St Mary's, Joseph Fison, was consecrated Bishop of Salisbury, in Southwark Cathedral; it was a service from which Mervyn absented himself – on the grounds that he would be on holiday in Ireland. 'There were times when he wouldn't turn up for a consecration because he wasn't going to be the star', Canon Roger Royle recalls. 'At Hugh Montefiore's consecration as bishop of Kingston in 1970 he told me "You must remember, Roger, I am the only bishop who is to wear a mitre". Then he said "I shall come immediately in front of the Archbishop of Canterbury". I said "I'm afraid you can't, the Bishop of London comes immediately in front of the Archbishop of Canterbury", and Mervyn said "I'm not being put out by the Bishop of London!" Mervyn was often very badly behaved when he was in the cathedral. Very badly behaved! At ordinations he was impossible.

'He would come to the rehearsal, on the Saturday morning, and this was usually conducted by the chaplain and myself, and it made Covent Garden look amateurish because it was so beautifully choreographed. And to give Mervyn his due, he put tremendous thought and care into his ordination services, but if he spotted anyone out of line he would bawl them out. He had no compunction about that whatsoever.

'We always entered to Parry's "I Was Glad". As we reached the chancel steps, where the throne was placed, it was generally at the part of the anthem where we were praying for the peace of Jerusalem, and by that time he was bored, and he would start to play up. There was one time when he took off his mitre, and that was passed to his chaplain. Then his books went to the chaplain. Then his crozier went to his chaplain – all in the middle of the anthem – and the chaplain – it was Martin Coombs – said "I can't hold any more" so Mervyn grabbed it all back. And then it all came my way!

'He didn't like having a sermon at ordinations because that meant he would have to listen to someone else. On one occasion the verger went to collect the preacher, to take him to the pulpit, and Mervyn said to me "I'm not having the sermon now", and I said "You are". "I'm *not* having the sermon now!" All this was in the middle of the Gradual being sung. This sort of hiatus was quite common. He was always frightfully on edge.'[18]

Canon Dominic Walker confirms that Mervyn regarded the Holy Week services in the cathedral, including the blessing of the oils on Maundy Thursday and Midnight Mass at Christmas, as 'his' services, and especially ordinations, at which he instituted concelebration by the newly ordained priests.[19] Canon David Hutt, who was Priest Vicar and Succentor at Southwark Cathedral from 1973 to 1978, recalls that 'Mervyn coming to the cathedral was an event in itself. He would arrive with a flourish and completely upstage everyone else. He was almost invariably escorted to the Harvard Chapel, where he would spend time sorting through his not inconsiderable collection of pectoral crosses, mainly given to him by the Orthodox, to decide which one to wear. On one terrible occasion the chaplain had left the whole lot behind at Bishop's House, so he borrowed a cross from a passing monk.'[20]

'Finances were always difficult', Canon Royle remembers. 'But Mervyn insisted there must be a great choir. He adored trumpets. At the drop of a hat trumpeters were brought in. He was not a musician, but he had a streak of vulgarity and he knew what worked. Then, when he did a Visitation to the cathedral, his great line would be – "The choir must go!"'[21]

'Bishop Faces Revolt Over Cathedral Cuts' was one newspaper headline in August 1970, above a story that claimed the Bishop of Southwark was 'facing a revolt within his congregation following his proposals for drastic economy measures at Southwark Cathedral, involving selling silver plate, disposing of old books and cutting down staff'. Three adult choristers had apparently resigned 'following cuts in their singing programme and a suggestion that they would lose their annual payment of £265'. Mervyn was quoted as saying 'The £3,700 cost of providing the cathedral's music was too high'.

By comparison to the great purpose-built cathedrals of England, Southwark is a humble affair, a former Augustinian priory and parish church with a thirteenth-century Early English choir and an altar screen dating from 1520. Originally the Priory Church of St Overie, after the Reformation it became the parish church of St Saviour, Southwark, and in 1905 the Cathedral and Collegiate Church of St Saviour and St Mary Overie. Shakespeare worshipped at Southwark and in 1607 his brother Edmund was buried somewhere in the cathedral. There are some fine eighteenth-century memorials, and a magnificent chandelier presented to the church in 1680. John Harvard, founder of Harvard University in America, was baptized in the church, on 29 November 1607, and it is the Harvard Chapel, in the north choir aisle, which contains the Reserved Sacrament and is maintained in his memory.

'The cathedral chapter', says Canon Royle, 'was divided between those who sided with Mervyn and those with the Provost. Ernie Southcott was someone who needed people on his side to support him. He was doing a tremendous amount of pioneering work and should have been better supported by Mervyn. In the cathedral, Mervyn the great innovator became very traditional and he didn't affirm the Provost. One of the problems was that Ernie Southcott wasn't stylish, he didn't entertain. His successor as Provost, Harold

Frankham, put the cathedral on a sound financial footing and did entertain, so Mervyn got on well with him.'[22] Frankham, 59 when he was asked by Mervyn, in 1970, to become Provost of Southwark, could not have been a greater contrast either to the radical and prophetic Ernie Southcott or to Mervyn himself. He was an avowed Evangelical and a born organizer, and once again Mervyn had recognized correctly the gifts required in a certain person at a certain time. Frankham, who died in 1996, brought much needed order and discipline to the cathedral chapter and steadied the nerves of the congregation by preaching sermons based on good old-fashioned biblical Christianity. He stuck to the job for a dozen year, eventually becoming a neighbour of Mervyn's when both were retired in Bath.

However badly Mervyn may have behaved in the cathedral, the fact remains that in the early years of his episcopate Southwark became a mecca for ordinands, young men who wanted to be involved in 'South Bank Religion', the term being related by Mervyn, in an article in the *Evening Standard* on 11 July 1963, to doctrine (he had in mind the writings of John Robinson), sexual ethics (a reference to the sermons of Douglas Rhymes) and pastoral methods. When the untried Southwark Ordination Course opened its doors there were 62 applicants, half of whom were accepted; by 1980, 200 men from the course had been ordained, half of them to the non-stipendiary ministry. But alongside the successes scored in Southwark Mervyn always had to measure the overall picture, the falling off of new priests and a national decline in church attendance. He always thought that Geoffrey Fisher had been appointed to Canterbury to deal with the survival of the Church of England as an institution; by 1974, when Michael Ramsey retired, Mervyn thought his successor, Donald Coggan, would need to concern himself with the survival of Christian faith as a philosophy, a religion and a way of life.[23]

Giles Harcourt remembers the informal manner in which, at Midnight Mass, Mervyn would administer communion, to his legal secretary in particular. 'The Body of Christ, the Body of Christ, the Body of Christ, David, come and see me afterwards, the Body of Christ . . .' Eric James's explanation for Mervyn's conduct towards Southcott was that 'they were personally incompatible. Ernie's body odour was like a polecat.' As well as having problems with Mervyn, with the cathedral chapter and with perspiration, Southcott had marital problems, and finally he had a nervous breakdown. Douglas Rhymes recalled Ernie being incapable of declining an invitation or a request, however trivial, and finally 'going batty saying Mass'. He spent some time in Guy's Hospital, where Mervyn was quite easily dissuaded from visiting him for fear of exacerbating his condition. When Denis Healey went to see him he thought he looked 'like a light bulb that has burned out'. He ended his ministry in a parish in Lancashire.

Notes

1 Very Rev. Murray Irvine, letter to the author, 21 March 1995.
2 Rev. Bill Skelton, in conversation with the author.
3 Ibid.
4 Letter from Chester Herald to the Bishop of Southwark, 11 December 1991.
5 Ned Sherrin, in conversation with the author.
6 A number of MS's *Evening Standard* articles were published as *Bishop's Journal* (Mowbray, 1964).
7 Edward Carpenter, *Archbishop Fisher: His Life and Times* (The Canterbury Press, 1991).
8 Fisher Papers at Lambeth Palace.
9 Dean Mayne, in conversation with the author.
10 Lambeth Palace archives.
11 Canon Eric James, in conversation with the author.
12 Eric James, *A Life of John A. T. Robinson* (Collins, 1987).
13 Canon Paul Oestreicher, in conversation with the author.
14 Canon Douglas Rhymes, in conversation with the author.
15 Douglas Rhymes, *No New Morality* (Constable, 1964).
16 Denis Healey, *The Time of My Life* (Michael Joseph, 1989).
17 Canon Roger Royle, in conversation with the author.
18 Ibid.
19 Canon Dominic Walker, in conversation with the author.
20 Canon David Hutt, in conversation with the author.
21 Canon Roger Royle, as above.
22 Ibid.
23 MS in *The Times*, 22 April 1974.

Chapter 9

A model pastor to his pastors

Scarcely had Mervyn Stockwood recovered his balance from mistakes for which he can fairly be blamed than he and his diocese became embroiled in a *cause célèbre* which was strictly none of their making and which was to leave Southwark and two of its bishops, Mervyn and John Robinson, synonymous with sensation. On 7 September 1960 Robinson received a letter out of the blue from a solicitor, Michael Rubinstein. Rubinstein had been instructed to prepare a defence for Penguin Books, for they were being prosecuted under the new and obscure 1959 Obscene Publications Act. Their alleged offence was the production of an unexpurgated edition of D. H. Lawrence's *Lady Chatterley's Lover*. Clearly the prosecution was being launched as a test case, and Mr Rubinstein wanted to know whether Robinson might, 'as an expert', be prepared to give evidence on his clients' behalf. John Robinson had never read the book and asked for a copy to be sent to him, but within 24 hours he had agreed in principle to help, on the grounds that he found 'the prosecution of this book very difficult to understand'.

He took advice from Martin Jarrett-Kerr, a scholar and a member of the Community of the Resurrection, who told him the matter might 'have considerable repercussions for the social and religious life of Gt Britain'. So having been assured by Mervyn that he was free to speak, John Robinson duly appeared at the Old Bailey in October. His evidence resulted in 'Christians Should Read Lady C. Bishop: "Essentially Something Sacred"' being splashed across the newspapers (it was essentially not what Robinson had said), and the jury acquitted Penguin of publishing an obscene article. Geoffrey Fisher was quick off the mark with a letter informing John Robinson, the wisdom of whose consecration at Mervyn's insistence, only a year before, he had so urgently questioned, that the distress he had caused to very many Christian people was so great he thought he must say something in public. And at his diocesan conference a few days later the Archbishop was in fine fettle. 'Anyone must know', he said, 'that in this sexually self-conscious and chaotic age to speak pastoral wisdom in public on particular questions is extremely dangerous. The Bishop [of Woolwich] exposed himself to this danger ... In my judgement the Bishop was mistaken to think that he could take part in this trial without becoming a stumbling block and a cause of offence to many ordinary Christians.' John Robinson told Fisher he was 'deeply sorry' if he had caused him embarrassment but denied – somewhat unrealistically – that he had given the press any 'handle whatever'. And he sent Fisher the draft of an article he proposed publishing in the *Observer* to clarify his views. It was sadly typical of Fisher that on 9 November he told Robinson he had had no time to do more than glance at his letter 'and at the first paragraph or two of your script', yet found time to dictate 500 words justifying his criticism of Robinson's decision to appear in the witness box.

A letter appeared in *The Times* which read: 'We regret that on one of the infrequent occasions when a bishop has caught the ear of the nation in a manner befitting a spokesman of the National Church he should have been publicly rebuked by the Archbishop of Canterbury.' One of the five signatures was that of another fearless exponent of morality, a canon theologian of Coventry and Dean of Gonville and Caius, Cambridge, Hugh Montefiore.

While the dust had been flying at the Old Bailey, Mervyn had been heading in the diocese for what he later described as 'a near calamity'. The cause was a clash with one of his clergy, the notorious William Bryn-Thomas, or Bryn Thomas as he is better known. Thomas was Vicar of Balham, and he and Mervyn had known one another when Mervyn was at Moorfields and Thomas had a parish in Gloucestershire. They preached for one another, and both wrote articles, in 1944, for the *Socialist Christian*. The first signs of trouble had occurred when Thomas was due to act as host during a visit by Mervyn to the Balham deanery, and absented himself on the grounds that he had to attend a Masonic meeting. This was unwise, for Mervyn had only just had a well publicized row over a request by relatives of a Freemason to hold a Masonic funeral in one of his churches. Thomas had certainly got his priorities wrong, but it was hardly a matter for discipline; by the end of 1960, however, it looked as though Thomas was riding for a fall when a woman laid a formal complaint of sexual impropriety. If guilty, Thomas might have to be unfrocked. But before an incumbent could be unfrocked it would be necessary for him to be tried in Mervyn's consistory court, and in this case Mervyn thought the evidence so damning that rather than Thomas have to endure the scandal of a trial, in a tribunal which ranked with the High Court, Mervyn tried to persuade him to resign – not just his living but Holy Orders. Fisher, however, ruled that resignation was intended only for those wishing to leave the ministry for some honourable reason; it was not intended as a method of escaping the jurisdiction of the Church in a grave moral matter. To any man with Mervyn's liberal instincts there were in any case grave objections to consistory courts, for they were presided over by the Chancellor of the diocese in the role of both judge and jury, without, at this time, even the benefit of assessors. The Chancellor Mervyn had inherited from Bishop Simpson was a very old friend, with whom he shared an interest in psychical research, Garth Moore, since 1947 a lecturer in law at Corpus Christi, Cambridge. By common consent he was the leading authority on canon law, and was one of those who had pressed Mervyn most strongly to accept the see of Southwark, which Moore had imagined they would between them rule with firmness and decision.

The case went to trial – in Holy Week, which seems almost unbelievable – and Mervyn rather childishly says he cried himself to sleep most nights. One reason for this may have been because it began to dawn on him that a verdict of guilty was very far from being an inevitable outcome. 'At one time', David Faull, Mervyn's Registrar and legal secretary, remembers, 'it looked as if Thomas had a perfectly good alibi.' The majority of cases heard in a consistory court have to do with faculties – permissions sought to alter the fabric of a church or install some new monument. Thomas's trial had the label 'sex' attached to it, Mervyn had already attained the status of a high-profile bishop, and he came to believe that if Bryn Thomas won the case it would be he, Mervyn, who would have to resign. In fact, Garth Moore found Thomas guilty, and Mervyn promptly deprived him of his living. So far, so good. Then arose the question of Thomas's unfrocking. Moore was adamant that this impressive if gruesome medieval ceremony should be conducted in public, in the cathedral, and there may have been pressure for this course of action from Fisher. Mervyn had good cause to look back on the incident with regret, to wish he had not taken his Chancellor's advice (which was undoubtedly very bad) and that he had performed the deed in private in his chapel. But for better or worse, armed with bell, book and candle Mervyn solemnly processed to the cathedral, providing a field day for the press, and there cannot be much doubt that the awful ceremony appealed to Mervyn's sense of theatre. The archives at Lambeth Palace reveal the oddest aspect of all: Thomas was unfrocked on 4 May 1961, whereas a formal Deed of Relinquishment had been entered before the Master of the Rolls in the Court of Chancery, by which Thomas resigned Holy Orders, on 10 April. The unfrocking need never have happened at all.

Having achieved, as he saw it, a famous victory for the letter of the law, Garth Moore now became a jealous guardian of the principle that not one stone shall be turned or window pane replaced without a faculty. There was a fine rumpus over some railings Eric James wanted to take down at St George's, Camberwell, which alerted Mervyn to the possibility that he had a Chancellor who might well be learned in law but who was not pastorally sensitive. Then it was discovered that a modern church had developed dry rot and was falling down. It was not until it had actually been pulled down that a faculty was applied for, whereupon Garth Moore declined to grant it, notwithstanding the building lay in ruins. Two things then occurred. Mervyn discovered he could in fact sit in his own consistory court, which for faculty matters he then proceeded to do; and from that moment he and Garth Moore, who remained Chancellor of the diocese during Mervyn's entire episcopate, never spoke again. David Faull tried to reconcile them, but in vain. Both Moore and Mervyn were autocrats, and their falling out was as much a clash of personalities as anything. But as far as Mervyn was concerned, the legal tangles he got into in those early days led to such severe doubts and depression that on a visit to the Holy Land shortly after the unfrocking of Bryn Thomas he talked incessantly to David Faull about resignation – simply because he felt he could not face ecclesiastical legalism.

Despite flaws in his character which sometimes made it difficult for Mervyn to behave well, his ambition was to be a Father in God to his clergy, and in particular he won laurels for the way in which he took care to draw into the life of the diocese Evangelicals, of whom there were a lot in Southwark, and whose beliefs and practices he did not particularly admire. He had got in some practice at wooing Evangelicals back in 1953, when he was invited to visit the

Christian Union at Monkton Combe, where one of the boys, now Canon Malcolm Widdecombe, remembers 'At Monkton we were all, with a few exceptions, strongly evangelical. So Canon Stockwood's visit was viewed with some trepidation. In actual fact he went down very well, especially when he said, "Unless your heart is ablaze with love for our Lord Jesus Christ do not dare to call yourself a Christian."'[1] Sometimes in Southwark he would pull the legs of the Evangelical clergy, calling them Father and plying them with unaccustomed liquor. Told by an Evangelical parish priest that he could not possibly pray for the dead, Mervyn retorted 'My dear, if I didn't pray for the dead I couldn't pray for 80 per cent of the Church of England'.

'What would you really like me to do?' Mervyn once patiently enquired of an Evangelical ordinand who had been complaining at inordinate length about some reference to the Blessed Virgin Mary due to be made in a hymn at his ordination service. 'Would you be satisfied if I took you out and burnt you at the stake?'

'I know you Tyndalle men', Mervyn once joked to an Evangelical who became a bishop, Colin Buchanan, 'all out in the garden with your telescopes, looking for the second coming.' Colin Buchanan first met Mervyn in 1964 when both were members of the Liturgical Commission. 'I was out on a limb theologically', he has written,

in that I had been chosen specifically to bring a conservative evangelical presence on to the commission. It was Mervyn who got me into the dynamics of it all – and he did it by ruthlessly pulling my leg. His main one: 'Let us have a sherry party and send Colin the bill', with reference to the supposed abstemiousness of evangelicals in the 1960s. The egocentric showman combined most amazingly with the genuine Christian pastor and preacher . . .

Staying overnight enabled me to share in his chapel worship in the morning. He was very humble and genuine in saying, 'Unless the clergy have reason to think that I am at my prayers, and with discipline each morning, then we have a situation where they may well abandon theirs.' And so he was having matins and communion, all on his own if I had not been there, and it left its mark on me.[2] It is not, of course, different from the way of life of other bishops and clergy, but it came across to me as a very disciplined and God-orientated exercise in the life of a man who did appear as a flamboyant showman so much of the time.[3]

Mervyn's reputation was for dodging episcopal chores like attendance at synods, and for seldom serving on a committee if he could help it, but when he thought something like liturgical revision important he gave an enormous amount of time to it. The only diocesan committee he chaired was the liturgical committee, and he was serving on the Liturgical Commission before he became a bishop; after a decade of attending its meetings he complained, in 1964, that he was still waiting to spend a whole day on the Eucharist. The result, when they did, was Series 2. Mervyn's interest in liturgical revision led him in November 1974 to write to the *Church Times* to express his distaste for Series 3. 'Of course', he wrote, 'I use it whenever I am asked to do so by my clergy, but I regard it as a merciful deliverance when Series 1 is put in front of me.' He thought Series 3 'an unhappy compromise' that would never satisfy 'most of us who come from a Catholic background', and having by then travelled a long way from his fracas in Carshalton he said he thought that those who wanted a more Catholic liturgy should be allowed to use 'the new Communion Services of the Roman Catholic Church'.

By then he had become impatient with what he saw as the snail's pace of reform, declaring in 1971 that children baptized but not confirmed might receive communion in his diocese. As this was illegal it was more than just another lurch towards liberalism. He had been sitting very loose to strict legality a decade earlier, writing in the *Evening Standard* on 4 July 1961, with evident pride, that it was illegal to hold a communion service in a private house, 'and in order to avoid prosecution I ought to ask the House of Commons for permission'. This comment appeared beneath a photograph of Mervyn celebrating Communion in the living room of a house in Purbeck Street – a good example not only of Mervyn's willingness to flout the law in a good cause but of his desire for personal publicity. (He once endeavoured to get himself photographed in the Tooting branch of Marks & Spencer purchasing a pair of socks.) The article began by commending the efforts of the Rector of Bermondsey – Bill Skelton – in taking the Church to the people, but instead of having Mr Skelton photographed in action he had summoned an *Evening Standard* photographer to record himself celebrating a house communion.

Mervyn learned also to sit loose to certain ecclesiastical conventions, making, as a result, the sort of imaginative gestures only a modern bishop quite sure of his role as an independent

Mervyn on holiday at
Llandudno in August 1932.
Although he was 19, he
pretended the snap had
been taken two years
earlier

Mervyn's sister
Marion
on holiday in 1929

Mervyn's elder brother Alick
who emigrated to Canada

Mervyn's mother,
Ethel Stockwood

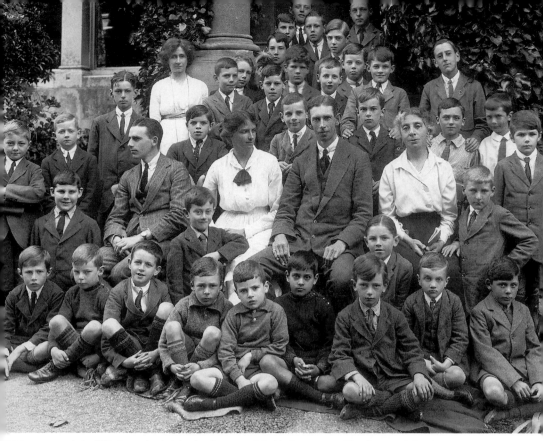

Mervyn aged six (fifth from the left in the front row) in his first year at The Downs School, Clifton, where he remained, with a break of two terms, until he was 13

On the left, aged 16, with two friends from Kelly College

Francis Longworth-Dames, at Westcott House with Mervyn, whose photograph, and the memory of his youthful good looks, Mervyn treasured for the rest of his life. Canon Longworth-Dames was among the mourners at Mervyn's Requiem Mass. Photograph: J. Ross, Dublin

With his fellow ordinands at Westcott House, Cambridge, in 1936. Mervyn is in the back row, third from the right. Fourth from the left in the back row is George Reindorp, later Provost of Southwark and successively Bishop of Guildford and Bishop of Salisbury. Seated in the centre is the Principal, B. K. Cunningham, and fifth from the right the future campaigner for nuclear disarmament, John Collins

In 1935 Mervyn, on the right, graduated from Christ's College, Cambridge, aged 22

Jimmy Hough, one of the boys Mervyn taught at Kingsland Grange in 1931, whose photographs he kept in an album all his life

With rod and line on Exmoor in 1941. Mervyn had taken up fishing when he was 18

Mervyn in his first year as assistant
curate at St Matthew, Moorfields

A Beautiful Baby contest
at St Matthew, Moorfields

The choir of St Matthew, with Mervyn in the centre and on his left his curate, John Robinson, later Bishop of Woolwich. The little boy in front is Tony Gingell, whose family Mervyn did much to support. He was one of the last people to see Mervyn alive, and received a legacy of £10,000

During the war, Mervyn, in the centre of the second row, joined the Shelter Wardens' Service. On his left is his old prep school headmaster, Wilfrid Harrison

With all sincere good wishes from R.B.B.

One of Mervyn Stockwood's most *outré* friends was his Bristol curate Richard Blake-Brown, by whose outrageous life-style and flamboyant personality he was fascinated

Mervyn returned to Kelly College for its centenary celebrations in 1977. On his left is the current headmaster, Dennis Ball, on his right his own headmaster, Norman Miller, to whose son he stood as godfather

Dick Chapman, the 17-year-old
Bristol Grammar School boy with
whom Mervyn fell in love

Roy Clevely, aged 15, the second of
Mervyn Stockwood's Boy Bishops.
One of his duties was to preach on
St Matthew's Day, and in adult life he
became a lay reader.
Photograph: Veale & Co., Bristol

With two fellow socialists, Michael Foot and the Earl of Longford

A youthful Charles Lansdale, on the right, in whose matrimonial prospects Mervyn took a personal interest.
Photograph: Harry's Photographers, Bristol

While Vicar of Great St Mary's, Mervyn frequently debated at the
Cambridge Union, on this occasion in January 1959

Mrs Mary Bevan, at her Elizabethan home, Longstowe Hall, where Mervyn was a frequent pampered guest

On a visit to Romania in 1976 there was 'much hand kissing, singing and flower throwing'.
Mervyn extends his episcopal ring to be kissed by a young Communist workman

With Queen Elizabeth the Queen Mother at St Giles, Camberwell in November 1967. The Queen Mother's visits to Bishop's House usually ended up in the kitchen

In 1979 Mervyn was spirited away from a diocesan conference at Margate to attend a Foyle's luncheon at the Dorchester for a book by Barbara Cartland, *I Seek the Miraculous*. On the left is Margaret, Duchess of Argyll. Photograph: Bill Bates-Van Hallan

A farewell blessing to his diocese when he retired in 1980.
The deacons at the Eucharist, celebrated on the Centre Court at Wimbledon,
were, on the left, Neil Heaviside, a minor canon at Southwark Cathedral,
and on the right his last domestic chaplain, Peter McCrory

In retirement at Bath with his cat Midge. The garden of 15 Sydney Buildings
had views over the Kennet and Avon Canal to Bath Abbey.
Photograph: Bristol United Press

arbiter in his own diocese would risk. Dominic Walker was a member of the Community of the Glorious Ascension, founded in 1960, and because in his house they had no priest brother to say Mass, in 1972 Mervyn ordained Dominic priest within only three months of ordaining him deacon. A much older man he ordained priest just one week after making him a deacon, without even sending him to a theological college. He very early on found a divorced and remarried curate out in the cold and gave him a living; needless to say, this elicited a note of protest from Geoffrey Fisher, who was moved to express his displeasure also on an occasion when Princess Margaret was invited to distribute Bibles to ordinands in the cathedral. It was presumably to her lay, not her royal, status that the Archbishop objected.

When Mervyn made that ill-judged foray into Carshalton to curb the use of the Roman Rite he became for a time, as Tom Driberg was to point out in the *New Statesman*, 'the hero of the extreme Protestants', but as David Bubbers more recently recalls, he also 'inevitably had skirmishes with the Diocesan Evangelical Union'. One such skirmish occurred when John Pearce-Higgins, the radical vice-provost of Southwark, declined to subscribe to the Thirty-Nine Articles. Mr Bubbers, now retired to Eastbourne, writes:

The Bishop invited us to meet him to talk the situation over and we were first advised we would be meeting in a church hall close to his house in Streatham. On the day, we were all welcomed into the Bishop's home ... Mervyn was in a most expansive and jovial mood, telling some very good jokes and keeping us all amused before there was even a breath on the subject that had brought us there. It was masterful, really, on the Bishop's part. He disarmed his critics, and even those who had come thirsting to attack felt that they could not be too outspoken as guests in the Bishop's home.[4]

Mr Bubbers's testimonial, coming from an Evangelical, is one of the most striking the author has received. He writes:

I developed a great regard and affection for Mervyn and this increased over the years. My wife and I knew him as a caring pastor and I greatly respected him for his knowledge of his parishes and clergy. He could be impulsive and unpredictable but he had the saving grace of a superb sense of humour, and I found him always ready to give his full support to men who were doing their job right across the spread of churchmanship.

He recalls that 'Soon after his arrival he issued to his clergy a pastoral directive virtually commanding us to say prayers in church daily according to the Prayer Book rubrics'. And as an example of Mervyn's spontaneous care of his clergy, Mr Bubbers remembers how on one occasion he himself had influenza, 'and on the Sunday, a day or two after, I came downstairs, and late one snowy afternoon the Bishop walked up to our vicarage door having had to leave his car at the bottom of the road because of the snow. He had come to see me and my wife and spent some time with us, conducting Evening Prayer in our lounge before he left. He was a model pastor to his pastors.'

But not everyone saw Mervyn at his best. Paul Oestreicher recalls that 'Twice I saw Mervyn at his worst'. On one occasion, a young cleric on secondment from Berlin, who had been found a job in the diocese by John Robinson because he was too radical for the taste of the German Lutheran Church, fell out with his wife. It was alleged that he had assaulted her, and he was summoned to Bishop's House where, with Oestreicher present as a witness, 'Mervyn wiped the floor with him, without listening to his side of the story at all. "I have no intention of entering into any kind of debate with you" Mervyn told the cleric. He treated this chap as though he was the scum of the earth. Maybe he deserved it, but Mervyn didn't bother to examine the case in any kind of detail.' An explanation for Mervyn's unpastoral conduct towards one of his pastors on this occasion may have been his abhorrence of violence or cruelty – a trait quite common in those who are themselves potentially prone to such vices; cruelty towards animals, in particular, Mervyn found impossible to tolerate. On 25 April 1961 he told his *Evening Standard* readers that seven boys aged between 12 and 19, conditionally discharged for impaling frogs on spears, should have been made to work hard for no pay on a diet of bread and water.

As parish priest of the Church of the Ascension in Blackheath, Canon Oestreicher also served as chaplain to Dartmouth House, a retreat house bequeathed by the sister of a former Bishop of Rochester. When Mervyn discovered that the newly appointed warden and his wife had decreed that only vegetarian meals were to be served, 'There was a tantrum. Mervyn demanded to know what right these young upstarts thought they had to dictate to the bishop and his ordinands what they were to eat? And the issue became one not of vegetarianism but authoritarianism. There was total impasse, and after six weeks the warden left with bitterness and tears. Because he had failed to reach a compromise, Mervyn felt himself a failure and could no longer bear to enter Dartmouth House, and although it was making a profit for the diocese he insisted on selling it. It went to the highest bidder and was turned into luxury flats.'

Dartmouth House was not the only 'institution' to which Paul Oestreicher ministered as chaplain. So dependent was Mervyn on supernumerary companions that he appointed honorary chaplains to himself, one of whom was Canon Oestreicher. Another was Bill Skelton. On 16 December 1975 a dozen honorary chaplains were entertained. They accompanied Mervyn on his Saturday walks, and one day, when the cook was ill, Paul Oestreicher was roped in to prepare the dinner. Mervyn's recruitment of Paul Oestreicher for the British Council of Churches in 1968 must rate as one of his most enlightened appointments, but despite Oestreicher's detestation of tyranny, his campaigning against apartheid and his work for Amnesty International he never quite measured up to Mervyn's expectations. 'He saw me as a critic. He thought I was critical of his life style. He would ask if I thought he was a socialist, because he needed reassurance, and I never quite gave it to him.'

Mervyn's mind was constantly at work, seeking causes to espouse, enterprises to encourage, bridges to build. In 1964 a parliamentary election was fought in Smethwick, won by Alderman Peter Griffiths on what Mervyn had no doubt was a racist ticket. Although the constituency was not in his diocese he had no hesitation in criticizing the campaign, which resulted in Michael Ramsey being obliged to field a letter of complaint from Miss Agnes L. Fenton, chairman of the Smethwick Conservative & Unionist Women's Luncheon Club. The same year (on 20 August) Mervyn was writing to Ramsey, for some reason marking his letter 'Confidential', to say

Three parsons who hold my licence or permission to officiate have had what they describe as a pentecostal experience which manifests itself, inter alia, in the ability to 'speak in tongues'.

They spent the day with me at Bishop's House recently in bible reading, prayer and study. We had a Mass of the Holy Spirit in my chapel and all of them spoke in tongues.

The three men who are of different ecclesiastical persuasions are well above the average – sensible, balanced, modest. All are happily married with families. What particularly struck me about them was an infectious goodness. Spiritual power seemed to radiate from them.

They are keeping in touch with me and we shall meet occasionally for further bible study and prayer.

Mervyn says in his autobiography he had many parishes 'in which men had been for years and were virtually useless'. He may have had in mind 'the sad case of St ——'s, Bermondsey', as he described one of his parishes in a letter to the editor of the *Church Times*, dated 9 November 1964 and not of course intended for publication.

For your private information the trouble is the temperament of the Vicar who lives in a state of constant quarrelling – with the congregation, the Borough Council, the Member of Parliament, the Press, the Diocese, the Bishop. It is a tragic story of a psychological misfit who ought never to have been ordained.

For years [it could not have been for more than five] I have tried to pour oil on troubled waters, but when Mr ——'s behaviour became quite outrageous last January I was compelled to tell him that until he lived peaceably with his brethren I should not visit his church. I have often wondered how another bishop would have dealt with the situation because he has certainly proved too difficult for the bishops, the archdeacons and rural dean of this diocese.

Mervyn had been driven to ask the *Church Times* to set the record straight in the wake of a 'mischievous and misleading' article in the *Sunday Express*. 'No doubt I could take legal action', he wrote, 'but, as you know, for a bishop this is not wise.' Mervyn claims that in his first year he called at 300 vicarages in the diocese – something of an exaggeration, surely; it would have meant very nearly one a day. What he actually did was set up a programme of systematic parish visiting, which might include a night spent in the vicarage, with a message sent ahead that if sherry was offered, the bishop liked it dry (at home he served Fells Manzanilla); the story that his chaplain was sent ahead, too, to test the bed springs is – one hopes – apocryphal. Donald Reeves, who took over as chaplain in 1965, says 'Mervyn was really a parish priest, which is why he enjoyed visitations. He would take sick communion to parishioners, pay visits to social clubs. But it was often rather intimidating for the clergy, who had to stay up with him until all hours of the morning. And he would come back absolutely exhausted. He would carry out a visitation every ten days.'

Once a year Mervyn would visit each deanery, or attend a residential deanery meeting at Wychcroft, and every four years he would go for five days to a Butlin's Holiday Camp with perhaps 400 or 500 clergy, leaving the diocese, he wittily remarked, 'practically without parsons – just a skeleton staff to bury the dead'. The first such camp took place in 1961 at Bognor Regis, when he invited the Bishop of Bradford, Donald Coggan, shortly to succeed Michael Ramsey as Archbishop of York, to give a lecture on preaching. Coggan later became, of the four archbishops under whom Mervyn served, the one he respected most. At Bognor, Mervyn wrote in the *Evening Standard* on 13 June 1961, Dr Coggan 'was outstanding. He combined ability, charm and commonsense to a remarkable degree, and I have rarely known a man win the respect and affection of an audience so quickly.' One of the attractions of the Bognor camp was a bar called The Pig and Whistle, 'the largest bar in the place', where on the last night Mervyn met Billy Butlin for a drink.

On a later occasion – there were five Butlin's Camps altogether while Mervyn was diocesan – Jilly Cooper dropped in on the Clacton Butlin's Holiday Camp to report for the *Sunday Times*, and asked one of Mervyn's clergy if it was compulsory to attend. He told her 'It's frowned on not to. The Bishop of Southwark put out a three-line whip.' An elderly vicar, while 'dipping a biscuit into his tea', told Miss Cooper the only excuse one was allowed to plead for absence was marital problems. 'Unfortunately I haven't had a cross word with my wife in years.' Getting in some practice for her future career as a novelist, she described Mervyn as 'a splendidly flamboyant figure with smouldering deep-set eyes. Urbane, very much the Prince Bishop.' She was equally stricken by David Sheppard, who in 1969 had succeeded John Robinson as Bishop of Woolwich, describing him as a real beauty, with 'black hair hardly touched with grey, exuding modesty and manliness like a John Buchan hero'. Another 'Stockwood Scorcher' who rolled up was the Vicar of St Peter's, Morden, 'who has curly hair, burning eyes and is the image of Terence Stamp'. Jilly Cooper did not fail to write up the Bishop of Kingston too. She found Hugh Montefiore 'suave and elegant in lavender flares and a striped shirt. Unusually tall, very donnish, he has one of those "frightfully, frightfully" voices.' A Redcoat told her they liked having the clergy: 'They're so well behaved and nicely spoken.'

Eric James confirms the personal touch that became a byword in Southwark. 'His detailed care was astonishing. He sent postcards

to everyone he had ordained until the day of his death.'[5] 'I understand you have had a son', was an archetypal note sent by Mervyn
to Tony Crowe on 25 April 1966. 'I hasten to send my best wishes
to you and your wife. I hope the child is flourishing. I am sure your
new parish will warmly welcome the arrival!' But rather more
cryptic, and not so much appreciated, were the notes he sent to
would-be ordinands who had failed to be selected for training. In
1960 Murray Irvine became a selection secretary at Church House,
and writes:

My colleagues and I did not regard Southwark as one of the easier
dioceses for ordinands. Mervyn had an excellent team of examining
chaplains but the bishop appeared remote and prelatical, even to an old
friend. The custom was (and is) for bishops to write to their candidates
on receiving the selectors' report. Mervyn would write curt little letters
to the men who suffered the often traumatic experience of not being
recommended by the selectors.[6]

Tony Crowe had no doubt that Mervyn supported his clergy 'If
you kept on the right side of him. If you had fallen out – and this
was one of his great weaknesses – he couldn't make it up, certainly
if he thought someone was a rascal or a shirker. When he let fly
it was uncontrolled.' At Crowe's induction to St Luke's, Charlton,
the rural dean failed to secure a parking space for Mervyn's car,
'and he tore him off a strip in the vestry in front of everybody'.
Shirkers were never among Mervyn's favourite people. 'He was
impossible, sometimes', his first chaplain recalls, 'because he
was very demanding, and his absolute bugbear was lazy clergy.'
On one occasion when Mervyn thought it necessary to discipline
a lazy clergyman, the unrepentant culprit said to him 'You are
only treating me like this because I am black'. 'Indeed I am', said
Mervyn. 'If you were white I should have deprived you of your
living.' On another occasion Mervyn decided he required someone's resignation but happened to be in bed with bronchitis.
Nothing daunted, and clad in purple pyjamas, he summoned to his
bedside, at dead of night, the Archdeacon of Southwark, his
Registrar and the errant cleric, who was steadfastly lectured into
the small hours until eventually he gave up the uneven struggle
and signed a deed of relinquishment. It never seemed to make any
difference to Mervyn whether a priest wanted to see him urgently,
in which case midnight was as good a time as any, or whether he

himself wanted to haul someone over the coals: midnight, again, would suit. The fact that he was in bed and unwell was neither here nor there.

Michael Mayne explains: 'Mervyn worked hard and he expected everyone else to work hard too. I didn't mind that because he was enormously thoughtful and he protected one's free time. I invariably had Saturday off. He never wanted to know what I did. He was an extraordinary combination of self-centredness in many ways, as we all are, but extremely thoughtful about small things, and imaginative about surprising you. If someone had been bereaved he would write on the anniversary.' On the fortieth anniversary of Mervyn's consecration Michael Mayne was to send him a greetings card. 'It is half a lifetime', he wrote from the deanery at Westminster, 'yet my memories of sleeping on a camp bed in the vestry of the Cathedral while you kept watch on the eve of your consecration are vivid, as are so many from those good and constructive years. And very happy too. Thank you for involving me in your memorable life and ministry, for which so many are grateful.'

Notes

1 Letter from Canon Widdecombe to the author, 27 February 1995.
2 It would have been illegal for MS to consecrate on his own, but at Bishop's House and in Bath he kept the Reserved Sacrament in a silver hanging pyx, so that had he been alone in the morning he would have been able to give himself communion from the Reserved Sacrament.
3 Letter from Bishop Buchanan to the author, 4 May 1995.
4 Letter from Rev. David Bubbers to the author, 20 March 1995.
5 Canon Eric James, in conversation with the author.
6 Very Rev. Murray Irvine, letter to the author, 21 March 1995.

Chapter 10

The Right Reverend Prelate

In 1961 Geoffrey Fisher retired, to the rectory at Trent, in Dorset, whence he bombarded all and sundry, including Mervyn Stockwood, with instructions not to support the Scheme for Anglican–Methodist Reunion. The enthronement sermon of the new Archbishop of Canterbury, Michael Ramsey, preached at Canterbury Cathedral on 27 June 1961, met with Mervyn's approval, for it called for greater freedom 'in the ordering and in the urgent revising of our forms of worship'. But he noted in an article in the *Evening Standard* that he had encountered a lot of smartly dressed people but no one from the working classes. He wondered if Christ would have been excluded from the service. It was hardly one of Mervyn's more penetrating attacks on social injustice, and all he wrote was:

After the enthronement service we had tea in the Assembly Hall of the King's School. The Establishment in more senses than one was present in full force. Hundreds of them in top hats and swallow coats. But I didn't run into a single working-class person.

I sometimes wonder what the Carpenter of Nazareth must think about His Church. And I wonder whether He would have been admitted to the Enthronement: probably not.

But this evidently scratched a raw nerve, and on 5 July Michael Ramsey was stung into a sharp response. 'In fact', the new Primate of All England took time off to explain,

the 'working class' people who were present, though not perhaps numerous, were all friends of ours both from Yorkshire and from County Durham who had come a very long way in order to be present, and, as you may know, 'working class' people have got quite a lot of money nowadays and do dress up smartly.

What was the purpose of your remarks other than a conventional piece of left wing sneering? As I have said, your words misrepresent the truth and are hard to relate to charity.

I would add that my 'working class' friends who came were specially given some of the best seats in the Cathedral.[1]

It was not an auspicious start to relations between Mervyn and his new Archbishop, and worse was to follow. Meanwhile, Robert Beloe, Ramsey's erudite lay secretary, was instructed to ask Mervyn if he could approach the *New Statesman* with a view to having them appoint an ecclesiastical correspondent, an interesting sidelight on the extent of interest shown at the time in Church affairs even by strictly secular publications. Mervyn contacted Tom Driberg, who on 23 June 1961 had contributed a long unsigned profile of Mervyn Stockwood to the *New Statesman*; Driberg told him he thought such an appointment unlikely. The profile had been headed 'Turbulent Priest', and recorded Mervyn saying apropos his expelling of the curate at Carshalton – 'with what seemed to some of his friends an excess of disciplinarian zeal, amid circum-stances of dramatic publicity and with the visible support of the civil law' – that 'if one had to play that hand again one might play it differently'. Driberg offered his readers a physical description of Mervyn, 'tall and lean, his strongly featured face . . . crowned by a mop of iron-grey hair, his voice . . . rich, deep and resonant'. As to his character, Driberg did not hesitate to write that 'humility and unselfishness seem always to be at war with a tendency to vanity, even arrogance (from which a self-critical sense of humour sometimes saves him), so in his public demeanour dignity and homeliness alternate with puzzling frequency'.

This dichotomy in Mervyn's character has been commented on by numerous people who knew him. Lord Soper is particularly forthright. 'He was a very imperfect human being, and the undoubted sincerity of his Christianity never seemed to make any difference to the habits of a basically self-centred man. I think he never grew up. I never felt there was a fully rounded quality to his beliefs and practices.' Canon Rhymes said 'He kept people at a distance and was very egocentric. You listened to him more than he listened to you. He was the best bishop I could ever have had, but if you asked me if I wanted Mervyn as a personal companion, the answer would be No. You sometimes loved him, sometimes hated him.' Canon Royle: 'There were times when Mervyn could show enormous kindness, but he was a mixture of generosity and meanness.' As for his alleged vanity, Giles Harcourt recalls: 'Mervyn spent a fair amount of time in front of the mirror. He was aware that he had a fine profile, and he always took care on big occasions to make sure his hair was well brushed.'[2]

It was in 1961 that Mervyn recruited a secretary, Mary Cryer, who remembers that at her initial interview Mervyn seemed incapable of looking her in the eye. Matters clearly improved, for Mary Cryer was to remain with Mervyn for 18 years – until the day he retired, when she moved on to Lambeth Palace to work as bursar. With the inevitable ebb and flow of domestic chaplains and house-keepers, with the eventual death of Mervyn's mother and changes of appointment among senior clergy in the diocese, Mary Cryer became the one symbol of permanence at Bishop's House, an anchor of whose steadfastness Mervyn may at times have shown a lack of appreciation but whose presence testified to the degree of loyalty he was capable of arousing. The relationship was very formal to start with, Mervyn addressing Mary as Miss Cryer, but when she had occasion to write Mervyn a letter and signed it Mary he took the hint and from then on made use of her Christian name. Mary always called Mervyn 'Bishop', and was very properly rewarded for her unbroken stint of discreet and diligent service with a legacy of £12,000.

On 24 January 1961 Mervyn had been lamenting in the *Evening Standard* the 'large slice of the week' that had been taken up with Convocation, 'which I dislike as it involves listening to interminable speeches on subjects in which I have little interest'. Its procedure, he wrote, was 'as picturesque as it is archaic, and it involved an appalling waste of time'. He complained of having to wear 'episcopal robes' and being compelled, before getting down to business, to listen to the Litany in Latin. He hoped the new Archbishop – Michael Ramsey – would 'tackle the problem', for although 'an enthusiast for reasonable traditions and pageantry', he wanted 'the Parliament of the Church to undergo a radical revolution so as to speak to contemporary England in a language and a dress that suggest the twentieth century and not the thir-teenth'. But when the 'Parliament of the Church' did undergo a radical revolution, half-way through his episcopate, by adopting synodical government, Mervyn was to experience considerable unease, telling his diocesan synod in June 1972 that instead of giving the Church greater freedom to win people to the faith, synodical government 'was becoming an octopus, whose tentacles were entwining themselves round the Church so that we are suffocating. There is', he said, 'a tendency for the General Synod to refer to the diocesan synods and back again as nobody wants to take the initiative.' In the autumn he intended issuing a Pastoral Letter to the churchmen in the diocese asking them 'to put ecclesiastical machinery into cold storage and to devote their attentions to the Christian Faith'.

Mervyn's impatience with ecclesiastical debate was well illustrated in the minutes of a previous meeting of his synod: 'The Bishop outlined the procedure for the day and stated that he hoped that speeches would be kept to a minimum length.'

Synodical government, introduced in 1970, was something Mervyn disliked almost as much as he disliked Freemasonry. Writing in *The Times* on 15 May 1974 he voiced the opinion that 'We have passed from episcopacy into what is supposed to be democracy. In the old days a bishop got on with his job. Today, a lot of ecclesiastical busybodies, who represent nobody but a small in-group of self-important party laity, take to themselves or try to take to themselves the governing of a diocese.' Nowhere more clearly than in that passage did Mervyn reveal the clash he always experienced between his high view of the episcopacy and his emotional allegiance to the claims of 'social democracy'.

In his *Evening Standard* article Mervyn went on to claim that he had tipped both Ramsey for Canterbury and Donald Coggan for York. 'The country may take a little time to warm to Ramsey', he warned his readers. 'He is not a popular figure like Temple; nor a statesman like Lang; nor a practical administrator like Fisher.' He was, in Mervyn's opinion, 'an eccentric with a massive spirituality', who would find a firm ally in Coggan. Unfortunately, Ramsey and Coggan were poles apart in churchmanship and social attitudes, and for a variety of reasons, for the next 14 years they tended to go their separate ways.

In January 1962 Mervyn had an opportunity to flex his muscles as a social reformer. Over the past 15 years a remarkable swing had taken place in the attitude of bishops towards capital punishment, a swing assisted by the introduction over that period of more liberal-minded prelates. When in 1948 a Labour-dominated House of Commons had voted in favour of experimental abolition, Fisher had spoken in the Lords in favour of retaining capital punishment, and indeed the only episcopal opponent at that time was George

Bell of Chichester. Opinion even among Tory MPs had shifted by 1956 to the extent that, on a free vote, the Commons again passed a motion for experimental suspension. This time, in the Lords, Fisher voted for abolition, with the proviso that the death penalty be retained for certain categories of murder, whereas Ramsey, as Archbishop of York, together with Bell and seven other bishops, voted for total abolition. A year later, the 1957 Homicide Act was passed, making distinctions of gravity between different kinds of killing, and when, in 1961, Ramsey succeeded Fisher at Canterbury, Mervyn decided the time was ripe for a push by the bench. Believing the death penalty to be a denial of the Gospel, he introduced in the Convocation of Canterbury in January 1962 a motion proposing that the death penalty be abolished for an experimental period. According to Ramsey's official biography, so persuasive were his arguments that every bishop in both Convocations save Maurice Harland, Bishop of Durham, supported Mervyn's motion. Ronald Williams, however, Bishop of Leicester since 1953, was an ardent opponent of abolition, and it seems unlikely he would have supported the motion.

As a result of Mervyn's debate, House of Commons campaigners received new impetus and a boost to their arguments for scrapping the Homicide Act, which was so unsatisfactory that even the Home Secretary and the Lord Chief Justice accepted that it was unworkable. With the advent of a Labour government in October 1964 and the appointment of a dedicated abolitionist, Gerald Gardiner, as Lord Chancellor, the chances of finally consigning the gallows to history seemed brighter than ever before. Lord Dilhorne, a diehard hanger, tried to dissuade Ramsey from piloting an abolition Bill through the Lords, and after some hesitation Ramsey realized he was unqualified for such a crucial role, and could in any case hardly spare the time. He continued to speak in favour of abolition, however, as did Mervyn, and the end result was a famous victory for those who believed capital punishment to be both socially and morally indefensible.

Within only four years of his consecration Mervyn found himself the 26th most senior diocesan bishop, and in consequence, in 1963, he took his seat in the House of Lords. In the bishops' robing room he soon set about encouraging the other bishops to address one another by their Christian names, much to the consternation of the Bishop of Chester, Gerald Ellison, and he disapproved of bishops wearing Convocation robes in the chamber as strongly as he objected to them wearing Convocation robes in Convocation. But he only once dared to defy convention by appearing in the Lords in a suit.

Mervyn was introduced into the House of Lords on 14 November 1963, and having led a pilgrimage to the Holy Land in April the following year he made his maiden speech, on 6 May 1964, on the subject of refugees and international aid. He was congratulated by a fellow cleric, Lord Sandford, who said he knew the Right Reverend Prelate well enough to say that 'whether we look forward to it or not, his contributions . . . are quite certain to be searching, trenchant and almost certainly controversial'. On 2 July Mervyn tackled overcrowding in prisons, and expressed particular concern about an increase in the numbers of people imprisoned for debt. He spoke on world population and family planning, the aircraft industry, the Consumer Council, licensing laws in Scotland and preparation for retirement. On 11 November 1964, however, he had to apologize for not being in his place to take Prayers, when the Lord Chancellor had been obliged to deputize. 'It was due to a false entry in my diary', he explained, 'for which I am wholly responsible.'

With some temerity, surely, he informed their Lordships they lived in a spiv age, in which 'expense accounts are elastically handled at all levels'. He called for better relations between police and public, and put in a plea for the abolition of capital punishment on the grounds that while murder was a terrible thing 'it was not for us to usurp the prerogatives of God'. Our task, he said, 'is to reclaim the murderer, as I know from personal experience can happen'.

In 1965 the Lords debated homosexual law reform, and Mervyn took the opportunity to tell of a 19-year-old physics student at Cambridge who committed suicide when the police got wind of his homosexual affair. He said he wanted the law proscribing all homo-sexual conduct changed because it was unhelpful and defeated its own ends. In tune with the times (all the bishops had to tread softly, for homophobia in the Lords was rampant) he lumped 'fornication, adultery, sadism, lesbianism, broken homes and homosexuality', somewhat incongruously, as 'domestic sorrow, failure and sin'. He brought his speech to a hasty conclusion because, according to *Hansard*, whose reporter presumably misheard him, he had 'an engagement made two years ago' which meant he had to be in Malvern at half past eight to take a service. He had risen to speak at

7.13 p.m., so presumably it was Malden for which he was heading. But he did not quit the chamber before declaring 'Very often in the past the Church has been accused by members of the Party now in power of dragging its feet, and not being socially aware, and being timid and being cowardly. All those charges I throw on to the Government.' He ended by accusing supporters of Harold Wilson's Labour administration (many of whom supported homosexual law reform) of 'sheer humbug'.

When the Sexual Offences Bill was again debated on 24 May Mervyn said 'In the sphere of personal behaviour, morality means freedom to choose between right and wrong in the context of personal responsibility'. But, he said, homosexuals had no such freedom. All were equally criminal. 'It is the opinion of many of us on this Bench that the law as it stands is one of the most misguided, the most vicious and the most evil in its consequences.'

Mervyn was certainly not afraid to throw his net wide. During the 1965–66 session he spoke on abortion, China, Greater London Transport, Southern Rhodesia and technical assistance to developing countries. During the 1966–67 session he contributed to debates, among other subjects, on the economic situation, House of Lords reform, the effect of television on young children, the problems of the countryside, race relations and world refugees. On 1 May 1969, the tenth anniversary of his consecration, he took up the cudgels on behalf of a resident of Purley, Dr Alfred Lawrence, a previous victim of Dachau concentration camp, who had been charged under the 1911 Official Secrets Act. Mervyn wanted to know why his home had been raided with publicity 'which did great damage to his standing in Purley as a resident and also in his position as an earner'.

Whether the time of a diocesan bishop is well spent speaking about the cleaning of the exterior of the Palace of Westminster or Sunday postal collections is debatable, and Mervyn was always at his most effective on important set occasions, as he was when he spoke at length on 16 April 1973 on accommodation for the homeless young. He said he was prepared to take any of their Lordships on an anonymous tour of south London at night to see for themselves what was going on. 'I put this question to your Lordships', he thundered. 'If these were your own youngsters, would your Lordships sleep comfortably in your beds at night?'

Another subject on which he was effective, because he knew what he was talking about, was The Church of England (Worship and Doctrine) Measure, debated on Michael Ramsey's seventieth birthday, his last day as Archbishop of Canterbury. Mervyn's contribution resulted in an altercation with Lord Sudeley.

Before the noble Lord [Lord Sudeley] sits down, and as he has devoted the earlier part of his speech to attacking my diocese in detail, may I say that had he observed the normal conventions of this House and informed me beforehand that he was going to criticise Southwark – and I am sorry that the noble Lord has not followed the usual conventions of good manners – I would have been able to give him some information which might have been helpful. I might indeed have saved him from the gaffe of talking about people who live in Twickenham, which is in the diocese of London, and complaining about what goes on in the diocese of Southwark. But my main point is that the noble Lord was talking about services being imposed on parishes in my diocese. I have watched these matters very carefully, and it so happens that I am not a supporter of either Series II or III. Nevertheless, where they occur I am told, and I have every reason to believe, that it was as a result of a democratic majority decision of the parochial church council. I know not of a single church in my diocese in which any service has been imposed on any congregation against the democratic will of the parochial church council.

In a debate on exorcism on 5 May 1975, Lady Gaitskell asked 'Is it not very worrying that high dignitaries of the Church not only accept exorcism and possession of devils as a fact, but also accept it as a therapy?' Mervyn retorted that exorcism might benefit many people, 'perhaps all of us, including the noble Baroness herself', at which point the Minister of State at the Department of Industry, Lord Beswick, wisely hurried the House on to the next business.

For Mervyn, attendance at the House of Lords was not only a duty and a pleasure, it was easy; he did not have to travel for hours from some diocese in the north of England. Even so, on 30 March 1977, when he spoke for 19 minutes on inner-city problems, he had to apologize for not being present at the start of the debate just after three o'clock because 'an inescapable engagement made that impossible'. In a heated exchange on the abduction of children in Rhodesia, on 31 July 1978, Mervyn claimed to have been 'pastor to the Foreign Secretary and responsible for his spiritual welfare for a good many years'. The Foreign Secretary was of course David

Owen. Mervyn was equally in his element during a debate on 13 February 1979 when he spoke during the second reading of the Marriage (Enabling) Bill, designed to permit marriage to a step-daughter, for he was able to ride a pet hobby-horse, the question of remarriage of divorcees.

When it comes to divorce, I should like to say to the noble Lord, Lord Mancroft, that it is not correct to say that it is against the law of the Church of England for a clergyman to marry a divorced person. He is fully entitled by the law of the land to marry a divorced person, even without consulting his bishop, if his conscience says so. He has the legal right to marry or not . . . I myself have married divorced people on a number of occasions, and so have many of my clergy friends. I have done so four times in the past 40 years, which is an average of once every 10 years, and when people tell me that if we have lax laws people will all be going over London Bridge to the south side of the river in order to get married in Southwark I say it is quite untrue; they are much more likely to go over London Bridge to get married in a more fashionable church on the other side of the river.

On 20 June 1979 Mervyn spoke on unemployment, pointing out that every unemployed person was costing the country £6,000 a year in benefits, in lost tax and lost production. The total, £90m a year, was more than the Government spent on education and health, and twice the bill for housing. 'It is time we made an all out effort to end this crazy situation', he said. On 30 April 1980 Mervyn again found himself on home ground, when the Lords turned their attention to a National Front march in Lewisham, and Mervyn asked whether the cost of policing could not be met by the whole community rather than by the ratepayers of a particular borough.

Within only seven months of becoming a member of the House of Lords Mervyn had found himself engaged in an acrimonious correspondence with a fellow socialist, Lady Summerskill, to whom, on 10 July 1964, he wrote a polite and conciliatory letter explaining the difficulty bishops had in attending the Lords as they had a full-time job, and that sometimes an important debate in Church Assembly clashed with an equally important debate in the Lords. 'Many peers', he wrote, 'when they think the intervention of a bishop might be helpful, write to him several weeks beforehand in the hope that he may be able to free himself and to prepare an informed speech. I have received several requests from peers on both sides of the House. If you were to extend us a similar courtesy I do not think you would be disappointed.'

Lady Summerskill, who was something of a battleaxe, retorted four days later:

My dear Bishop, Please try to be a little more objective.

When we see the Bishops' bench full to discuss doctrine, vestments etc. and not a word is heard on slums, widows, the sick, and the fatherless child, some of us get a little hot under the collar.

If you could see the picture from our side you might express yourself differently.

The only chance of a religious revival in this country is for the Christian ethic to be preached on ALL occasions.

Furthermore, you should not have to be told to do it as you suggest in your last sentence; the debates are given in the Order Paper.

No wonder Robert Beloe told Mervyn that Lady Summerskill could be 'incredibly irritating'. In a further attempt to explain why bishops were not always present in the Lords when she would like them to be, Mervyn wrote to Lady Summerskill on 17 July to say:

Yesterday, for instance, I was present at a debate on Penal Reform [a subject on which Mervyn was entitled to his opinions: both Brixton and Wandsworth prisons were in his diocese] only by cancelling engagements that I had made several weeks before and disappointing those who had expected to see me. Even so I had to leave before the end of the debate because I was scheduled to go to Eltham to open a centre for teenagers. My day began at 6.30 am and when I went to bed after midnight at least two dozen letters remained unanswered. This sort of programme goes on day after day. I am not asking for pity, but I do hope that you will appreciate that a diocese of 2½ million people, 400 churches and 600 clergymen make tremendous demands upon a bishop.[3]

A week's engagements taken from about the middle of Mervyn's episcopate give a fairly typical flavour of the daily round and common task into which had to be fitted non-ecclesiastical chores like attendance at the House of Lords, and more importantly, pastoral emergencies:

Monday, between 11 a.m. and 12.30 p.m., half-hour interviews with three clergy. Further meetings at 5.30 p.m. and 6 p.m. At 8 p.m. a centenary Sung Eucharist at St Philip, Battersea.

Tuesday, between 11 a.m. and noon meetings with three clergy, and at 12.30 p.m. a meeting with a churchwarden. In the evening a party at Bishop's House for St John's, Lewisham.

Wednesday, a staff meeting at 10 a.m., an interview at 3.30 p.m., an Institution to St Paul, Wimbledon Park and a clergyman to dinner.

Thursday, at 11 a.m. a meeting at the Church Commissioners followed by lunch at the House of Lords, and a private dinner in the evening.

Friday, meetings with clergy at 11 a.m. and noon, a lunch party at Bishop's House and an evening of relaxation as the guest of Lady McLeod before arriving in Oxford on Saturday to marry his chaplain at Keble College.

Sunday, back to the diocese, where Mervyn was due to preach at a centenary parish communion at St Anne, Bermondsey, to entertain guests at lunch and at 6.30 p.m. to make a Visitation to St Mary, Balham.

The chaplain in question was Martin Coombs, who had first met Mervyn 'in a crowded pub' in Bristol in 1956, had been ordained by Mervyn at a service with 48 ordinands, had served as a curate for three years at St John the Divine, Kennington and had then been appointed chaplain at Emmanuel College, Cambridge. When he took up his duties as chaplain to Mervyn in 1968 he found his file at Bishop's House, on which Mervyn had written to the Dean of Emmanuel, 'Martin will be quite good as chaplain but not as good as his predecessor', which may not have done much for his ego and would have come as a surprise to the predecessor, Donald Reeves. Martin had been attracted to the idea of working for Mervyn because while chaplain at Emmanuel he had invited Mervyn to talk to the undergraduates about the Rhodesian crisis, a subject on which he was 'very riveting', and because he also did the devil's advocate with a number of rather pious would-be ordinands, demanding to know of them why they wanted to be ordained. 'After all', said Mervyn, 'there is nothing you can do as a priest that you can't do as a layman except celebrate the Eucharist and absolve and bless.' Such a head-on approach to the question of vocation was fairly radical at the time. Mervyn's other ploy would be to challenge young laymen by demanding to know why they should *not* be ordained.

Mervyn did not restrict his trick questions to ordinands. He was particularly good at getting young people to sit up and think. Preaching at his old school in 1985 he spoke of the persecution of Christians behind what was then called the Iron Curtain, and concluded his sermon by asking the boys 'If there were police outside this church on Easter Day, what would you do? If they were to arrest you for being a Christian, would there be enough evidence to convict you?'

Martin Coombs, now a member of a team ministry in Oxfordshire, was tougher than his gentle manner might indicate, and seems to have survived fairly well. 'I was not a soul mate of Mervyn's in any way, but basically I liked him. He could be impossible, but when he was I didn't find that too intolerable. The pressures on him were horrendous. Working for Mervyn cured me of any ambition ever to be a bishop! He once said that he spent most of his time just clearing up messes.'

Martin experienced an uncomfortable occasion when Mervyn decided, late at night, to clear up his backlog of letters, an example of the 'two dozen letters remaining unanswered' to which he had referred in his letter to Lady Summerskill. Martin recalls the incident in vivid detail. 'He came in after midnight, and said "Now we'll go through my letters". I was absolutely exhausted, and I said "Sorry, I'm going to bed". And I walked off. And he followed me. I think it was the only time he ever followed me into my flat. And I shut the door and said "No, I'm going to bed, I can't do any more".

'So he shouted back "You're sacked!" To which I replied "I don't care, I'm going to bed". Next morning I joined him in the chapel, and had breakfast separately, as I always did. All Mervyn had for breakfast was a cup of black coffee. By nine-fifteen I had all the letters open and ready for him to see, and went in wondering what my position was – if I had a job any more. I said "Here are your letters", and he just looked up and said "We'll forget about last night".'

And yet, Martin Coombs can say today 'As a bishop I rate him very highly. I think he was absolutely outstanding as a pastor. He could make the clergy laugh. He would really make it all fun. As a public figure, he made a lot of difference to people's morale. We felt he was a prophet who would say what he felt.'[4]

In May 1972, when Martin Coombs was Vicar of St John the Evangelist in Dulwich, he experienced a Visitation from Mervyn, surrendering to him for two days the cure of the parish. Mervyn paid visits to two hospitals, two schools and an old people's home. He also went to a convent, and took communion to the sick. He met those who ran voluntary organizations as well as the parish council, warning them of his concern about the financial future of the Church long before it had dawned on anyone else that the Church Commissioners were living not only off the dead but on borrowed time.

The year that Mervyn began his 17 years' membership of the House of Lords was the year also in which his whole diocese was swept off its feet by a hurricane in the form of a harmless-looking SCM paperback. Its title was *Honest to God*; its author, the Bishop of Woolwich, was just about the only person ever to fail to understand what all the fuss had been about. Anticipating some sort of trouble, however, in a preface to the book he wrote 'What I have tried to say, in a tentative and exploratory way, may seem to be radical, and doubtless to many heretical. The one thing of which I am fairly sure is that, in retrospect, it will be seen to have erred in not being nearly radical enough.' Late in 1961 Robinson had been confined to bed, flat on his back, and to avoid strain on his eyes he had his wife read to him. Their chosen subject was Paul Tillich's *The Shaking of the Foundations*. By June 1962 copies of the manuscript of a book in large part inspired by Tillich was eagerly being read and approved by such eminent theologians as Dennis Nineham, Max Warren and John Wren-Lewis, and the fact that the initial UK print run of *Honest to God* was a modest 6,000 testifies to the fact that no one, least of all the publishers, was planning a sensational runaway best-seller. It was, however, helped on its way by a pre-publication article by Robinson in the *Observer* on 17 March 1963, summing up the book and with the headline 'Our Image Of God Must Go'. Two days later the first edition sold out on publication day. The author received 4,000 letters, not all of them, needless to say, from people who had read what he had written, and eventually *Honest to God* was translated into 17 languages and sold over a million copies. By any standards, it was one of the publishing phenomena of the century.

One person who read it – with dismay – was Michael Ramsey, a biblical theologian who ought, in the opinion of Harry Williams, 'to have seen it coming and seen it more clearly'.[5] Fr Williams thinks 'John Robinson was quite conservative in many ways and *Honest to God* was not an original book'.[6] But for Michael Ramsey, the publication of *Honest to God* was his first real test of leadership, and, as he tended to do on the spur of the moment he reacted in a heavy-handed manner, only to repent at leisure and too late. Twelve days after publication of *Honest to God* Ramsey went on television to say: ' . . . it is utterly wrong and misleading to denounce the imagery of God held by Christian men, women and children, imagery that they have got from Jesus himself, the image of God the Father in Heaven, and to say that we can't have any new thought until it is all swept away.'

'As his diocesan bishop, I have been bombarded with letters about [John Robinson's] book', Mervyn told readers of the *Evening Standard*. He said he had read *Honest to God* three times, and it had taught him much. Although he himself might be described as a liberal in his theological views, he was basically orthodox, some-one for whom the traditional language of the Church presented few difficulties. He realized, however, that when he addressed audiences in factories, technical colleges or universities he was forced to admit that the language he used often failed to register and gave rise to misconceptions. This was the barrier the Bishop of Woolwich was trying to break through. Mervyn said he could not pretend to keep abreast of John Robinson's thinking, yet there was no man in the Church for whose mind he had a greater admiration or for whose integrity and single-minded devotion he had more respect. This article constituted a vigorous and very proper support for his suffragan, especially as, in the opinion of Ruth Robinson, 'Mervyn didn't really understand *Honest to God*'.[7]

Mervyn had begun this *Evening Standard* article by recalling that when seeking ordination, William Temple had at first been rejected because of his unorthodox views. 'Maurice, Gore, Henson and Inge, like Temple, were among the more famous who received their measure of abuse as heretics', he wrote. This was too much for Ramsey, who like many of his generation revered Temple, and on 17 April 1963 he informed Mervyn that to say that Temple 'received his measure of abuse as a heretic' was 'a travesty of fact', a 'sheer falsification of history'. He was grieved that the issue of orthodoxy had arisen, but he would be anxious to affirm the proper place of thought and freedom in the Church. The Archbishop wrote:

But it is impossible for the Bishops of what claims to be a part of the Holy Catholic Church just to run away from their pledges, or else we cease to be a teaching Church and become a club for the discussion of religious opinions.

Any solution, *any* action or inaction now is going to be unhappy in one way or another, and this need not have been so if there had been at the outset a sense of responsibility about these matters, all of which could have been foreseen.

Ramsey was overlooking the fact that he was among those to whom John Robinson had sent a copy of the manuscript; he had also been asked to a supper party at which those who were present had been invited to say whether in their opinion the book should be published. Ramsey had apparently been too busy to attend but had sent 'warm good wishes'. Robinson had followed up his initial act of courtesy by sending an advance copy of the book to Lambeth Palace, and typically, for administration in Ramsey's day was often chaotic, with letters mysteriously vanishing if they contained unwelcome news, the book got lost, and a message was sent to Robinson requesting a second copy. This was duly dispatched, but never acknowledged.

Mervyn replied to Ramsey's letter on 19 April, by hand, explaining that he was just about to leave for Ireland for a week (to go fishing, in fact). He admitted he should have described Temple as 'less than orthodox'; he was going to convene a meeting of his examining chaplains at the end of May to advise him on what steps he should take; meanwhile, he was, he told the Archbishop, deeply conscious of the distress the book had caused,

to you as Archbishop, to me as bishop of the diocese and to many Christians of all denominations. My permission was not sought and had it been I should probably have asked the Bishop to submit it to three or four theologians of my choosing for advice. And perhaps a rather different book would have been the result.

In spite of the difficulties I am faced by the publication of the book, I am compelled to admit that many people have found it helpful, particularly the younger generation. [*Honest to God* had been dedicated to Stephen and Catherine 'and their generation'.] As I write I have on my desk a long letter from the Prime Minister [Harold Macmillan] who liked the first half of the book & disliked the second.

At a party in 1984 to celebrate his eightieth birthday, Ramsey, by now living in retirement in Durham, told Mervyn 'I made two major mistakes in my primacy. One was the way I reacted to John Robinson.'[8] While still in an agitated state, Ramsey had retreated to his study to produce an instant critique, a short pamphlet he called *Image Old and New*, rushed out by SPCK ostensibly as a reasoned contribution to the debate fired by *Honest to God*. Although it directly criticized certain passages, it showed some understanding of John Robinson's approach to interpretive theology, and Ramsey would have been well advised to let his reactions, pretty fairly balanced in *Image Old and New*, rest there. But he now informed Mervyn that he intended to make a statement about *Honest to God* when he addressed the Convocation of Canterbury on 7 May. Mervyn wrote a carefully argued letter to Ramsey warning him of the danger should he state publicly that the doctrines of God and the deity of Christ as stated in John Robinson's book were incompatible with the doctrines of the Church, a danger that might 'lead to estrangement between my Diocese and the Province with the possibility of the Archbishop and the Diocesan Bishop on different sides, and perhaps open conflict'.

But Ramsey could be incredibly stubborn when he felt his authority under threat. He too would have been bombarded with letters, demanding action. Hence he remained determined to reiterate in front of the clergy in Convocation the criticism he had made of Robinson on television, criticism which had hardly measured up to the considered language expected of a former Cambridge Regius Professor of Divinity; it had been the facile conservative reaction of a public figure trying to steady a rocking ship of state, and had not begun to reflect either on the truth about religious imagery or on what John Robinson was trying to say. Now he did not even see fit to let Mervyn read the text of his address in advance, and Mervyn was so affronted that in protest he absented himself from the meeting.

'I was very cross with him and hurt when he never consulted me', Mervyn recalled in retirement. 'Apart from anything else, common courtesy demanded that he spoke to me before publicly rebuking one of my suffragans.'[9] Mervyn set great store by loyalty (by which, admittedly, he sometimes meant being in agreement with him: 'You have not been loyal to me', he would say to someone who had not taken his advice), and he was genuinely shocked that Ramsey should not have supported a fellow bishop in public whatever he may have felt he needed to say in private – a fellow bishop whom Mervyn was to describe, on his relinquishing the bishopric of Woolwich in 1969, as 'one of our truly great men'.[10] Ramsey never had the courage to discuss *Honest to God* and the consequences of its publication with the author face to face, and for a time the rupture between Ramsey and Mervyn was so severe that Canon Max Warren of Westminster Abbey had to act as a go-between.

Notes

1 Lambeth Palace archives.
2 Lord Soper, Douglas Rhymes, Roger Royle and Giles Harcourt, all in conversation with the author.
3 Lambeth Palace archives.
4 Canon Martin Coombs, in conversation with the author.
5 Michael De-la-Noy, *Michael Ramsey: A Portrait* (Collins, 1990).
6 Ibid.
7 Mrs Ruth Robinson, in conversation with the author.
8 See *Michael Ramsey: A Portrait*.
9 Ibid.
10 MS in the *Evening Standard*, 24 February 1969.

Chapter 11

High pheasant and marvellous claret

Mervyn Stockwood's time at Southwark coincided not only with a marked decline, nationally, in church attendance, and in the number of candidates coming forward for ordination, despite a surge in theological debate and a real sense of excitement engendered by ecumenical progress, but with a loosening within society of strict moral values. 'The permissive society' was an easy but misleading catch phrase; in many ways society remained very restrictive, but blind adherence to authoritarianism was certainly on the way out. Theatre censorship was generally recognized to be absurd; so was the regulation of private sexual behaviour. Through this confusing minefield of changing ethical attitudes Mervyn trod a wary but usually enlightened path.

One of the most riveting political scandals for many years broke in 1963, for it concerned not only the adultery of a cabinet minister, John Profumo, but his links thereby with the Russian Embassy, and it ended, after revelations had landed day after day on the nation's breakfast tables, with Profumo lying to the House of Commons and resigning as Secretary of State for War. With his government tottering, Harold Macmillan spent the best part of a morning at the height of the Profumo scandal discussing who was to be the new Dean of Wells. Mervyn, perhaps sensing the imminent departure of an exhausted Conservative administration, called for a clean-out of the 'national stables', and followed this up with a lecture delivered through the good offices of the *People*. He told the newspaper's readers that 'For a member of the Government to tell blatant lies and break faith with Parliament is reprehensible, and it will be a sad day when moral values descend to a level that such conduct ceases to shock'. Denying that much of the present outcry was 'a hangover from the moral outlook of Victorian England', he concluded: 'The fact that a man is an adulterer . . . does not minimise the offence [of lying] – except, perhaps, for those who equate "enlightenment" with the practices of the farmyard.'

*

January 1964 saw the publication of a seminal report, Leslie Paul's *Deployment and Payment of the Clergy*. This presented a coherent plan for redistributing the clergy to match shifts in population. At the present time, 41 per cent of the clergy were dealing with 11 per cent of the population while 14 per cent of the clergy had charge of 34 per cent of the population. Mervyn's diocese was classically one of those containing inner-city parishes where one or two clergy were struggling to minister to a large and largely unchurched population, and he thoroughly approved Leslie Paul's proposals. He had to stand by and watch Holy Trinity Church, near the Elephant and Castle, falling down stone by stone because the London County Council would not permit him to hand it over to the Church Missionary Society; he wanted to build a new church on the Croydon Airport estate but bureaucracy even prevented him selling the site of Holy Trinity to pay for it. 'In the last century', Mervyn wrote in the *Evening Standard* on 21 January 1964, 'the country cleaned up its political life by dealing with rotten boroughs and private patronage. The Church still has to grasp the nettle.' He thought Leslie Paul's recommendations for overhauling the present system of patronage, the parson's freehold and the distribution of the clergy 'sheer commonsense' and the present system itself 'plain daft'. He even went so far as to suggest that 'If a majority in my diocese thinks I am failing them it should be able to sack me. Just as a bishop should be able to sack those of his clergy who are lazy or incompetent. And there is much to be said for appointments having to be renewed by election every five years.'[1]

But opposition to the Paul Report was led by Gerald Ellison, since 1954 Bishop of Chester, who believed that Paul's proposals would 'radically alter' the character of the Church of England – which was precisely what they were intended to do. His reward, in 1973, was the see of London, a preferment for which, after 14 years in Southwark and a decade in the House of Lords, Mervyn himself might perhaps have been considered a serious contender. There was by this time, however, an omnipotent influence in the Establishment that was to ensure no translation of any kind for Mervyn. 'Who can tell', Paul Welsby asks in his authoritative history of those years, 'what the course of the Church of England might have been if it had had the will and the vision possessed by some of those it dubbed radicals.'[2] Mervyn could by no means be regarded as radical in every area of life, but in his desire to see the Church unravel its medieval parish system, so largely dependent on private patronage and the parson's freehold, he could only gnash his teeth in impotent rage as he watched the Paul Report being watered down stage by stage. By the day in 1969 when the Convocations of Canterbury and York rejected the Scheme for Anglican–Methodist Reunion Mervyn had about despaired of any serious desire on the part of the Church of England for pastoral or ecumenical progress; he returned to Bishop's House in such a state of suppressed anger and shock he hardly seemed to notice he had dinner guests and just paced up and down in utter dejection.[3]

Somehow it seemed inevitable that it would be in Southwark that publicity would first be given to the disturbing fact that running parallel with unprecedented hope and excitement among the Church's intelligentsia was a failure to fill the pews, or at least, to fill them at a rate any management consultant might regard as cost-effective. In 1963 a member of the cathedral's general chapter had declared that the diocese was 'seething because of the present trends', a remark which seeped in to the *Daily Mirror* via the *Church Times* and drew a vigorous denial from 13 rural deans, who wrote to both *The Times* and the *Church Times* on 28 June 1963 to say 'We believe that this is a dangerously misleading statement. As Rural Deans we are in close touch with the clergy of our deaneries, and we believe that the great majority are wholeheartedly behind the Bishop of Southwark in his aims and approach.' (Eight years later, when a *Panorama* programme on television spawned a lively correspondence in *The Times*, Trevor Huddleston, then Bishop of Stepney, stepped in to say 'I think it grossly unjust to call the diocese of Southwark "a centre of disillusion and defeatism in the Church of England". On the contrary it is a diocese in which bold, contro-versial and constructive experiments are being made for the glory of God and the renewal of his Church.') One of the signatures in 1963 was that of the Rural Dean of Lewisham, Francis Longworth-Dames, Mervyn's fishing companion from less hectic undergraduate days, and with approval and backing like that Mervyn was not prepared for an article on 6 December 1964 in the *Observer*. It was billed on the cover of the *Observer Magazine* as 'Woolwich: A Church's Failure' and headlined inside 'A Mission's Failure'. The author was Nicolas Stacey, Rector of Woolwich, a former chaplain to the Bishop of Birmingham and by any standards one of the most dynamic of the young clergy Mervyn had encouraged to come to his diocese.

But after only four and a half years, and supported by a remarkably able team ministry (one of his clergy was a Triple First), Nick Stacey was dismayed that his congregation had only doubled to 100. He described the area that Mervyn – and many of his clergy – had taken on: 'The picture was one of derelict churches . . . bleak-hearted clergy . . . and disheartened congregations.' They had raised a fortune and spent it, and had 'quite obviously failed'. He sealed off the galleries in his 'enormous Georgian parish church' (St Mary's) and created a coffee house and a lounge. The local branch of the Samaritans moved into the crypt. In effect, the church was thrown open for weekday secular use. Mervyn must have rejoiced to read that 1,500 people used the church building every week, and it is doubtful if he was too concerned about the size of the Sunday congregation. He had told Stacey to 'build up a team of clergy and for God's sake do something to show the people of Woolwich that the Church exists'. Both of these injunctions Stacey had carried out. But he says he never received any response from Mervyn over the article, and that Mervyn never forgave him for it.[4]

It is unlikely he and Mervyn would ever have enjoyed any real rapport. Both were ecclesiastical divas. An Old Etonian and married to the daughter of a peer, Nicolas Stacey was hardly the run-of-the-mill parish priest with whom Mervyn felt at home. Mervyn twice made a Visitation to St Mary's, Woolwich, having his chaplain, as usual, send ahead a note of his requirements, not perhaps realizing that Anne Stacey was perfectly well versed in the social graces. Convinced the Church would never make greater use of his talents than to elect him rural dean, in 1967 Nicolas Stacey quit the parochial ministry and became deputy director of Oxfam. In his autobiography,[5] he has said there were few people for whom he had more sympathy than Mervyn.

He has always been accident prone, has worn his faults on his sleeve and has laid himself open to criticism. He is obviously and painfully torn between heart and head. Intellectually he is a Radical Socialist dedicated to the building of a fairer society with a lively concern for the underprivileged. Emotionally he is a high church Tory who finds compensation for his bachelor life in the trappings and glamour of episcopal office and the prestige of a seat in the House of Lords.

On one hand he can see through the hypocrisy and cant of much of the Establishment, and yet on the other, he needs the security it provides. Inevitably the radicals are suspicious of his prelatical heart and the Establishment suspicious of his Socialist head. And so his is a lonely life. In view of the disappointments and frustrations of much of his work in Southwark it is to his lasting credit that he has prevented his heart from completely controlling his head. There are many occasions when Mervyn Stockwood has infuriated me and many times when I believe he has deserved criticism. But there are also times when I realise he was a scapegoat for my own frustrations.

The paranormal was one of Mervyn's favourite subjects, and writing about it in *The Times* on 2 May 1969 he recalled that on one occasion someone in his diocese had come to see him 'at his own request. As he entered my study I said: "I know what you want to tell me. You are about to become engaged." He was astonished. So was I. I knew nothing about his matrimonial affairs, nor that he was interested in a particular girl.' The person in question was Mervyn's chaplain, Michael Mayne, who had steadfastly seen him through his first often very stressful six years in Southwark. It is no disrespect to the half-dozen chaplains who followed in Mayne's footsteps to say that Mervyn always looked back upon Mayne's period at Bishop's House as utopian. For his part, Michael Mayne has said: 'I loved being chaplain and would not have missed it for anything. I learned a huge amount about how the Church works, some of it for good, some of it for ill. And I learned what a very lonely person Mervyn was, what a vulnerable person he was, and what an isolated thing it is to be a diocesan bishop if you are unmarried.

'Mervyn's sexuality was never in doubt, but neither was his celibacy. I don't believe he was ever anything other than celibate, and he was very disciplined in that whole area. But he needed desperately the friendship of someone with whom he could share in a totally trusting way anything that was on his mind. I was there as a trustworthy listener, and as someone whose opinion he wanted and needed. There were certain times when I was with him when things were acutely painful. He really went through hell over the Thomas affair.'[6]

The area in which Michael Mayne thought Mervyn most vulnerable was to criticism, by which he was often hurt. He attributed his loneliness 'to his childhood and his relationship with his mother, and his repressed sexuality – although he was capable of very deep friendship'. Not that Mayne found, any more than anyone else did, that Mervyn 'shared the complex emotions that arose from his childhood'. He noticed always 'a very uneasy relationship between his mother and the current housekeeper. Mrs Stockwood was a very demanding person and I think Mervyn found her extremely difficult. But he was very good to her and used to visit her every night. But she didn't make his life easy. He never talked about her. One was simply aware there was a tension.'[7]

Like all his chaplains, Michael Mayne was well aware of Mervyn's dependence on alcohol, but he says 'I never saw him what you would call drunk. I never saw him incapacitated, but on a good many occasions, at a dinner party, as the evening wore on he became a little slurred in his speech. But I never knew drink to affect his ministry to people. I never saw him the worse for wear in the morning.' It says a lot for Michael Mayne's six-year tour of duty that his most serious misdemeanour occurred when one day Mervyn asked him to fill up a decanter, and Mayne poured half a bottle of sherry into half a decanter of whisky. 'That', he says, 'took a lot of getting over!'

As for Mervyn's reaction to Mayne announcing his engagement, 'He was entirely positive, very kind and thoughtful'. And he married Mayne and his bride in the cathedral. At this time, Mayne's stepfather died, and Mervyn had Michael Mayne's mother to stay. 'Beneath the showman', says Mayne, 'there was consistently a pastoral heart, and a pastoral care for people that went very deep.'

Hearing that Michael Mayne was to leave, Andrew Henderson moved into action, and introduced to Mervyn a 31-year-old curate from All Saints', Maidstone, Donald Reeves, now Rector of an important West End church, St James's, Piccadilly. He had met Mervyn briefly in Cambridge when he had been an undergraduate, and in 1965 he had been a priest just two years. 'The job description was not very clear', he recalls. 'I accepted Mervyn's offer to become his chaplain partly because I was ambitious, partly because I was intrigued by South Bank Religion.' Donald Reeves would be the first to agree today that in some ways it was not a very appropriate or happy appointment. 'I remember feeling that I never really unpacked at Bishop's House, that I never really had a room to myself. I had no real privacy. Psychologically I never felt at home there. I always felt I was in a hotel, in a way. And as soon as I was established as chaplain I promptly proceeded to lose my faith. Mervyn didn't know about this.

'But he had quite enough to put up with because I found the whole ecclesiastical round pretty tiresome. I underwent a very expensive session of psychotherapy, and he was quite puzzled by me. I used to go round the diocese on Sundays preaching sermons on loneliness! I was much more meek and mild when I was with Mervyn than I am now and there was a sense in which he was a bit of a bully. If you didn't stand up to him he could ride over you. It was part of his desire to have a relationship with you. It was his very clumsy way of reaching out to you.'[8]

Donald Reeves has some amusing recollections of the way the diocese was run. 'Mervyn had nothing to do with the management of the diocese. There would be one meeting of the finance committee a year, when Mervyn would be heavily briefed. This meeting usually ended with salmon, high pheasant and marvellous claret. Nothing had been decided, but everybody felt fine and off they went.'

Reeves says there were a lot of things about Mervyn he liked, 'but I'm not sure he was really a likeable man'. The most difficult aspect of Mervyn's personality with which Reeves, young, inexperienced and very unsure at the time of his own emotions, had to cope was Mervyn's ambivalent attitude towards Reeves as his chaplain. 'His relations with his chaplains was something to do with his need to have a relationship with somebody. Mervyn never had a lover so far as I know, but he wanted to belong to somebody, and he hoped his relationship with his chaplain would somehow come to that. I was not prepared to belong to him in that way. I saw it as a job, and his confusion of roles meant that when he appointed chaplains his judgement was a bit awry.' Mervyn even confused Donald Reeves with Michael Mayne, sometimes disconcertingly calling him Michael. At one point Reeves became so disheartened he felt he should leave, and went over to Cambridge to discuss the matter with Hugh Montefiore, since 1963 Vicar of Great St Mary's. Montefiore told him to stick it out.

'A part of me really disliked Mervyn', says Reeves. 'He used to go to Cuddesdon for bishops' meetings with his whisky and sleeping pills and I wished he wouldn't come back. I also very much loved him and would have done anything for him. I wasn't the most efficient chaplain, and sometimes he would arrive for an appointment an hour late, or even a week late, and he would be sweetness and light. But we once went to a chapter meeting at Petersham and I hadn't packed the crozier, so he sent me all the way back for it, because he said he couldn't give a blessing without it.

'He sacked me once or twice, once because I got back late after Christmas. He was really angry and I burst into tears. So he just said "That's enough now, we'll meet at dinner", as if it had never happened. But with people with whom he was not involved he was rather good. A priest in Surbiton was found in bed with someone he shouldn't have been in bed with, and the parochial church council wrote a letter of complaint, saying this young man should be sacked. So Mervyn summoned the PCC to Bishop's House, read them a lecture about motes and beams from the Sermon on the Mount, and asked which of them could speak from a position of purity. Then he sent them off with a flea in their ear, got the curate in, and said to him "Don't be such a bloody fool, just behave yourself, will you". It was the way any intelligent headmaster would have coped. There was something about the headmaster in Mervyn. What I liked and admired about him, which you don't see in bishops today, was that he enjoyed his job.'[9]

It seems that Donald Reeves served as chaplain – from 1965 to 1968 – during a period when (perhaps because he was missing Michael Mayne) Mervyn was drinking very heavily indeed. 'I had to sing carols to Winkie, the cat, and I used to have to wait around, and when Mervyn had drunk a lot I had to get him to bed. He would then take more whisky and sleeping pills, and then wake at three in the morning, to go to the lavatory, and he would just collapse and fall over, to the sound of crashing glass. I really got desperate. But it didn't incapacitate him as a bishop at all. Next day he would be in chapel for morning meditation and prayer, listening to gramophone records, as bright as a button. I think the drinking was something to do with his failure to have a primary relationship. I wouldn't have thought he had a vocation to celibacy, and as a result he developed voyeuristic tendencies. When I went off for therapy he used to detain me so that I would arrive late, and he used to say "I am not in the least interested in my chaplain's private life" and then, on my return, interrogate me. "What do you actually *do* when you have this therapy?"'

It is hardly surprising that Donald Reeves remembers 'I was perpetually tired when I was with him'. Mervyn Stockwood was indeed a demanding man. 'At inductions of the clergy to their parishes he would just alter the arrangements as he went along. At ordinations in the cathedral he would say to me, very loudly, "Brush my hair".' Yet at table at Bishop's House Mervyn would wait on Donald. 'I never knew if I was a butler, or a son, or a surrogate lover – or an archdeacon in disguise, because by the end of my time I was receiving confidences. Or a skivvy.'

Towards the end of 1965 Mervyn had an opportunity, available to all the bishops but ignored by most (honorable exceptions included Michael Gresford Jones of St Albans and Mark Hodson of Hereford), of extending much needed moral support to Michael Ramsey. With Rhodesia on the brink of rebellion and civil war, the British Council of Churches, of which Ramsey was President, happened to be meeting for two days in Aberdeen. During a debate on Ian Smith's intention to declare independence, Ramsey said 'If the British government thought it practicable to use force for the protection of the rights of the majority of the Rhodesian people, then I think that as Christians we have to say that it will be right to use force to that end'.

What Ramsey wanted for Rhodesia was justice, and Mervyn, described by one of Ramsey's biographers as 'the most urbane and the most radical of bishops',[10] did not hesitate to support the Archbishop's modest attempt to steel a weak and irresolute British Government to take unpalatable action if it had to. Yet Ramsey, who, without realizing he was about to do so, had positioned himself at the centre of a major political and constitutional crisis, was depicted in the crudest terms as a warmonger. His measured language was actually described by the *Daily Express* as a tirade. On 31 October 1965 Quintin Hogg, who had renounced his hereditary peerage in the vain hope of becoming prime minister, decided to weigh in against Ramsey in the *Sunday Express*, accusing him of blunders that would ruin the career of any politician. Hogg levelled similar charges against Mervyn, Fisher (Hogg did not like the idea that he had opposed the introduction by Macmillan of Premium Bonds) and John Robinson (his crime had been to give evidence in the case of *Lady Chatterley's Lover*). Hence, in a cartoon by Cummings, Mervyn had the honour of joining Ramsey, Fisher and Robinson, who were all depicted jumping up and down and waving their clenched fists in the air. Britannia has her hands over her ears, exclaiming, à la Henry II, 'Who will free me from these turbulent priests?'

By 1967, four years after taking his seat in the House of Lords, Mervyn's diligent attendance had become cause for comment at Lambeth Palace. At a luncheon for the Church Commissioners, Richard Crossman asked Michael Ramsey for his views on

Anglican bishops retaining seats by right in the House of Lords. Ramsey would have been perfectly content for the number of seats to be reduced from 26 to 16, and he told Crossman that the bishops' pastoral duties made it impossible for them to attend regularly – and that if they did, it might not be desirable. Crossman took this to be a veiled reference to Mervyn, 'who attends regularly and is too political'.[11] From a geographical point of view it was of course easy for Mervyn to attend, and hardly fair to blame him on that score. As for his politics, he saw the support he gave to political issues like race and sexual law reform as part of his commitment to the social gospel.

In his autobiography, Mervyn says that his mother died at a great age; and that is all. There is no account of her death, or of the effect it had upon him. Ethel Stockwood died, in fact, on 7 July 1967, at the age of 87, and the effect her death had on Mervyn was profound. Mary Cryer arrived for work at Bishop's House to find the place in uproar; Mrs Stockwood, it seems, had suffered a stroke, and to rescue her it was necessary to break down the bathroom door. 'With Mervyn's help', says Donald Reeves, 'I fished her out of the bath, and we put her to bed and got a doctor.' Mary recalls that Mervyn was crying, took off his pectoral cross, laid it on his mother and repeatedly kissed and blessed her. 'He was incredibly upset.' All Mrs Stockwood managed to say was 'Winkie' – the name of her cat. She was moved to St Anthony's Hospital in Cheam, where she was visited each day by Mervyn and Donald, who said the Offices with her. Marion was unable to visit her mother, for she too was in hospital at the time, undergoing an operation. Mervyn was so shaken he started smoking Mary's cigarettes, and when eventually Mrs Stockwood died, he took ten days off. 'I went into the drawing room', says Donald Reeves, 'and I can remember Mervyn crying. I remember seeing him from a distance, with his back to me and his shoulders heaving. He was clearly very, very distressed, and I remember saying to myself, I must go and put my arms round him, but I couldn't do it. I reproach myself for that. However, I think if I had he would probably have collapsed completely. And then probably pulled himself together – which is what he did as soon as he saw me.'[12]

It is doubtful whether Ethel Stockwood had ever entertained any great interest in religious matters, but she was given a very grand, ecumenical funeral at St Leonard's, Streatham, with the Bishop of

London and the Roman Catholic Archbishop of Southwark in attendance. Afterwards, at her own request, she was cremated and her ashes were scattered in a garden of rest. Mary Cryer, who liked Mrs Stockwood, had nevertheless found her 'quiet and secretive', and remembers how she was 'spirited away' when Mervyn was entertaining. 'She was very proud of him but couldn't say so.'[13] David Tankard, who met Mrs Stockwood on his youthful visits to the vicarage in Moorfields, recalls that although Mervyn was 'polite and cordial with her, I felt that he insisted on distancing himself from her. He would humour her rather than treat her as an equal.'[14] A Cambridge chaplain who saw a lot of Mrs Stockwood when Mervyn was at Great St Mary's thought her 'a difficult woman, very demanding, who wanted to be part of things she couldn't be. I found her tiresome and irritable, and I admired Mervyn for the way he handled it.'[15] 'A very powerful influence in his life' is how a Southwark cleric saw Mrs Stockwood in relation to Mervyn. 'But she was a bit kept in the attic. She was the kind of person for whom nothing was ever right. She was very contrary. Nothing could please her.'[16]

At the age of 54 it must have occurred to Mervyn that so far as family was concerned, he was well and truly alone, and that in a sense he always had been. The grief he found so hard to express and which he largely bottled up was for a mother whose love he felt he had never had, a sentiment that may well have been reinforced when he discovered that in a will she signed on 8 June 1961 she had left £9,559, every penny of it, including all her personal possessions, to Marion. Mervyn had given his mother a home for years, and she did not even bequeath him a keepsake.

'In some ways', says Donald Reeves, 'Mervyn found his mother very irritating. He didn't like her very much. He had times in his diary earmarked "Mother" to remind him to go and see her. I rather liked her. She very much had a mind of her own, and was not in the least taken in by Mervyn's prelatical ways.' It may have been this seeming lack of appreciation of his achievements on the part of his family, on the part of his mother in particular, that Mervyn found hard to accept. She never actually gave him a pat on the back and said well done when he became a bishop. 'At some level', says Reeves, 'I think Mervyn's mother prevented his growth as a person. The relationship was close but ambivalent.' If one requires an explanation for Mervyn's homosexual disposition, which was almost certainly a consequence of environmental factors rather than genetic, there is no need to look further than to the absence of a male role model together with the lack of any physically affectionate woman from whom to learn about female allure. In the opinion of Donald Reeves, 'Had Mervyn resolved some of that underlying loneliness he would have been a very great bishop indeed. But his misogyny was something I found very, very difficult. He really disliked women, unless they were women like Elizabeth Cavendish or Mary Cryer, who mothered him a bit. Lunches for the clergy and their wives could present real problems.'[17]

So far as his brother and sister were concerned, they, like Mervyn's mother, had shared in none of Mervyn's ecclesiastical interests. His brother he seldom saw as he lived in Canada. Marion was a frequent visitor, both to Bishop's House and later to Bath, but her relations with Mervyn struck observers as being on a very formal footing. It was unfortunate that his bereavement and the awful void it must have opened up coincided with a drama in the diocese with which for two months that summer Mervyn became pastorally involved. A letter in the *Guardian* signed 'Approved School Teacher' had alerted the Home Office to irregular adminis-tration of corporal punishment at Court Lees, an approved school near Godstone. The teacher in question was Mr Ivor Cook, who alleged there had been excessive canings at Court Lees once or twice a week over a period of five years. The Home Secretary, Roy Jenkins, asked the Recorder of Oxford, Mr Edward Gibbens QC, to conduct an enquiry. He found that since 1961 a large, un-authorized type of cane had been used to punish boys who absconded, and that on four occasions in 1967 corporal punishment had been administered with excessive severity. The headmaster, Mr D. Haydon, frequently withdrew the boys' shirts from their trousers before thrashing them. A boy of 14 had received six strokes of the cane for absconding and after the second stroke had had to be held down. Three eminent medical witnesses confirmed injuries to the boys of 'quite unusual severity'.

Much to the indignation of the board of management, Roy Jenkins closed down the school. On 25 August *The Times* published a short letter from Mervyn, thanking them for a 'helpful' leading article they had printed six days previously 'on the sad business of Court Lees'. Like many others, Mervyn seemed to think there were two sides to the question, but, he wrote, 'Certain things have happened that ought not to have happened, and I neither condone nor excuse them'. He was, he said, prepared to raise the matter in the House of Lords, but it was in fact Earl Jellicoe who did so, on 25 October 1967. When Mervyn got up to speak he recalled that in August he had met those members of the staff of Court Lees who had wanted to talk to him, and he was anxious to see justice done to individuals. While he was against the use of corporal punishment, with withering scorn he tore to shreds the evidence of Mr Cook, whom he thought an unreliable witness. Mervyn challenged the photographic evidence of the boys' injuries, and drew the attention of the House to the fact that Cook had been an unsuccessful applicant for the headmastership and had himself been instrumental in 110 beatings. He concluded his speech by saying 'It is my opinion that the Home Secretary has not yet given us sufficient grounds for complete satisfaction, and I now ask him, in the interests of freedom and of fair play to all the persons concerned, to initiate a full and impartial Inquiry'. Winding up the debate, Lord Jellicoe echoed Mervyn's concern about the position of the headmaster and his deputy, and said he for one had been 'deeply impressed by the speech of the Right Reverend Prelate the Bishop of Southwark, who knows the school more intimately than any other Member of your Lordships' House'.[18]

The year 1967 was altogether a watershed; it witnessed the passing of the Sexual Offences Act, which legalized homosexual conduct in private between two consenting males over the age of 21. Hence by the early 1970s, liberal-minded clergy felt able to conduct private services of blessing for gay couples they believed to be in, or wishing to enter, a stable, loving relationship. One of the most striking aspects of this unorthodox liturgical development, which later grew into publicly acknowledged services with a carefully planned ritual, was that Mervyn himself conducted a gay blessing – for the headmaster of Bristol Grammar School, John Garrett, whose partner was an Anglican priest, still alive and living in seclusion in Ireland. It was Garrett, of course, who had introduced Dick Chapman to Mervyn. The blessing took place in Henbury parish church, on the north-west outskirts of Bristol. Mervyn was very strongly in favour of such things being done in private; because he only wore a suit, he was also able to convince himself that nothing he had done was of sacramental validity. But he had a genius for splitting off parts of his persona. Eric James, for instance, can remember sitting in the garden at Bishop's House when Mervyn would suddenly announce 'There's something I want to say to you,

Eric'. He would then escort Eric indoors, and sit behind his desk in his episcopal high-backed chair adorned with his coat of arms, 'because it was something he wanted to say as bishop'. It follows of course that if Mervyn was prepared to bless a gay relationship he was content to turn a blind eye to its consummation, and indeed one of his suffragans, Hugh Montefiore, has said 'He didn't mind his clergy having it off as long as there wasn't a scandal'.[19]

Mervyn's unorthodoxy took any number of directions. In a letter to his Cambridge curate, Robin Howard, he said that while in hospital he had been greatly helped 'by some of the more positive' teaching of Christian Science. 'Although much of it is heretical nonsense', he added, 'yet it does encourage me to have a hopeful, confident approach to life',[20] an attitude echoed in a letter Mervyn wrote on 13 August 1964 to the editor of the *Church Times*: 'Like the Patriarchs of old, I continue to set out in hope! As you know, I am a born optimist.' According – again – to Bishop Montefiore, Mervyn 'had a very lovable habit of making friends with criminals'. There was a wealthy self-made businessman who lived close by, who provided fishing facilities for Mervyn; he went to prison. An alleged property developer who gave Mervyn holidays in Majorca and hampers of turkeys and champagne at Christmas ran an office in Gray's Inn Road much on the lines of the office routine favoured by Lloyd George's honours broker, Maundy Gregory, bogus telephone calls from the great and famous being put through by a secretary in the next room. When the Inland Revenue descended on Gray's Inn Road with a bill for some enormous outstanding sum Mervyn ducked beneath the parapet. 'Mervyn was a bad judge of character', in the opinion of David Faull. 'He sometimes sailed very close to the wind. The trouble was, he was fascinated by people with money, and did not always ask where it had come from. He was both worldly and gullible. My only real criticism of Mervyn is that he could be a fair-weather friend. When things turned awkward he would tend to distance himself very quickly.'[21] One crook of whom Mervyn certainly did not approve was Roger Gleaves, the self-styled 'Bishop of Medway', whose penchant for giving succour to young boys endeared him for a long time to the police and welfare agencies, so gullible were *they*. No tears were shed when he went to prison, following investigations inaugurated by the *Sunday Times*, and Mervyn dubbed him the only evil man he had ever met.

As far as the official recognition of gay relationships was

concerned, Mervyn took the opportunity of making his views plain in 1979 in a letter to Tony Crowe. He said the Archbishop of Canterbury (Donald Coggan) had written to him about a report in the *Kentish Times* 'with regard to the alleged "gay" weddings that take place, or are said to take place in your church'. Mervyn said he imagined that the report was 'more than a little inaccurate', or perhaps he was hoping it was. 'Of course', he wrote, 'there can be no such thing as a wedding between homosexuals as it is a contradiction in terms. The dictionary is explicit when it says that marriage is "the condition of man and woman legally united for purpose of living together and usually procreating lawful off-spring".'

It was odd that Mervyn should have fallen back on a dictionary definition to delineate a theological concept, and indeed Tony Crowe and other clergy, like Michael Peet, team Rector of Holy Trinity and All Hallows in Bow, or Malcolm Johnson, a former Rector of St Botolph's in the City of London, have never sought to emulate a form of heterosexual marriage when conducting a service of blessing for gay couples.[22]

Mervyn went on to explain to Tony Crowe:

As you know, I have a liberal attitude towards these matters . . . but I try to take into consideration those who hold contrary views. That is why I think one has to treat the subject with great delicacy and not to be insensitive.

I regret much of what is done by the Gay Liberation Movement, especially in the Church. If two men believe that they are justified in living together, and if they wish to ask God's blessing on their commitment, I think it best for a priest to say prayers with them privately. The time may come when the Church will take a different attitude, but at the moment a public ceremony can do nothing but make a difficult situation even more difficult. It is true we have a duty as priests towards homosexuals, but we also have a duty to those who sincerely take a different point of view.

Tony Crowe assured Mervyn he had never used the word marriage to describe a union between a couple of homosexuals or lesbians, but had not denied to his local paper that a ceremony of blessing had taken place – for two men who had been living together for 19 years, both of whom were active members of his congregation. A few months later, Crowe's parochial church council debated the issue and gave him the go-ahead to perform blessings. Over the years, Tony Crowe's services became well known (he conducted 28) and received publicity on television, and he became convinced that because of his activities Robert Runcie blocked his transfer to another parish.[23] The issue of Crowe's career became a cause of trauma in February 1993 when he and a friend went to Bath to take Mervyn out to lunch. Apparently having had too much to drink, Mervyn let fly about Crowe's 'lack of *gravitas*' and told him he had been 'bonkers' to court publicity in the way he had. Thanking Crowe later for his hospitality, Mervyn wrote 'I hope you did not find me too unsympathetic about "the marriages" which achieved such publicity'. He attributed difficulties in finding a new parish for Crowe to objections from churchwardens. 'As you know, I did a lot to help in this matter during my episcopate, but I never appeared in print or joined a campaign.'

In 1968 Mervyn was on one of his not infrequent pilgrimages to the Holy Land when, in the Panorama Hotel in east Jerusalem, he encountered the second chef and part-time barman, a Palestinian called Munir Abul Elhawa. Less than enchanted by his succession of housekeepers at Bishop's House, and genuinely anxious, at the time of the Six Day War in the Middle East, to extend a symbolic helping hand, he suggested to Munir that he might like a job in England as his cook. Munir at that time had very little English (today it is fluent), and agreed to come to England for a six-month trial period. The rest, as they say, is history. Munir attended cookery classes at Marylebone in the afternoons, and went to a language school to learn English. By 1972 he was not only in charge of the kitchen but became Mervyn's official chauffeur, returning briefly to Palestine in 1975 to marry. He now has four children, and to this day remains a legendary member of the Bishop's House establishment, driving the present bishop and keeping alive memories of royal dinner parties for which he was responsible. During Mervyn's episcopate Munir first drove a Ford Executive, and then a Granada, which Mervyn purchased from the Church Commissioners on his retirement. It was a large car and not one which Mervyn handled with any particular dexterity. In June 1974 Mervyn was driving himself to Oxford, to attend a residential bishops' meeting at Cuddesdon, when he was involved in a head-on crash with a lorry. He ended up in Hillingdon Hospital, where he received a visit from Cardinal Heenan.

Mervyn's jaunts to the Middle East were apt to take an unexpected turn. He was once on holiday with Elizabeth Cavendish, which puzzled the management of the King David Hotel in Jerusalem, who assumed that Lady Elizabeth was Mervyn's mistress and could not comprehend why they did not share a bedroom. As the hotel filled up, with a consequent lack of spare accommodation, ever more pressing hints were made that it would be greatly appreciated if Lady Elizabeth would kindly vacate her room and move in with the bishop.

It was in the year of the car crash that Munir received instruction from Dominic Walker, appointed chaplain in 1973, and was baptized and confirmed in the chapel by Mervyn, who gave a party on 23 December to celebrate the occasion. In appreciation of his services, Mervyn was to leave Munir a legacy of £5,000. Perhaps part of Mervyn's intention was to compensate Munir for the terror he had experienced when the ghost of Bishop's House materialized, as it first did one day when Munir was alone. He heard mysterious footsteps; Mervyn's cat heard or sensed them too, and arched her back. When this happened a second time Mervyn got in a medium, who went out of the room to investigate and returned two minutes later to announce there was undoubtedly a spirit on the first floor, a woman walking up and down the corridor in great distress, stopping apparently at the door leading to the new extension. Mervyn then went through all the rooms, accompanied by Munir, sprinkling holy water, and it seems that he quietened the ghost, who, according to local gossip, was the Polish sister-in-law of a previous owner. Mervyn was a firm believer in spooks, as was his vice-provost John Pearce-Higgins, more in touch, it was said, with the dead than the living; he and Mervyn would swap notes on whom they had managed to contact. One day Mervyn paid a visit to Pearce-Higgins accompanied by Martin Coombs, who rashly said to Mervyn he thought belief in the paranormal was all a load of rot. 'I trod on something very precious there', Canon Coombs recalls. 'I could see I had really hurt Mervyn. There was some personal search he was making.'

In May 1969 Mervyn contributed two long articles to *The Times*, on successive days. The first was entitled 'Explaining The Apparition At Bishop's House', the second, 'Can We Communicate With The Dead?' In the first article he went further than the account of footsteps, provided by Canon Coombs; he said he had twice seen the ghost, 'an elderly, sad-looking woman'. He recalled too that one night in Cambridge he had woken up with a sense of horror. 'I was so frightened that I turned on the light. One thing was clear to me – I must call on the Dean of King's College as soon as possible. I got up early and arrived at the college gates soon after 8 a.m. I was met by the porter, who said that the dean had committed suicide during the night by throwing himself from the turret of the chapel.'

Among his papers, Mervyn preserved a report of a committee appointed by the Archbishop of Canterbury in 1937 'To investigate the subject of communications with discarnate spirits and the claims of Spiritualism in relation to the Christian Faith'. And in 1954, only a year after it was founded, Mervyn hastened to enlist in the Churches' Fellowship for Psychical and Spiritual Studies, an ecumenical body set up 'for the study of the wider reaches of the paranormal and extra sensory perception in their relation to the Christian faith'. No one could accuse Mervyn of joining a gang of crackpots; his fellow members included Graham Leonard when he was Bishop of London, Lord Soper, Bishop Montefiore, the distinguished Dean of Westminster, Edward Carpenter, and Michael Ball, Bishop of Truro. Until his death, Mervyn served either as a vice-president or a patron; he took part in numerous conferences, and contributed to the Fellowship's journal. On 26 February 1958, in Cambridge, he entertained the famous clairvoyant Ena Twigg, and as late as 1989 he was enthusiastically reviewing a reprint of *Testimony of Light* by Helen Greaves for *The Christian Parapsychologist*, edited by Michael Perry, Archdeacon of Durham.

In August 1964, five years after his arrival in the diocese, John Robinson wrote to Mervyn at great length. He said he needed a six-month sabbatical and he also told Mervyn he would like to see explored 'as a matter of some urgency' the possibility of 'getting an extra suffraganship in this diocese'. He had in mind a bishop 'whose frontier would not be geographical so much as missionary', and he cited as areas of work in need of oversight the South London Industrial Mission, 'all the new work connected with our priest-workmen, Southwark Ordination Course, lay training, religious sociology, clinical theology, press and publicity etc.' Mervyn discussed Robinson's suggestions with the Archbishop of Canterbury and the immediate outcome was sabbatical leave for Robinson but no additional suffragan bishop. By 1969 John Robinson had served ten years as Bishop of Woolwich, and on 7 January 1969 Mervyn was writing a testimonial for him, commending Robinson as Dean of Chapel at Trinity College, Cambridge. 'Taking the larger view and setting aside personal considerations', Mervyn wrote, 'I know I must encourage him to go.' To Robinson himself he wrote on 24 January:

As I told you on the telephone I have made my own grave! I hate the idea of losing you, but I am cheered by the conviction that the decision is right. You have so much to contribute to the life of the Church and I know that, at this juncture, it can best be done in Cambridge rather than in Woolwich. You must be free to grapple with the deep theological problems on which everything in the last resort depends.

You have always been a wonderful friend and colleague and my life in Southwark would have been intolerable without you.

John Robinson died very peacefully from cancer in December 1983, six months to the day after he had been told he had six months to live. At his Thanksgiving Eucharist in Southwark Cathedral on 4 February 1984 Mervyn recalled that Robinson had told him that after ten years in academia he had hoped to 'return to full-time ministry in the Church of England'. And he informed the congregation, 'I approached the likely authorities in Church and State. I think that charity demands that the rest should be silence.'

So the hunt was on for a replacement as Bishop of Woolwich. Mervyn did not cast his net very wide. It was while he was camping out in Lennox Gardens that he had already met the man he had in mind, a good-looking young Evangelical parson called David Sheppard, and from Lennox Gardens he had taken Sheppard out to dinner, and ticked him off for conducting a wedding in a Baptist church. They had communicated by letter over liturgical reform, and had in common an experience of inner-city deprivation. Like Mervyn, Sheppard had wanted to be a public school chaplain; like Mervyn, Sheppard had built up a Christian community from near collapse, in his case the Mayflower Family Centre in Canning Town; and like Mervyn, Sheppard detested the South African regime, and had said in 1960 he would never play cricket against South Africa so long as the country was governed by apartheid. Sheppard had in fact played for England 22 times, and represented the archetypical public school sporting hero Mervyn would perhaps have liked to have been himself. Once David Sheppard had been consecrated, people noticed that Mervyn was forever speaking with admiration about him. 'Mervyn was physically attracted to David Sheppard', says Eric James, 'and would go on for ages about him. The fact that Sheppard was heterosexual made no difference at all!'[24] But first Sheppard and his wife had to undergo trial by marital luncheon party. 'On All Saints' Day', David Sheppard recalls, 'we went to an expensive restaurant in East Grinstead for Grace to meet Mervyn. We had heard he was a woman-hater, and in fact on one occasion Grace was summoned to Bishop's House to open 100 oysters for dinner, and didn't get a single one to eat herself!'[25]

Sheppard was only 40. He had undergone conversion at Cambridge, served his title at a famously Evangelical church in Islington, where his vicar was the future Bishop of Norwich, Maurice Wood, and could not claim any wide experience of ecclesiastical life. His appointment was in part by way of a gesture of goodwill to the Evangelicals in the diocese, but before finally making up his mind Mervyn reminded David that another Evangelical, Christopher Chavasse, Bishop of Rochester, had once remarked that he had never seen a converted man unemployed. What did David think of that? Fortunately for his future career in the Church, David agreed it had been a terrible thing to say.[26]

Like Donald Reeves, who had found himself being addressed as Michael, David Sheppard had to get used to treading in a former paragon's footsteps, and would constantly catch Mervyn referring to 'John and I . . . '. He was glad to find his fellow Evangelicals telling him they thought they got the fairest crack of the whip of any diocese they knew, and having become a bishop, David was sent by Mervyn to the Rural Dean of Camberwell, 'to be taught to swing and sing'. At the time of his consecration David still had no episcopal ring of his own so Mervyn lent him a spare; having proved Mervyn's amazing gift for spotting talent by being appointed Bishop of Liverpool in 1975, David Sheppard, to mark his time in Southwark, on leaving gave Mervyn the gift of a new episcopal ring, later bequeathed back to him in Mervyn's will. One of the notable hallmarks of David Sheppard's episcopate in Liverpool was his collaboration with the Roman Catholic Archbishop, Derek Worlock, partly as a result of the encouragement in ecumenicism he received from Mervyn. He says Mervyn also taught him not to chair committees.

In an article for the *Evening Standard* on 24 February 1969 Mervyn provided his own idiosyncratic reason for choosing David Sheppard as John Robinson's successor. 'Curiously enough', he wrote, 'Enoch Powell was responsible for my choice.' The previous year Powell had delivered a notorious speech on immigration, predicting 'rivers of blood'. Mervyn said he was determined to appoint a suffragan bishop who, 'uncompromising on the race issue, would be a friend and pastor to all'. Foolishly, Mervyn went over the top, spoiling his article by writing: 'Enoch's evil speech last summer was the equivalent of a foul smell. I have crowds of coloured people in my diocese, more than 40,000, and until Powell let off his fart white and coloured lived happily together.'

It has been argued that it is sometimes necessary to resort to provocative language when writing for the popular press in order to get a point across, but the fact remains that use of the word 'fart' sits uneasily on episcopal lips; it is hardly the fastidious turn of phrase that makes a piece memorable, and all that people remembered about the article, which had been intended as a song of praise for the departed Robinson and his newly arrived replacement, was the word 'fart'. Before sending his copy to the *Evening Standard* Mervyn showed it to his chaplain, Martin Coombs, who wisely advised him to delete the offending expression, but Mervyn just 'looked very mischievous and said he was going to keep it in'. Presumably he knew what he was doing. On his next visit to the House of Lords a number of his fellow peers cut him.

However foolish or wrong-headed Mervyn may have been at times he never lacked moral courage, and would often venture into areas from which more timid creatures would shy away. Michael Ramsey and Cardinal Heenan both declined invitations to see a production at the Round House called *Oh! Calcutta!*, famous for its nudity, the invitations having been extended by a Tory member of the Greater London Council, who had hoped to rope the two prelates in to his campaign against the revue. But Mervyn accepted an invitation from the *Guardian* to attend, and on 19 August 1970 he recorded his impressions, gathered as they were through a haze of tobacco smoke and from the vantage point of a 'horribly uncomfortable' seat. He pronounced the evening to have been one of 'sheer, stark boredom, and of a sick variety'. He doubted whether, had the cast worn clothes throughout, the show would have survived a week, for he could not remember 'a more tedious evening, a more excruciating two hours'.

He said he could not get excited about nudity on the stage. It was a matter of degree. 'In *Hair* – a production which I found challeng-ing and full of good things – there seemed to be a sensible balance.' In *Oh! Calcutta!* the frequent excursions into nakedness reminded him, evidently with a shuddered remembrance of distaste, of 'bath night drill at boarding school'. He was against suppression of such shows on pragmatic grounds – 'If the State puts them down in one place they will reappear in another' – and he thought, in any case, the public would soon tire of 'this sick sort of sex'. In 1971 his article was reprinted in *The Bedside Guardian* No. 20.

Mervyn had a genuine love of the theatre, but sometimes theatrical treats failed to go according to plan. Thinking to lay on an amusing evening for the Archbishop of Canterbury he invited Dr Coggan and his wife in 1973 to see a new farce by Alan Bennett, *Habeas Corpus*. Also in the party were the Bishop of Kingston and Mrs Montefiore, and Lady Elizabeth Cavendish. Alan Bennett has described his play as 'an attempt to write a farce without the paraphernalia of farce – hiding-places, multiple exits and umpteen doors. Trousers fall, it is true, but in an instantaneous way as if by divine intervention.' Although *Habeas Corpus* remains one of his favourite plays, Bennett now admits that some of the jokes make him wince.[27] The author has more to answer for than perhaps he realizes, for Lady Elizabeth recalls the evening as a complete disaster. 'It was', she says, 'impossible to raise a single smile out of the Coggans!'[28] Many people assumed the bishop depicted in John Mortimer's play about hell, *The Prince of Darkness*, to have been based on Mervyn, but Mr Mortimer says 'I didn't think the Bishop in *The Prince of Darkness* was Mervyn Stockwood. I only met him once . . . '[29] In the play, Mr Mortimer has also recorded, 'the Prince of Darkness turns up as a curate to a trendy South London vicar. This vicar takes the view that miracles are the sort of vulgar conjuring tricks which a deeply caring, rational and Socialist God wouldn't stoop to. To his anger and dismay, when the Bishop comes to dinner unexpectedly, the miracle of the feeding of the multitude takes place in his fridge.'[30] With the scene set in south London it is hardly surprising the bishop was taken for Mervyn.

Less than a year after David Sheppard's appointment Mervyn heaved a sigh of relief at the news that his recalcitrant Bishop of Kingston, William Gilpin, wished to retire. Now he was able to acquire the third suffragan of his own choice. It is inconceivable that anyone other than Mervyn would have contemplated offering a bishopric at this time to the Vicar of Great St Mary's, Hugh

Montefiore. Montefiore was prone to rash decisions. In 1954 he resigned as vice-principal of Westcott House, where he had taught New Testament Studies and Doctrine, without having another job lined up to go to, and he admits in his autobiography 'This [was] a lunatic thing to do'.[31] He became in fact Dean of Caius College, Cambridge and was one of Mervyn's first parishioners at Great St Mary's, where, when the benefice fell vacant in 1963, Montefiore was Trinity's second choice as vicar (Simon Phipps was the first, and turned it down). According to a letter from Sir Frank Lee to Mervyn, a number of people advised that Montefiore, although excellent as Dean of Caius, would not be a suitable appointment for Great St Mary's because he was primarily interested in theological scholarship.[32] It was while at Great St Mary's that Montefiore dropped his bombshell regarding the possible sexual orientation of Christ, speculating that because he had remained unmarried, a most unusual occurrence for a Jew of his age and time, he might have been homosexual. He did so in 1967 during the course of an open lecture to the Modern Churchman's Union at Somerville College, Oxford, and like many a naïve don before him, failed to take into account the way such speculation would be handled by the press. The result was what the bishop has himself described as 'a colossal scandal'.[33]

The first to cover his tracks, for he had preached the opening sermon, was Michael Ramsey, who issued a *non sequitur*: 'There is no evidence whatsoever to support Canon Montefiore's reported views. Christians believe that Christ's dealings with both men and women were those of a perfect man' – whatever the Archbishop intended the expression 'a perfect man' to mean. He later wrote to Montefiore to say he was sorry he had been involved in a turmoil which he hoped would soon die down. But no damage-limitation exercise was mounted, by way of a press conference to explain exactly what Montefiore had said and had meant, and a bad mark went against his name in the office of the Prime Minister's appointments secretary.

Hence, exhausted after seven years by his duties at Great St Mary's anyway, in 1970 Hugh Montefiore was not looking like promising episcopal material. Yet he was desperate for a change of occupation, and was only keeping going, he tells us, on sodium amytal and Mogadon. Apparently at dinner one night Rab Butler, Master of Trinity, said to Eric James 'What can you do for poor Hugh?'[34] Butler is supposed to have intimated that the Queen would 'never consent to his getting a bishopric', by which he must have meant a diocesan bishopric, for in the event she did not censor Mervyn's nomination of him to Kingston; the Queen, in any case, is not in the habit of rejecting the advice of her ministers, nor is she known to be particularly fussed, any more than are her mother and sister, about matters pertaining to homosexuality. Had Montefiore's name landed on the Prime Minister's desk as a suggestion for a diocese any time between 19 June 1970 and 4 March 1974 it would have been a former news editor of the *Church Times*, Edward Heath, who would have decided whether to send it to Buckingham Palace to be rubber-stamped by the Queen. He, like the Queen, is not known to be homophobic. However, what we are led to believe happened occurred thus: Butler pressed Eric James to do what he could, so at lunch at Bishop's House the following day Eric James recounted to Mervyn his conversation with Butler. '"Poor Hugh," said Mervyn pensively.' As Eric left, Mervyn said to him 'I'll have a word with John [Robinson] about Hugh. We can't just leave him.' A few days later, Mervyn telephones Eric and says 'I thought you'd like to know as a result of our conversation I've decided to ask Hugh to be my suffragan. Whether I shall succeed in getting him is another matter.'[35]

This story remained unrelayed to Montefiore until after Mervyn's death. In acknowledging Eric's version of events, sent from the Reform Club, Montefiore wrote, on 19 January 1995, 'Absolutely riveted by your letter. So *that's* how it happened. I often wondered why Mervyn thought of me.'

John Robinson duly took Montefiore out to lunch, and primed by Mervyn, asked if he would like to be Bishop of Kingston. Robinson told him that Michael Ramsey, previously consulted by Mervyn, approved. The next ploy devised by Mervyn was to get David Sheppard to meet Montefiore and report back, for Mervyn thought there was no point in appointing someone with whom David would not get on. They met at the house in Sussex of David's mother, and fortunately they clicked. Hence in September 1970 Hugh Montefiore was consecrated, and proved to be yet another of Mervyn's inspired appointments; in 1978, against all the odds, he was the first diocesan bishop recommended by the newly constituted Crown Appointments Commission, and was enthroned as Bishop of Birmingham. So much for the Queen's alleged aversion to him.

Hugh Montefiore is refreshingly candid about the matter of his

appointment to Kingston. 'I was at the end of my tether', he says.[36]
'I was really desperate. I don't think I ever thought I wouldn't
accept.' He accompanied Mervyn on one parish Visitation, watched
Sheppard at one confirmation, and was given special pastoral care
of a stretch of the diocese from Church Ditton beyond Kingston
and on towards Guildford, south of Reigate and eastwards to
Waterloo, a large but fairly green chunk of south London, compris-
ing the boroughs of Lambeth, Streatham, Wandsworth, Richmond,
Kingston, Merton and Reigate. He had 148 parishes in his care
and two archdeaconries, and with a population of over a million
the area was as large as a small diocese. He disgraced himself
by arriving two minutes late for his first staff meeting. 'As I came
in, Mervyn said in a rather authoritarian voice, meaning I think
only to show disapproval, "Bishop, we don't usually allow anyone
to join us who comes in late." I thought that two could play at that
game, and I replied, "I am very sorry, Bishop, but I misjudged the
traffic", and walked out.'[37]

As Hugh Montefiore's name quite obviously indicates, he is a
Jew, 'déraciné; an exile from the Jewish community', as Montefiore
has described himself, and most diocesans would have hesitated
to share their episcopate with someone who – again to quote
the bishop himself – did not really feel accepted in the Christian
community. 'I was sensitive about criticism', he has written.
'I realised that I was not altogether likeable, otherwise my peers
would talk to me more and befriend me. I felt I always had to take
the initiative. I might appear to be brash and self-confident
(I was certainly impetuous); but this often hid an inferior feeling of
unacceptedness.'[38]

As far as Mervyn's attitude towards him was concerned, Bishop
Montefiore has said 'He didn't treat his suffragans as equals, but he
didn't talk as an equal to anybody. He just talked! I don't think he
ever heard more than he wanted to hear. He would ask for advice
from his staff team on serious matters, but all major decisions were
made on his own. But he certainly gave us freedom. I told him I had
been asked to chair a commission on transport which would take up
a day a week and he said "You must make your own decision about
that".'[39] But the Bishop of Liverpool recalls: 'Whenever there was
a crisis he drew us all in. There was something about Mervyn
that almost relished a crisis.' Like so many others who knew and
worked with Mervyn, David Sheppard also recalls 'He found it very
difficult to say sorry, or that he was wrong'.[40]

In 1970 there was another change of chaplain. Derek Watson, who had been ordained by Mervyn and was now chaplain of Mervyn's old Cambridge college, was invited to Bishop's House to consider taking over from Martin Coombs. In the afternoon he made himself scarce, and on his return he was impressed to find the household quaffing champagne. This was following a visit to the chapel for the laying on of hands of Mervyn's chauffeur, Gary Reader, who was about to go into hospital for a minor operation. (It was on Gary Reader's departure – he went to live in New Zealand and was left £2,000 by Mervyn – that in 1972 Munir became Mervyn's chauffeur.) Derek was so impressed by this combination of spiritual and material concern ('It just felt like fun, it was very much Mervyn's style') that he did not hesitate to accept the offer of a job. By this time, Mervyn had been a bishop eleven years, and Derek Watson says 'You were in a very privileged position and learnt an enormous amount, from a very experienced old bird. But most of us congratulated ourselves on surviving. There were many times when I wondered whether I could continue. It was very demanding, living in your place of work with a very powerful character who wanted so much attention. I'm afraid I opted out of the late night sessions. I simply couldn't cope with the alcoholic anecdotage. He was a lonely man, and the drinking was fuelled by loneliness. Bachelor late-night drinkers are almost by definition lonely.'[41]

Nevertheless Mervyn was able to make light of his bachelor status. When another episcopal bachelor, Launcelot Fleming of Norwich, who later became Dean of Windsor, married in 1965, Mervyn sent him the following clerihew:

Launcelot, you face
A disgrace
For leaving Cuthbert and me
Free.

Cuthbert was Cuthbert Bardsley, the jovial Bishop of Coventry, who lived for many years with his sister, but who sprang a surprise by getting married in 1972. To Bardsley, Mervyn then wrote:

Cuthbert, like ex-Norwich, you face
A disgrace
For leaving Southwark alone on the bench
With no wench.

Like Paul Oestreicher, Derek Watson, together with the Arch-deacon of Southwark, was once roped in to do the cooking – for a dinner given for the Chinese chargé d'affaires, at a time when Mervyn was keen to visit China, a trip which in the event he never made. But by and large, Derek Watson considers he got least involved of all the chaplains. 'The extent', he says, 'to which we got involved with Mervyn depended really on our own needs. My predominant need was to get out!'

It was also in 1970 that another diocesan pilgrimage was planned to the Holy Land. On 11 June 1970 Mervyn was told by the Archbishop in Jerusalem, George Appleton, 'I understand that your diocesan pilgrimage is being criticised as likely to indicate moral support for the Israeli Government within the present situation in the Middle East'. He wondered whether Mervyn might consider spending two or three days in Amman as 'this would show our desire to understand both sides of the question', but Mervyn told Tony Crowe 'I am not all that keen about staying in Amman, but perhaps you would like to act as Chaplain on my behalf to the El Fatah'.[42]

One of those who accompanied Mervyn on this pilgrimage was Roger Royle, who was currently very much in favour. 'Mervyn chose you as a friend', Canon Royle explains, 'you didn't choose him. And you could have a sell-by date. He lost interest in you if you were no longer any use to him. You were considered of use if you were prepared to have a meal with him, or go for a walk. He loathed anyone he thought was a bore.' (Mervyn's Saturday walks were not exclusively recreational. Once a year he would promenade David Sheppard to talk about his performance rather than have a chat with him in the study.) The pilgrimage was organized by Inter Church Travel, and while most of the pilgrims, a planeload of 200, transferred to a fleet of charabancs, Mervyn installed himself in a Mercedes. His behaviour throughout seems to have left something to be desired. At the fourth station of the cross it came on to snow, and 'Mervyn decided to return to the hotel. "I might catch a cold", he explained.' Roger, acting as chaplain for the duration of the pilgrimage, exploded, reminding Mervyn that 'Our Lord got killed!' At Hebron, Mervyn wandered round the market. 'At first he had been incredibly cold, so he had a nip of brandy. At Hebron he felt incredibly hot, so he had another nip of brandy. We then drove to the Dead Sea over a very bumpy road, and he turned to me and said "Roger, I think I'm going to be sick", and had *another* nip of brandy!' At Evensong in the cathedral in Jerusalem Roger was suddenly sent out to scour the area for drinks, as it had occurred to Mervyn that he ought to invite the Archbishop to a party.

Roger Royle explains why he was again invited to accompany Mervyn overseas, this time on holiday to Majorca. 'He liked me because he thought I was efficient and good company. At nine o'clock one morning he said, "Roger, I think I've been recognised. I'm absolutely certain I've been recognised."

'I said, "I should think they imagine you're Harry Worth."

'"That", said Mervyn, "is very, very rude."'

Even on holiday, the honorary chaplain in tow was expected to join Mervyn for Matins on the balcony. They travelled with two bottles of sherry in the glove compartment, stopping every hour on the hour for a drink. One Sunday Mervyn decided to celebrate the Eucharist in the countryside, and somehow managed to get hold of a server. The server held the book and Mervyn began: 'Almighty God, unto whom *all* hearts be open, *all* desires known, and from whom *no* secrets are hid – I want the book higher, *higher* . . . ' Roger thought 'Why doesn't the server slap him round the ear?' But, he says, 'However much you got infuriated with Mervyn there was something about him that was very attractive. He wanted to add a brightness to life. And there were times, if he was in the right mood, when he could make you feel good. But if he started to reject you, that could be painful, and you didn't really know why it had happened.'

Mervyn did pretty well for holidays, generally escaping from England in February for sound medical reasons, taking himself off for Lent in 1971, for example, with John Betjeman and Elizabeth Cavendish to Spain. This was the year that Kenneth Woollcombe took up his duties as Bishop of Oxford. On his arrival at Cuddesdon he found on his desk, 'after only a short interregnum, complaints against several clergy about their sexual behaviour. I hadn't expected them and was quite unfamiliar with the Ecclesiastical Jurisdiction Measure, which I had fondly imagined would be rarely used.'[43] Remembering Mervyn's daunting brush with Church law when he had to unfrock Bryn Thomas, Bishop Woollcombe rang him up. '"Don't do anything until I come," he almost shouted down the 'phone, "and don't tell the lawyers!"' Within two hours Mervyn had got Munir to drive him to the Bishop of Oxford's residence at Cuddesdon, 'and spent the rest of the day with me explaining how to use the Measure pastorally, but *not* in open court. I did exactly what he told me & stuck to his good advice for the next seven years. It meant, of course, that sinners had to be punished – but *not* pilloried.'

It was in 1972, on the occasion of the marriage of Cuthbert Bardsley, that Bishop Woollcombe joined in the episcopal poetic stakes, sending to Mervyn the following:

If, like Launcelot, you found a Guinevere, Stockwood,
The shock would
Be to the rest of us rather unnervin',
And possibly to Mervyn.

Someone else who was inspired to write verse by his knowledge of Mervyn and his diocese was the Poet Laureate himself, Sir John Betjeman. Despite once falling asleep at dinner he was a frequent and welcome guest at Bishop's House, and loved and admired Mervyn. To say that Betjeman was church-orientated would be a fairly absurd understatement, and in Southwark he found that whole range of ecclesiastical architecture and churchmanship in which he revelled. For Mervyn he wrote a poem called 'The Diocese'. It began:

The Diocese is quite my scene,
With Tooting Bec and Canon Dean.
In scarf and hood at Table's end,
The North, of course – no modern trend
Like wafer bread or Series Two.
WE stick to 1662.

Not far away is Father Smith,
A very different kind of fish.
He bows and bobs and shows his arse
When genuflecting at the Mass.
To Rome he has a private line –
H.H. Pope Paul, Vat 69.

And so it went on for a further eleven pertinent stanzas. Writing to Mervyn on 10 January 1977 to thank him for dinner the night before, a dinner party also attended by Lady Elizabeth Cavendish, Charles Lansdale, Vicar of Benhilton, and one of Mervyn's former chaplains (Dominic Walker), Betjeman said 'It certainly is a wonderful thing that has grown up since your appointment and that thing is the diocese. Before you came it had very little character. Now', he added, his tongue firmly in his cheek, 'Southwark has more character than any Diocese, always excepting Sodor and Man.' He added, 'That was a delicious dinner. Tell El Fhata how beautifully they cooked the dinner. Yours in the sure and certain hope etc.' And he added a postscript, in his appalling handwriting, 'Dominic is obviously a saint. So is Charles. Neither . . .' and the rest is illegible. When in 1980 Mervyn resigned the see, John Betjeman went on record as saying he thought Mervyn, as a father to his clergy, the perfect bishop, and very loyal to old friends. 'The older and more dissolute they are', he said, 'the more he likes them.'

Notes

1 MS, *Bishop's Journal* (Mowbray, 1964).

2 Paul Welsby, *A History of the Church of England: 1945–1980* (OUP, 1984).

3 The Scheme foundered over the controversial Service of Reconciliation. Only five bishops voted against, but a majority of 75 per cent in favour of the Scheme was required in the Convocations, and neither of the Lower Houses attained it.

4 Rev. Nicolas Stacey, in conversation with the author.

5 Nicolas Stacey, *Who Cares?* (Anthony Blond, 1971).

6 Very Rev. Michael Mayne, in conversation with the author.

7 Ibid.

8 Rev. Donald Reeves, in conversation with the author.

9 Ibid.

10 Owen Chadwick, *Michael Ramsey: A Life* (OUP, 1990).

11 *The Crossman Diaries* (Mandarin Paperbacks, 1991).

12 Mary Cryer and Donald Reeves, each in conversation with the author.

13 Mary Cryer, in conversation with the author.

14 Letter from David Tankard to the author, 8 July 1995.

15 In conversation with the author.

16 In conversation with the author.

17 Donald Reeves, as above.

18 On 4 September 1995 Jean Overton Fuller wrote to the author to say 'I have just finished writing a book entitled *The Canings at Court Lees*, in which Stockwood comes out terribly badly'. No explanation was vouchsafed.

19 Bishop Hugh Montefiore, in conversation with the author.

20 Letter from MS to Robin Howard, 16 March 1957.

21 David Faull, in conversation with the author.

22 See Michael De-la-Noy, *The Church of England: A Portrait* (Simon and Schuster, 1993).

23 It is not in dispute that Lord Runcie, when Bishop of St Albans, declined to ordain a deacon, Richard Kirker, now secretary of the Lesbian and Gay Christian Movement, to the priesthood because he thought Mr Kirker was involved with homosexual concerns to the exclusion of a priestly vocation.

24 Canon Eric James, in conversation with the author.

25 The Bishop of Liverpool, in conversation with the author.

26 Christopher Chavasse, Bishop of Rochester from 1940 to 1960, had run in the 400 metres at the 1908 Olympic Games, won a Military Cross and the Croix de Guerre and lost a leg in a boating accident. In 1928 he became the first Master of St Peter's College, Oxford. His father was a bishop too, and two of his brothers were killed in the Great War, one of whom, Noel, was awarded the VC and bar.

27 Alan Bennett, *Writing Home* (Faber and Faber, 1994).

28 Lady Elizabeth Cavendish, in conversation with the author.

29 John Mortimer, in a letter to the author, 1 July 1995.

30 John Mortimer, *Murderers and Other Friends: Another Part of Life* (Viking, 1994).

31 Hugh Montefiore, *Oh God, What Next?* (Hodder and Stoughton, 1995).

32 Letter from Sir Frank Lee to MS, 14 March 1963, in Lambeth Palace archives.

33 Montefiore, *Oh God, What Next?*

34 Letter from Eric James to Hugh Montefiore, 16 January 1995.

35 Ibid.

36 Bishop Hugh Montefiore, in conversation with the author.

37 Montefiore, *Oh God, What Next?*

38 Ibid.

39 Bishop Hugh Montefiore, in conversation with the author.

40 The Bishop of Liverpool, in conversation with the author.

41 Rev. Derek Watson, in conversation with the author.

42 Letter from MS to Tony Crowe, 12 June 1970.

43 Letter from Bishop Kenneth Woollcombe to the author, 11 March 1995.

Chapter 12

Not the right man

When Derek Watson left Bishop's House in 1973, to work in a parish in Surbiton, and in 1978 to become a canon of Southwark Cathedral (he now is currently Dean-designate of Salisbury), Mervyn Stockwood went to dinner at St Matthew's clergy house in Westminster with the parish priest, Gerard Irvine. It was with the express purpose of vetting Fr Irvine's curate, David Hutt, now Canon Steward of Westminster Abbey. In the event, Canon Hutt declined to serve as chaplain to Mervyn, and recalls today how he 'narrowly avoided that fate'. Instead he was appointed Priest Vicar and Succentor at the cathedral, and speaks of Mervyn with some asperity.

At Bishop's House, where he first signed the visitors' book on 17 August 1973, Canon Hutt remembers 'imitation flowers banked everywhere. I think Mervyn was both aesthetically sensitive and extraordinarily insensitive. He was a fairground person, in a way. He would store daffodils in the deep freeze and bring them out out of season.' He says he stayed two nights to be further vetted, and there was a dinner party each night. 'No one drank port after dinner except Mervyn, so every four minutes he would top up his glass, and by one o'clock in the morning he was completely pie-eyed. After 48 hours I thought I couldn't manage this at all. I just couldn't. Mervyn wasn't quite clear whether he wanted a kind of live-in nurse, or live-in boyfriend. And it is clear to me with hindsight, even clearer than it was then, that Mervyn lived in that strange ambivalent world of bishops who are gay and have a private life – a private sexuality and a public persona. I would say that Mervyn was desperately in need of affection, and he needed more touch and more reassurance than most people I know, and I think how he got it was by surrounding himself with rather sycophantic clergymen who would go along with his role-play, would never oppose him, but give him a sense of security. And it actually wasn't enough for that man. I think that he was emotionally starved. He was someone who had never experienced unconditional love. Everything had to be earned, and love came as a reward. It was an evangelical concept very much to do with his generation. I think that complexity about liking frozen daffodils and imitation flowers extended into his sexuality. He was someone who really needed a permanent, stable, loving relationship. I wasn't going to place myself in the situation of being either nursemaid or live-in friend. So I made my excuses and took my leave.'[1]

Someone else who knew Mervyn well but did not want his remarks on this matter attributed to him has a further revealing insight to offer about Mervyn's possible need for a permanent homosexual relationship, and why he never had one – quite apart from the virtual impossibility of such an arrangement for a bishop, then or now. 'I think Mervyn would have been an impossible person to live with, as a partner. He was very much caught up with himself and what he was doing. He had a low boredom threshold. I think it would have been very difficult for him to cope with one other person. And I think it would have been very difficult for another person who wasn't a saint to cope with him. So I don't think a partnership would have been a practical possibility.'

Charles Lansdale, now a team rector in the diocese of Chichester, found himself embarrassed by Mervyn's chronic inability to sort out friendships and potential love affairs, or his roles as friend and bishop. And interestingly enough, he and Mervyn shared a similar disturbed childhood; Fr Lansdale's mother had been killed in the blitz when he was four, and at five he, like Mervyn, had been shunted off to boarding school. He trained as an ordinand at Mirfield, and first met Mervyn at Artillery Mansions when investigating parishes in Southwark in which to serve his first curacy. He remembers that Mervyn was very charming, 'and kept asking if I liked the poor. We weren't really engaging, because I was rather more into mysticism and the Early Fathers than the poor, but he was kind and thoughtful and put me at my ease.'[2]

Eventually Fr Lansdale went overseas, to work in the diocese of Zululand and Swaziland. 'Prior to that', he says, 'Mervyn had not shown a great deal of interest in me, except that from time to time he would invite me to go out with him on his day off. My incumbent was very impressed! Why did he invite me? Mervyn was interested in personable young men. But I didn't realize it at that stage. We would go walking somewhere and usually ended up in a pub. When I went to Swaziland Mervyn kept in touch by letter.' When, in 1972, Charles Lansdale became too unwell to continue working overseas, Mervyn took him off on holiday, as 'chaplain', to Greece and Crete. 'As soon as we arrived in Athens he was ringing up everyone under the sun. He was incredible at arranging one thing after another. Every moment was occupied. One day we were in a taverna on Crete and in walked the Archdeacon of Southwark and the Vicar of Lewisham. Their eyes popped open somewhat!'

In the end Mervyn paid the Bishop of Zululand to release Fr Lansdale and gave him a parish, All Saints' at Benhilton, only some 20 minutes by car from Bishop's House. 'He was always ringing up. Could I come to this or that? My main job was to pour out the wine. There was always this confusion between his being a friend and an employer. I felt I had been caught in a spider's web. I was very fond of him, he became a father figure, but one moment he spoke as a bishop, the next as a friend. I wasn't flattered by all this attention so much as a little worried by his motives, because he was a very overpowering person, quite frightening in many ways. I sometimes found it very difficult to assert myself and continue to be myself when he was so dominating. I was always saying that I felt under enormous pressure from him and that I found this difficult to cope with, and he would argue that true love liberates and doesn't manipulate.

'He wanted this done and that done. He wanted *us* to do this and *us* to do that. I think he genuinely wanted my happiness, he always knew my heterosexual tendencies, and always claimed that he would find some suitable young lady for me. I felt he was being voyeuristic. He was always telling me about the marvellous relationships homosexuals had. On holiday he would size up the waiters. Why was he so fond of me? Maybe he thought I hadn't discovered myself. And that was part of the pressure. I won't say there was an element of fear of him in my relationship but it wasn't far off. I felt it very difficult to say No when he invited me out so frequently. And I was never quite sure whether I was being invited on an official level, as a sort of chaplain, or as a friend.'

Fr Lansdale adds: 'I don't think he had many close friends. I think I probably ended up being his closest.' Surprisingly, he retained Mervyn's friendship when in 1987 he got engaged – not to one of the 'smart gals' Mervyn had selected for him to meet but to a young woman of his own choice in his own parish. 'I thought my getting married would be the end of our friendship. He had been brokering it for years, but when it happened he didn't like it. I think he thought of it as a betrayal.' Mervyn wrote Fr Lansdale rather a pathetic letter, ostensibly breaking off their relationship, the sort of letter an emotionally wounded prep-school boy might have penned to some chum who had gone off with another boy. But he retained his wits sufficiently to send £50 in Premium Bonds as a wedding present, and he eventually baptized the Lansdales' child, asked Charles to preside at his Requiem Mass and bequeathed him £10,000.

No one encountered the sharply contrasted sides to Mervyn's character and personality in greater detail than Charles Lansdale. 'He told me about his depression in the mid-1970s. I think he saw it as a dark night of the soul, and he just kind of endured it. He was very good at not showing to the public or his staff how he felt. There was something of the stoic about him. He had enormous determination and tenacity. Nothing would thwart him. People who opposed him were crushed by the juggernaut of his personality. At the same time he was genuinely compassionte. One of his priests had been fiddling some alms house accounts and committed suicide by jumping off Beachy Head. Mervyn took the funeral, and handled the press superbly, focusing only on the priest's good qualities. Often he would draw a veil over the clergy's weaknesses and cover up for them. At my worst moments with him, when I was very, very angry, and I was really horrible to him, he was extremely patient.'

Mervyn was also extremely generous and hospitable, taking Charles Lansdale with him to Romania, the Holy Land, Spain, Majorca, and in this country on holiday to Devonshire – all in addition to inviting him to countless meals at Bishop's House, on one occasion to meet Princess Alexandra, on another occasion to celebrate his birthday; he may have placed Fr Lansdale under pressure, but there certainly seem to have been compensations. Lansdale's view is that Mervyn would have liked a relationship with another man, and he very much admired people who did have one. But he came from an era when this was not acceptable and 'The lid was kept on because of that. He didn't want to damage the Church and be disloyal to his calling. That was a very powerful force in his life.'

This is a conclusion echoed by Canon Hutt. 'I have no evidence that Mervyn was other than a non-practising homosexual. Part of Mervyn was that old *Boys' Own* story line, about Edwardian chums, stories shot through with homoerotic overtones, but not actually doing anything genital. He belonged to an ethos in which to show any emotion was unmanly. You were not allowed to cry. Mervyn was actually asking for help, for a great deal of warmth and affection which is entirely appropriate for a small child, but of course it was overlaid by this great persona that he had accumulated. That was his shell. He needed the externals of religion, but I don't really remember him as a man of profound spirituality because he was so restless.'[3] This restlessness has also been remarked upon by Giles Harcourt, chaplain from 1976 to 1978. 'At prayer, Mervyn was not a calming influence. He raced through things. Even when meditating he would make notes in his notebook. He hadn't the ability to be totally still, and for him to listen to God was difficult because Mervyn really wanted God to listen to him.'[4] It is small wonder that Mervyn once wrote to Charles Lansdale to say that to become a monk was 'never *my* line of business!' He asked Dominic Walker, who had experience of two religious orders, how long he thought he would last in the monastic life, to which Fr Dominic replied 'I would give you until lunch'. Even making a private retreat was anathema to Mervyn. Canon Hutt says 'I think he would have been terribly unhappy in retreat because it would have meant silence, and he couldn't cope with that. He needed lights and sounds and activity to give him the vitality that he so badly needed. He wasn't someone who, before a great service, made an act of recollection, as most people do. Mervyn was always on the go. It helped to keep reality at bay.'[5]

As to Mervyn's stoicism and sense of duty, he preached at his godson's ordination 'in spite of having a high temperature and flu at the time', and Giles Harcourt remembers one occasion when Mervyn had a temperature and was due to take a confirmation at St Lawrence, Catford. He insisted on going, and 'was brilliant. There is no other word for it. His timing was impeccable. He produced all the right touches. But he was sweating profusely, and by the time he got back into the car he was almost ready to pass out.'[6] One of Mervyn's personal touches at a confirmation was to name each candidate as he laid hands upon them. One evening he got a boy's name wrong. 'Defend, O Lord, this thy child Samuel with thy heavenly grace . . . ' at which point he was interrupted by the lad, who complained that his name was Daniel. 'Tonight you're Samuel', Mervyn informed him.

The indifferent health from which Mervyn suffered throughout his life should not be underestimated. He endured numerous operations, in England and overseas, for sinus problems. 'Went to drinks with Mervyn Stockwood ... He looked awfully pale and drawn', Tony Benn noted in his diary on 29 March 1960. 'He doesn't enjoy good health.' He was on sick leave during April and May 1964. In January 1971 he failed to attend his diocesan synod 'on doctor's orders'. He always carried a nebulizer with him to help with breathing, and Dominic Walker was with him when one day, in order to recover from a bronchial attack, Mervyn had to take refuge in a vicarage and lie down on the floor.

Someone besides David Hutt who resisted Mervyn's blandishments was a handsome young American, David Sox, who says that in 1977 he was offered by Mervyn a residentiary canonry, and turned it down 'because I didn't want to be beholden to him. I didn't want to become one of Mervyn's boys. I preferred to keep my distance.'[7] Sox, who had been introduced to Mervyn in 1973, was nevertheless a frequent guest at Bishop's House, and it was David Sox who took the photograph of Mervyn at Chanctonbury Ring that appeared on the dust jacket of his autobiography – without acknowledgement. Sox was initially on an exchange visit to the Church of England with the Vicar of St John's, Peckham, and during his time there the parish received a visit from Princess Margaret, patron of the Peckham Settlement. Sox recalls the Princess, who has a considerable personality of her own, firmly stamping on Mervyn in the vicarage dining room. 'Oh, do shut up', she said to him. 'You bore me!'[8]

An indirect consequence of Hugh Montefiore's arrival in the diocese as suffragan Bishop of Kingston was one of the most dramatic fallings out Mervyn ever went through with one of his clergy. In 1971 there was, according to Bishop Montefiore, 'the father and mother of a row'.[9] Yet he makes only passing reference to the row in his autobiography.[10] It involved all three bishops and had its origins in education, for which, as already noted, the previous Bishop of Kingston, William Gilpin, had been responsible. When Gilpin retired, Mervyn asked Canon Eric James to scour the country for 'the best man there is' to be appointed a residentiary canon with the education portfolio.[11] Using his experience since 1964 as roving director of Parish and People, a task which had given him an almost unrivalled insight into the problems and personalities of the Church of England, Eric James came up with the name of Patrick Miller, the holder of a First in theology at

Mervyn's old college, a former curate at Great St Mary's under Joseph Fison, and currently head of the department of religion at Manchester Grammar School. He was duly installed as a canon in 1969 (he succeeded Douglas Rhymes as Canon Librarian), and commenced an enquiry into secondary church schools. According to Eric James, Montefiore was displeased with the appointment of Miller, displeased with Eric's hand in it, and 'was saying very negative things about Patrick all round the Diocese'. Eric James's version of events continues: 'Things got worse and worse and it became clear that Mervyn was now ceasing to give Patrick the backing he needed. Mervyn was embarrassed, and realised there wasn't room for two people at the head of education. His appointment of Hugh with his educational knowledge on top of his appointment of Patrick with his was a disaster.'

In his autobiography, Bishop Montefiore says he thought Patrick Miller's commission of enquiry 'worked, perhaps necessarily, in rather an inquisitorial manner'. When, in 1971, Mervyn took the Montefiores off to Spain, it was left to David Sheppard to chair a meeting of the Bishop's Council, at which Canon Miller's Commission was authorized to extend their enquiries into the diocesan primary schools. Montefiore writes:

I was distressed that this had happened in my absence without asking me or the Schools Committee of the Board of Education, especially as I found that the primary school head teachers, whose morale badly needed boosting in the inner city, were very nervous about the whole undertaking; and on the advice of the Schools Committee I would not have sanctioned it. When I came back from Spain and discovered what had happened, I refused to join in, and the project had to be dropped. This caused grave distress to the Senior Advisor on RE [Patrick Miller] and to one of the Residentiary Canons [Eric James], both of whom left the Diocese feeling that they had been badly treated. It took me a long time to get over the distress generated by this episode; but I am still convinced that I did the right thing.

Miller's enquiry was to be financed by the Action Society Trust, of which John Vaizey, Professor of Economics at Brunel University and 'a devout High Anglican' according to his entry in the *Dictionary of National Biography*, was a trustee. Eric James has written: 'The climax came when Hugh told John Vaizey, behind the scenes, that the money . . . must not be given to Patrick. That cut

Patrick's work at its roots. (John Vaizey was scandalised by Hugh's action.) I felt, having got Patrick into his post, I *had* to defend him.' So Eric 'took the matter to staff meeting and battled with Hugh and Mervyn on behalf of Patrick, but it was clear I could not win. David Sheppard made it clear to me that the power was all with Hugh and Mervyn and it would be wiser for Patrick to leave and for me to take a sabbatical and think out my future, too.'

Patrick Miller did resign, and was appointed Director of Studies at Queen Mary's College, Basingstoke, while Eric took himself off on a six-month tour of India, South Africa and Australasia. On his return to Southwark he was greeted with rumours that he had gone away because he had had a nervous breakdown, and, even more bizarrely, 'I had had a homosexual affair with Patrick Miller (who was married and had two children)'. Eric James has never made any secret of his own homosexuality, and adds 'As a homosexual, any *innocent* friendship I had was always vulnerable to the charge', a charge he strongly denies but one which was passed on to Michael Ramsey, presumably with a view to wrecking Eric's ecclesiastical career. It was left to Robert Runcie to come to Eric's rescue, by installing him in 1973 as a residentiary canon of St Albans. Six years later he was appointed Director of Christian Action.

In conversation, Eric James has supplied a general explanation for the hiatus: 'Mervyn thought hierarchically. Hence he thought he had to support Hugh, and the only way he could do that was by getting rid of Patrick and me. He was marvellously loyal to his fellow bishops, but over against vicars, and loyal to vicars over against the laity. He had a very hierarchically structured mind. When I tried to talk to him about the whole matter he just said, "I don't want to discuss it", and got into a great temper.'

There are a number of puzzling postscripts to the events Hugh Montefiore has described as 'the cause of the greatest sadness during my time in Southwark'.[12] First of all, Eric James can still say 'What astonishes me is how much affection one had for Mervyn'. A reconciliation was eventually contrived in 1976 at the Bloomsbury flat of Jim Storey (a wealthy left-wing cleric and barrister who acted for Trade Unions, was a close adviser to Mervyn and left him £1,000 with which he bought a canal boat for use in retirement, which he named the *Jim Storey*). Even so, one wonders why, after apparently being treated so badly, Eric James should have wanted to burden himself with the task of writing Mervyn's biography, but he did ask if he might do this. Mervyn stalled.[13] In August 1993, however, while contemplating his final will, dated 30 November 1993, Mervyn evidently approached Eric to see if he was still interested in the project, for on 22 August 1993 Eric wrote to him to say 'I think it would be impossible for me to take on doing anything with *your* papers', citing as the reason the fact that he was already committed to writing a biography of Bishop Trevor Huddleston. Nevertheless Mervyn proceeded to bequeath his papers to Eric, writing also, on 24 August, to David Sox, to ask if *he* would be interested in writing his biography. Nothing came of that suggestion, and when, after Mervyn's death, Eric was informed that he had been left Mervyn's papers, he wrote to the present author to say 'I hope *you'll* do his biography. He has left me as his "Literary Executor" in his will but I made it clear to him that I could *not* be that! Typical!!'[14] But Mervyn did not actually appoint a literary executor.

By 1974 Mervyn had been Bishop of Southwark for 15 years. At 58 he was in his prime, and despite all the vicissitudes of his episcopate he had acquired an undoubted *gravitas* and a reputation as a pugnacious champion of social justice. So he might have expected some recognition of his achievements from 'the powers that be'. It was the year in which the bishopric of Winchester (the fifth most senior bishopric in the Church) together with the arch-bishoprics of Canterbury and York happened to fall vacant. Mervyn's name was not considered for Winchester, as it had not been the year before for London, the diocese for which in some ways he would have been best suited. Winchester is historically significant, for the holder of the see is *ex officio* Prelate of the Order of the Garter (hence there is plenty of fun to be enjoyed at Windsor Castle), but the diocese itself would probably have bored Mervyn to tears, and in the event the see was filled with distinction by John Vernon Taylor. But when it became known that on his seventieth birthday Michael Ramsey proposed retiring, at least one person, the theologian and philosopher Sir Malcolm Knox, seems to have suggested Mervyn for Canterbury. Harold Wilson wanted Donald Coggan of York to succeed Ramsey, which he did – contrary to the advice offered to Wilson by Ramsey himself. But Coggan was only translated after Wilson had taken account of a very wide range of views 'both inside and outside the established church', as he told Sir Malcolm in a letter dated 5 June 1974. 'Since you mention Stockwood', Wilson continued, 'I doubt if there would have been an outcry but I know him very well indeed, and I did not feel he was the right man.'

One reason Wilson did not think Mervyn the right man for Canterbury may be discerned from Mervyn's autobiography. 'In 1973', he writes, 'I became impatient with the attitude of Harold Wilson towards the European Community. He seemed to shilly-shally, the epitome of indecision and vacillation . . . I regretted the growing difference between us because we had had happy relationships for several years and I knew him as a man who was capable of much personal kindness.' In being thought not the right man for Canterbury Mervyn was in good company; Wilson also rejected, as imaginative outsiders, two distinguished theologians, presumably because they were not in episcopal orders (neither was Thomas Becket): Owen Chadwick, Dean of Christ Church, and his brother Henry, Regius Professor of Modern History at Cambridge.

Anxious, as he so often seemed to be, to get on the right side of the headmaster, Mervyn made no secret of the fact that when sounded out by Downing Street regarding Ramsey's successor at Canterbury he had recommended Coggan; he boasted of it in an article in the *Daily Mail* on 15 May 1974 headlined 'The Magnificent Donald – And Why He Got My Vote'. On the same day he told readers of *The Times* why Dr Coggan was 'equal to the challenge of the scientific age'.

As the weeks ticked by following the announcement that Donald Coggan was to move to Canterbury Mervyn waited anxiously for a letter from the Prime Minister, asking if he might suggest his name to the Queen for the vacant archbishopric of York. 'We had a long talk about York', David Faull recalls. 'Mervyn could not understand why he had not been offered it. He became very upset.'[15] The question of Mervyn's not being offered York is particularly pertinent because before Wilson managed to fill the see with a less than efficient replacement, Stuart Blanch of Liverpool, it had been declined by Bishop John Howe, Secretary General of the Anglican Consultative Council, by Patrick Rodger, Bishop of Manchester and by Robert Runcie, Bishop of St Albans. 'The fact is', says Mr Faull, 'he simply wasn't trusted by the establishment. You could never be sure how he would react, and he often reacted very violently. He knew they were having difficulty finding someone, and that Blanch had not been the first choice.'[16] Had Mervyn known he had been regarded in this way, he might have been subjected to even deeper depression than he was shortly going to suffer anyway.

In 1975 Mervyn took sabbatical leave, during the course of which, while in Spain, he slipped a disc, and he has recalled that 'soon after my return to duty in July 1975 I was hit by a very deep depression which did not lift until my resignation five years later'. He says he often had a temperature and had to change his clothes 'because they were wet with perspiration'. Then he developed eczema, which like so many skin complaints is liable to have its roots in some psychosomatic cause. He attributed these symptoms to his increasing detestation of the machinery of organized religion and, more realistically, perhaps, to loneliness, to which it requires a certain courage to admit. He makes no mention of his being over-looked for any kind of preferment, and for Mervyn to have made such a mention himself would have been in poor taste, but this must surely have been one cause. It is interesting that for all his assiduous wooing of royalty he was never even offered a royal plum. In 1970, when Robin Woods left Windsor to become Bishop of Worcester, Mervyn might have been considered a suitably pastoral replacement as dean. He was not made Clerk of the Closet or Lord High Almoner. Another cause of Mervyn's deterioration in health, in particular his depression, could have been physical – his exorbitant intake of alcohol; and perhaps Princess Margaret had warned the Queen that Mervyn might start knocking the furniture about, for he was incapable of drinking in moderation at Kensington Palace. He must in fact have been quite naïve to have imagined he would have been seriously considered for York, and perhaps the depression came on when he eventually put two and two together and realized that his over-indulgence had come to the notice of the two most influential people where his future was concerned, the new Archbishop of Canterbury and the Prime Minister. Neither were what one might call bon-vivants, and as far as homosexuality was concerned, Tom Driberg thought Wilson a 'deeply prejudiced' puritan.

There happened also to be a senior layman, with the ear successively of Michael Ramsey and Donald Coggan, whose influence upon the appointment of bishops, and as often as not the withholding of appointments, was quite simply crucial. He was not a member of Mervyn's fan club, and whether or not Mervyn ever realized how much extraordinary power this layman wielded, he certainly never went out of his way to ingratiate himself. On the contrary, he appeared to treat him with some disdain, displaying an antipathy which was mutual. Hugh Montefiore has said 'Mervyn was shattered he didn't go to York. But I don't think the establishment would ever have been happy with Mervyn in a position of major power because he was so mercurial. He was impulsive and could always be on the verge of a scandal that never actually occurred. Had I been in charge of events, I would have taken the risk!'[17] (In 1980 Mervyn hoped that Montefiore might have been chosen as a lively successor to Coggan at Canterbury – and if he had been, there is little doubt that all the bitter debates about homosexual clergy would have been deftly disposed of.) Giles Harcourt thinks 'York would have been ideal for Mervyn, and Mervyn for York. It was the drink that prevented it.'[18] Michael Mayne thinks Mervyn would have been 'a powerful Archbishop of York. But the Establishment didn't appreciate him.' To Mervyn's credit, while he never campaigned on homosexual issues he made no secret among many of his diocesan clergy that he was homosexual, and looked with favour on permanent homosexual relationships, believing, rationally enough, that for homosexuals, homosexuality is as natural as heterosexuality is for heterosexuals. Lord Coggan has recalled that Mervyn was a generous man, 'a man with a big heart & a great need for affection & appreciation – a lonely man, I would guess. It would not surprise me if there were evidence that he hoped for a move from the extremely difficult & heavy diocese of Southwark – & the sadness of his closing years there point in that direction. He may – probably *did* – feel "by-passed."' Lord Coggan adds: 'He sometimes opened his mouth without having given adequate thought before doing so. That is a weakness which becomes more serious the higher the office occupied by the speaker.'[19]

One thing which is quite clear about Mervyn's drinking is that he was not an alcoholic. He was abstemious when alone, he never drank secretly, or to excess before the evening. He gave up drink for most of Lent, fasting the whole of Good Friday. Not everyone would agree with Dominic Walker's assessment that 'when Mervyn was drunk his mind was more acute than when he was sober', but Fr Dominic insists that whereas Mervyn quite often forgot what had been said during the day, first thing in the morning he could remember everything said the night before. One explanation for his ability to survive on so little sleep is that he had the enviable ability to catnap. But drink and sexual orientation apart, it is unlikely that Mervyn and Coggan would have made a well-matched pair. Concerned, as were very many people, with the growing secularization of society and with violence and racial tension, on 15 October 1975 the two new evangelical archbishops issued a somewhat simplistic 'Call to the Nation', upon which Mervyn was swift to pounce. He felt that the Call placed too much emphasis on the responsibility of the individual and did not say enough about the structures of the society which conditioned the individual. For some inexplicable reason, however, he decided, on 31 October, to open a debate in the Communist *Morning Star*. The mild conciliatory sop he offered Dr Coggan at the start of the article was swiftly forgotten by a famous paragraph which read as follows:

... those of us who have visited Socialist countries in Europe know that if a Communist government were to be established in Britain the West End would be cleared up overnight, and the ugly features of our permissive society would be changed within a matter of days. And heaven help the porn merchants and all engaged in the making of fortunes through the commercial exploitation of sex.

This was tantamount, being published in the *Morning Star*, to a recommendation of Communism, and the heavens duly opened. Fifty Members of Parliament signed a Commons motion supporting Coggan. One backbencher told the *Guardian* 'The Marxists seem now to have penetrated the higher echelons of the established Church'. A close reading of Mervyn's *Morning Star* article reveals the pen of a very tired man. Mervyn's literary style was often in need of the ministrations of a sensitive sub-editor, but this article was particularly badly constructed, and as *The Times* rightly pointed out in a leader, it was 'written in a language that is often ambiguous, so that some parts of it seem to have little meaning'. Mervyn's Registrar – David Faull – came to his defence in the letters column of *The Times*, while his old adversary, Garth Moore, still Chancellor of Southwark, accused him of stabbing the archbishops in the back. Mervyn's championship of Communist methods got short shrift from a group of 16 Labour MPs, who signed a motion 'marvelling at the innocence of Dr Stockwood in imagining that a communist government would end our permissive society "within a matter of days"'.

While Mervyn's ill-considered article never amounted to an

attack on the archbishops, in the shorthand of journalism that is what it became. Headlines read 'MPs Protest And The Bishop Is Told To "Belt Up"', 'Bishop's Attack On Dr Coggan Starts Storm'. Once again an enormous amount of emotional energy had been expended to very little purpose, except that it furnished Harold Wilson with a quip at the conclusion of a Cabinet meeting. He said he did not want to introduce a note of piety as it would get a blast from the Bishop of Southwark.[20] By 6 January the following year the Archbishop and Mrs Coggan were at Bishop's House for lunch, and in 1978, somewhat perversely, Mervyn made further amends by dedicating *The Cross and the Sickle* to Donald Coggan. In a Foreword, David Owen explained that at Cambridge Mervyn had taught him both Christianity and Socialism, and that 'to understand the underlying philosophy of Communism should be an important objective for any thinking Christian'.

Mervyn's personal encounters with Communism included an extraordinary incident that took place in Moscow while he was on a parliamentary visit, in the company of six members of the House of Commons and one other from the Lords. His electric razor proved useless, and decked out in purple cassock, his episcopal ring prominent as ever (not looking, it has to be said, remotely like an Orthodox bishop, for they wear neither purple nor a ring), he appeared in a barber's shop to be shaved – by an enormous and ebullient woman. The room was full of Muscovites being shaved too. His visit to the barber's shop coincided with the Orthodox Easter, and the woman shaving him, spotting the ring and the purple, asked if he was an Anglican bishop. On being assured that he was, with one hand she raised Mervyn's right arm, and flourishing her razor in the other proclaimed 'Christ is risen!' To which her fellow Communists responded, to a man, 'He is risen indeed!'

Yet a further cause of the onset of Mervyn's depression in 1975 may very well have been the shock he received when on 28 February that year he found himself pilloried in the *New Statesman* as No. Six in a series devoted to The Defectors. The root of this damaging article, the burden of which was that Mervyn was not really a socialist at all, was his decision two years previously to support Dick Taverne's election campaign in Lincoln. Since 1962 Taverne had sat as the Labour member for the constituency. In October 1972 he resigned the Labour whip and fought the seat the following spring on a Democratic Labour ticket, standing and winning against an official Labour candidate – and Mervyn's decision to support him was hardly an action likely to endear him to Harold Wilson. Mervyn addressed a packed hall on the subject of Europe; there was an overflow of 200 people outside; and Dick Taverne was so impressed by Mervyn's performance that after the election he invited Mervyn to lunch to thank him. He said he had been surprised to discover that Mervyn was so well briefed on Europe. Mervyn admitted he knew very little on the subject really; the speech had been written by Oswald Mosley, who had suggested that Mervyn should deliver it for him.[21]

To too many people, the *New Statesman* declared, Mervyn Stockwood 'seemed to have gone over to the enemy'. They cited as only his most recent crime his decision 'to go and support Dick Taverne at Lincoln – sharing a platform with Bernard Levin and, inevitably, being prominently reported in Rees-Mogg's *Times* for his pains', adding 'to some of his friends it appeared to mark the culmination of what had already begun to look uncommonly like a collapse with relief into the arms of the Establishment. The former turbulent priest twice tossed out of the Bristol Labour Party for left-wing deviations had long since ceased to remind anyone of a socialist firebrand.' The article was weak on its facts, stating that Mervyn was the seventh Bishop of Southwark (he was the sixth) and that he had taught for two years at 'one of the most conventional of all English public schools, Shrewsbury'. What would have cut a deeper wound in Mervyn's already shaken psyche was the assertion that his awakening to socialism in Bristol had been 'an intellectual rather than a temperamental conversion'. They were on safer ground, alas, when they dug up incidents like Mervyn's rebuke to the magistrate who died, his locking a cleric out of his church and his public unfrocking of Bryn Thomas, and called him an authoritarian prelate. 'The unifying theme in all three episodes lies perhaps in Mervyn Stockwood's determination always personally to be seen to hold the centre of the stage; and it is this which may explain why he has been, if anything, an even greater disappointment to church reformers than to political ones.' Referring to Mervyn's aversion to synodical government, this damning indictment of his episcopate went on to say 'If the wind of democracy has at last started to blow through the Church of England, it has done so in the teeth of the strongest possible opposition from the Lord Bishop of Southwark'. Presumably the anonymous author of the profile knew nothing of Mervyn's work behind the scenes to make effective the Pastoral Measure, which has served the Church of England in one way or another for the past 20 years, work which has prompted David Faull to regard Mervyn as 'a great reforming bishop'.[22]

The *New Statesman* went on to take a swipe at Mervyn's legendary hospitality ('sampled, among others, by Princess Margaret, Sir Oswald Mosley and the Duke of Windsor'), but again, in the course of grubbing around for ammunition, they had slipped up on their facts: the Duke was never at Bishop's House. Unfortunately, Mervyn convinced himself that the author of the article was Eric James. It was in fact the editor of the *New Statesman* himself, Anthony Howard. Like Michael Ramsey, Mervyn was not only vulnerable to criticism but seriously unnerved by it, and he instructed David Sheppard to seek the opinion of Lord Goodman. 'Mervyn was', the Bishop of Liverpool says, 'bitterly, desperately upset. He wanted a confrontation.'[23] David Sheppard had breakfast with the great libel lawyer, and as no writ transpired his advice, presumably, was to let the article wrap up the fish and chips. But to keep Mervyn's emotional reaction at the time in perspective, it is necessary to realize that in 1975 the *New Statesman* still remained a periodical of stature; it was in fact the Labour Party's house paper, in the way *The Times* was that of the Establishment, and after the balanced profile contributed earlier in Mervyn's career by Tom Driberg, Howard's must have seemed like a particularly vicious volte-face.

One of David Sheppard's services to Mervyn and the diocese in 1971 was to recruit as rector and team leader of the new Thames-mead housing estate the chaplain at Cuddesdon Theological College, James Thompson. Thompson arrived in fact as the first 1,000 residents were being housed, and it was to his council house on the estate that Mervyn was invited to dinner. At the age of 35 Thompson still seems to have been rather innocent, and admits he knew nothing about drink, but at least he produced a bottle of whisky after dinner. This seems to have revived Mervyn's flagging spirits, and in 1975 Mervyn returned to lay the foundation stone of the new St Paul's, Thamesmead. Thompson recalls that 'Mervyn could act in totally arbitary ways, and if you got on the wrong side of him he could be unbelievably fierce', but clearly Mervyn's opinion of Jim Thompson's heroic efforts to weld together an ecumenical team who celebrated, before St Paul's was built, 'in an old people's club room, reeking of beer and cigarettes', was high, for in 1978 he urged Gerald Ellison to appoint Jim Thompson suffragan Bishop of Stepney. When in 1991 the good news broke that Thompson was to succeed George Carey as Bishop of Bath and Wells, Dr Carey telephoned Jim to say that he and his wife were praying for him. Two minutes later the telephone rang again. By contrast it was Mervyn, ringing to say he had a glass of wine in his hand and was drinking his health.

In 1975 David Sheppard accepted the bishopric of Liverpool. Once again Mervyn had to find a new suffragan bishop of Woolwich. The first person he invited to accept the post declined. He had worked with Mervyn previously, and felt 'it would be like becoming his curate again!'[24] So he cast his eye in the direction of one of London's most famous Anglo-Catholic churches, All Saints', Margaret Street, and its youthful vicar, Michael Marshall. As an undergraduate at Christ's College, Cambridge, when Mervyn was Vicar of Great St Mary's, Michael Marshall had been a lapsed Roman Catholic. He was also a member of the right-wing Pitt Club, and at the time of Mervyn's open air meeting to protest about the invasion of Suez, Marshall had gone along to jeer. By the Lent term of 1957 he had become one of Mervyn's converts. Since Marshall's induction to All Saints' in 1969 Mervyn had been to preach for him, and no doubt had gathered that, in his turn, Marshall was an outstanding communicator of the Gospel. Despite the fact that he was very young – only 39 – Mervyn offered him the bishopric of Woolwich, and to Mervyn's consternation (he had already had one candidate slip through his fingers) Marshall kept him waiting a considerable time while he considered whether he ought to accept. While negotiations went on, and furtive restaurant meetings were arranged, Mervyn saddled him with the name of Mr Pilkington, just as Hugh Montefiore had been told to call himself Mr Johnson. Once Michael Marshall had been consecrated, Mervyn accompanied him to one confirmation and on one Visitation, and was thankful, in turn, to accept from Marshall some post-consecration training in High Church ritual; being left-handed, Mervyn tended to get into a muddle when censing the altar. Michael Marshall was impressed by the way that Mervyn always opened a staff meeting with bible study and prayers for the sick, but like so many others, he was soon aware of 'a dark side' to his nature; Mervyn actually confided to Marshall that he thought people were going to shoot him.[25]

It was also in 1975 that Giles Harcourt was recruited as chaplain. Mervyn would have been impressed by the fact that his guardian was a nephew of the Queen Mother. Harcourt thinks Mervyn 'was a man in whom all the aspects of darkness and light met'.[26] He remembers him in particular as the son of outdoor games players who was himself 'a great indoor games player. He loved social games, and watching how you reacted. He was fiercely loyal, seldom forgot an injury or a friend, and was for ever doing the unpredictable. If he had self-knowledge he chose to ignore large sections of it. That was what he called his divine dispensation.'

Alongside the depression, which commenced at the time that Giles Harcourt arrived at Bishop's House, Harcourt recognized the donnish way in which Mervyn would engender humour as he went along. One morning Harcourt was summoned to Mervyn's bedroom. It transpired that the Bishop of Southwark had mislaid his false teeth. 'These teeth', he explained, 'have to make a speech in the House of Lords this afternoon and I know not where I have laid them.' Giles found them in Mervyn's bed – quite possibly mislaid on purpose, to cause an attention-seeking distraction from the tedium of the day. Giles Harcourt thought Mervyn had great qualities but was not a great man. 'As a bishop, he was first class, because of his pastoral care of the clergy.' He says he always thought that if Mervyn had married, that would have 'rubbed off some of the hard edges. Children would have softened him. What he lacked were people close to him who he couldn't control, in the way he could always control his staff.' Giles Harcourt was 39 when he joined Mervyn's household, and says 'I didn't realize at the beginning that he was homosexual. One of the abiding tensions between Mervyn and myself was the fact that I was strongly heterosexual. And it wasn't that I couldn't appreciate all the gifts he had, but by the time I went to work for him my mind was too independent. I didn't mind when he was emotionally angry or unjust – and his treatment of people on the telephone was some-times appalling. But he once had an all-male party for 70 people and it was quite obviously a homosexual gathering, and some of the guests were very overt. I had to entertain them, and I did find that a bit overwhelming.'

It was Oliver Tomkins, the Bishop of Bristol, who encouraged Giles to go to Southwark. 'He said he couldn't offer me a job in Bristol that would offer such a range of experience, and I did in fact learn something every day. Tomkins said "Mervyn will drive you to distraction but you'll learn a lot from him. Basically he is a caring and pastoral man."'[27]

In 1976, the year that he received the Freedom of the City of London, Mervyn was off again on his seemingly inexhaustible quest for first-hand knowledge of Communist regimes, this time to explore the delights of Romania, a country being governed at the time by a mass murderer. He was there from 7 to 22 September. Mervyn had been to Romania two years before, no doubt delighting readers of the *Daily Telegraph* by telling them on his return: 'It might be good for some of our social misfits, who think they can get away with anything in this country, to spend a year in Bucharest. If they burgled a house, raided a bank, attacked a policeman, failed to return a purse dropped in the street, they would receive a sentence which would quickly convince them that anti-social behaviour does not pay.' As in the furore over the 'Call to the Nation', Mervyn appeared to be chanting the praises of Communism, and indeed, in his autobiography he tells us he was reluctant to criticize the President, Nicolae Ceauşescu, because 'it is difficult for us who have comparative freedom to appreciate the circumstances of those who live under a dictatorship'. The idea that the freedom enjoyed by English people was in any way comparable to oppression in Romania was simply ludicrous. But Mervyn's judgements were frequently wide of the mark. The relationship between the Orthodox Church in Romania and the Government, he wrote in the *Telegraph*, was one 'which members of the Church of England might well envy!' Were it not for lack of evidence, one might be tempted to suggest that Mervyn was being paid by Moscow to write this sort of rubbish.

After flying, in 1976, via Sofia, where he had to wait in the transit lounge while the plane was searched, Mervyn was met at Bucharest airport by the assistant bishop of Bucharest, an interpreter and various other dignitaries, including the Trade Councillor from the British Embassy. By the time he had dined and slept at the Patriarch's palace he must have felt as though he was on a state visit. A fellow guest was a bishop from the Egyptian Coptic Church, and he and Mervyn attended the Liturgy in the cathedral on the Feast of the Nativity of the Blessed Virgin Mary, Mervyn being invited to give his blessing afterwards from the steps of the palace. There were visits to seminaries and monasteries, including the monastery at Cozia where Mervyn had stayed in 1974, and he was presented by the abbess of a convent with a rosary. A visit to attend the Liturgy at Sibiu, in the Transylvanian Mountains, ended, according to Dominic Walker, who kept a log of the jaunt, with 'much hand kissing, singing and flower throwing'. Mervyn managed to return with a photograph of a handsome young man, signed on 26 September 'with my love and affection, George, aged 25'. He would have felt at home when he arrived at the Archbishop of Cluj's residence to find the names of John Betjeman and Elizabeth Cavendish in the visitors' book. Mervyn discovered that in Romania, every Wednesday was a fast day, and as meat was forbidden he had to make do at lunch with caviare and champagne. No doubt he fared better at a reception at the British Embassy given for the Lord Chancellor and Lady Elwyn-Jones. It was the year after this visit that the University of Bucharest conferred upon him an honorary doctorate of divinity, and he was back in Romania, accompanied by the Bishop of Woolwich, Michael Marshall, in 1979.

In 1977, only two years after the departure of David Sheppard, Hugh Montefiore left the diocese to become Bishop of Birmingham, and Mervyn had to look around for a replacement as suffragan Bishop of Kingston. He alighted on yet someone else destined to become a diocesan (of Lichfield, in 1983), someone, moreover, who could not, in his churchmanship, have been a greater contrast to the Anglo-Catholic Michael Marshall. Keith Sutton had been brought up in the Southwark diocese, at Clapham Park, and he had become an Evangelical while an undergraduate at Jesus College, Cambridge. Since 1973 he had been Principal of Ridley Hall. But Mervyn also wanted as a senior partner in the diocese not just a man of contrasting churchmanship but someone with experience overseas, and between 1968 and 1973 Sutton had served as tutor and chaplain at Bishop Tucker College in Mikono, Uganda. He recalls that by the time he arrived in the diocese 'Mervyn was very tired. I think he would have benefited from a move, but he was certainly not bitter about it. One of the great things he continued to do for Southwark was give the clergy a godly pride in their vocation. I would say that on the whole he was better with the clergy than the laity.'[28] Keith Sutton recognized immediately Mervyn's 'passionate belief in the local church', and his sense of the ridiculous. Referring to Bishop's House 'he used to say he lived in an absolute hovel'. For Mervyn's last year in office Keith Sutton found himself virtually running the diocese, in tandem with Michael Marshall, for by this time, in addition to spending two weeks in Westminster Hospital, Mervyn was sedated and close to almost complete collapse.

On 27 March 1974, still at this time in buoyant mood, Mervyn had written to David Tankard to say 'I have now been at Southwark for 15 years and I feel I have become a part of South London. I remember saying when I was a younger man that I could never work in London as I loathed and detested the place. However I now find it difficult to envisage not living here.' Three years later, on 28 February 1977, on House of Lords notepaper, Mervyn was writing to David to say 'I should love to retire but I cannot afford to do so'. Nevertheless events occurred to keep his depression at bay. On 9 June 1977, for instance, Mervyn joined the Queen on board the royal yacht, moored in the Pool of London, for a meal of poached asparagus and hollandaise sauce, Suprême de Volaille Kiev and raspberry flan.

The last of Mervyn's seven domestic chaplains, Peter McCrory, arrived in 1978, and in anticipation of a successor to Mervyn who might have a family and need all the available accommodation in Bishop's House, lodgings for Peter were found outside. He was thus spared many of the tensions endured by his predecessors. That year Mervyn attended his second Lambeth Conference, managing to avoid regular attendance at any of its sessions. Donald Coggan had transferred the venue from Church House in Westminster to the somewhat spartan environment of the University of Kent in Canterbury, so Mervyn nobly volunteered to do a month as duty bishop in the House of Lords, which says something about his enjoyment of the Upper House and a good deal about his interest in the Anglican Church overseas, which was not very great. He closed the year, on 15 December, by declaring open the new London Bridge Station.

At 8.00 p.m. on 30 April 1979 a special service of Holy Communion was celebrated in the cathedral to mark the 20th anniversary, the following day, of Mervyn's consecration. By 7.15 p.m. the nave was already full. The service was attended by Princess Alexandra and her husband, the Archbishop of Canterbury, who preached, and the Roman Catholic Archbishop of Southwark. The Bishop of London was there too, and no fewer than a dozen bishops concelebrated. After the Peace, 'the Bishop of Southwark', according to one parish magazine account of the event, 'gave an amusing little talk', and then startled the Princess, Dr Coggan, the Bishops of London and Woolwich and the Archbishop of Southwark by presenting them all with bunches of flowers. The anniversary coincided with a General Election, and on 1 May itself Mervyn informed Baden Hickman of the *Guardian* that the way the country had been going in the last few months was 'very, very sad'. There had been selfishness and greed. The Wilson administration, he pronounced, had done more to debase the coinage of political morality this century than 'anyone since perhaps Lloyd George'. Three days later, James Callaghan, who had taken over from Wilson in April 1976, and had faced a wave of strikes in 1978, was to surrender power to Britain's first woman Prime Minister. Mervyn celebrated this historic milestone in his own inimitable fashion, by sitting for a favourite photographer of the Establishment, Cecil Beaton.

The summer of 1979 saw Mervyn attending his last Butlin's clergy camp, at Margate, and having given strict instructions that under no circumstances was anyone to leave the camp until the proceedings were over, he was suddenly spirited away to attend a Foyle's luncheon at the Dorchester, for the launching of a book by Barbara Cartland, *I Seek the Miraculous*. He would not have been disappointed, on consulting the seating plan, to find that he had been positioned between the ebullient Miss Cartland and the equally newsworthy Margaret, Duchess of Argyll.

In November a letter – by no means the first – arrived from Prince Charles. The Prince had first met Mervyn when he arrived at the Prince's hated school, Gordonstoun, wearing a purple tie prior to preaching. By the time Prince Charles had entered Cambridge University he was evincing an interest in parapsychology, a subject that was to knit prince and prelate close together, and Mervyn's knowledge of the subject was eagerly sought. Mervyn was writing to the Prince in 1969, at the time of his investiture as Prince of Wales; and in these early days of what was to develop into an almost filial relationship Prince Charles was still addressing Mervyn as 'Dear Dr Stockwood'. By the time Prince Charles was enjoying the hospitality of Bishop's House, on 27 July 1976, he was addressing his thank-you letter to 'Dear Mervyn'. Prince Charles receives letters on a wide variety of subjects, and when any arrived with queries about spiritual matters or parapsychology, and the Prince felt ill-equipped to deal with them, he would sent them to Mervyn for his advice. From an early age, Prince Charles took his own religion, and the natural doubts it sometimes raised, extremely seriously, and it seems that he gravitated for guidance more towards Mervyn than towards clerics like the incumbent Dean of Windsor, traditionally close to the royal family. Prince Charles was particularly shattered by the murder of his great-uncle Earl Mount-batten, an occasion relatively early in his public life when outside events carried a backlog of unanswered correspondence. Yet, as he once told Mervyn, he felt that if there was something one could do to help it was worth trying. These were sentiments reciprocated by Mervyn, who went out of his way to recommend books for the Prince's reading list. It would have been understandable for Mervyn to have felt flattered by the Prince's reliance upon him, but he never made capital out of it. Indeed, he treated his friendship with Prince Charles in such a matter-of-fact manner that he thought nothing of punching holes in the Prince's letters when they were filed, and even of sometimes giving them away, once as a gift to one of his chaplains.

It was in November 1979 that Mervyn made up his mind to retire, and announced that he would resign the see of Southwark in October the following year. He was tempted to go at the end of his twentieth year in the episcopate, but 1980 was the seventy-fifth anniversary of the founding of the diocese, and he was, fairly easily, persuaded to stay on to take part in that. On 2 December he issued a Pastoral Letter, explaining that as his contribution to the cele-brations he would visit each of the 21 deaneries to spend two days in each. On 10 December he received a generous tribute in *The Times* from Clifford Longley, who wrote that Mervyn was 'one of the few really "spiritual" leaders of the Church of England at present', and that the Church needed 'more, not fewer, Stockwoods'. Back in August 1962 the Editor of the *Church Times* had written to Mervyn to say his paper had 'the greatest sympathy with the great problems which confront the Church in Southwark, and great admiration for the way in which they are obviously being tackled'.[29] In their issue of 31 October 1980 the paper now stated its belief that when Mervyn 'goes off to his retirement home in Bath' he would leave the ecclesiastical world 'a duller and a drabber place'. They were certainly making amends for their howler when on 31 March 1964 the editor had addressed a letter to 'The Right Reverend M. Southwark'.

On his travels through the deaneries, Mervyn predicted that in 20 years' time the Church's manpower might be reduced to 'half of what it is today, perhaps a quarter'. His farewell charge to the clergy contains a paragraph blocked out in episcopal purple. It included the remark, possibly liable to cause offence, 'There are a hundred and one reasons why so few people in this country go to church, but one of them is the sheer boredom with what happens inside the building'. On 16 June 1963 Mervyn had published an article in *Punch* entitled 'Why I'm Not An Agnostic', annotating his own copy 'This is basically my religious faith and has been for years', but in his 1980 charge to the clergy he said

We cannot hope to do more than to 'see through a glass darkly'. An honest Christian must admit to a degree of agnosticism. When I am asked whether I am a believer my reply is 'Yes, for two seconds out of three.' How can it be otherwise? . . . The traumatic experiences that are part and parcel of human experience are difficult to reconcile with the concept of a loving and purposeful creator.

Over the years Mervyn had addressed the deaneries on evangelism, the liturgy, Christian unity and on social issues. In 1972 he had turned his attention to prayer, saying 'Perhaps it is my ordinariness, my pedestrian approach, that qualifies me to speak to those of you who like myself are on the lowest rungs of the ladder of prayer'. Exhorting his clergy to begin the day with Matins, because 'it means that the day begins rooted in Scripture', he added 'I do not believe that a Christian will make the grade unless he thinks the bible, breathes the bible, understands the bible and loves the bible'. As an aid to contemplation, he recommended use of the rosary. 'When I find myself at some excruciatingly boring meeting', he said, 'I take out my rosary and reflect upon the great biblical joys and sorrows of Our Lord's life.'

Meanwhile, plans were being drawn up to celebrate the seventy-fifth anniversary of the diocese, which inevitably coincided with the seventy-fifth anniversary of Birmingham, now presided over by Hugh Montefiore, and oddly enough, also the 100th anniversary of Liverpool, in the charge of David Sheppard. The jubilee began officially on 1 December 1979 with a diocesan synod meeting held in the cathedral, and was due to culminate on 13 July 1980 with an open air Eucharist on the centre court at Wimbledon. A competition was held to write a hymn, which produced four prize winners. T-shirts were manufactured. A rugby match between Parsons and People was staged at Mitcham. On 3 May a Jubilee Fun Run was launched in the Sutton deanery. Canon David Diamond, recruited to Deptford by Mervyn in 1969, where he ran a spectacular ministry, put in a plea for street parties. For the great Wimbledon service, 11,000 people, many wisely equipped with picnics, packed the stadium. Three dozen clergy, together with the two suffragans, concelebrated, and communion was administered by another 100 clergy. Two of the archdeacons were observed to nod off, but presumably they awoke to the sound of Mervyn's triumphal exit; waving to the cheering throng, like the great showman he was he relished every moment of a sincere and heart-felt send off.

During the last year of his episcopate Mervyn expressed a desire to visit both East and West Berlin, to meet a variety of Lutheran bishops, and he roped Paul Oestreicher in to organize the trip and of course to act as chaplain and interpreter. He was entertained by the British Military Commandant, and housed in a very beautiful flat run by an order of nuns. As Donald Coggan was also in Berlin, Mervyn's timing was not too tactful, and Canon Oestreicher recalls 'By eleven each night he was razzled'. Yet he adds 'I wish there were more like him. Eccentricity is a virtue, not a vice.'[30] Back home, a group of well-meaning clergy and laity performed a somewhat amateur version in a church hall of the popular television programme *This Is Your Life*, sprung on Mervyn as a surprise, but as he did not care for surprises being sprung on himself, and he was by this time fairly heavily sedated, the occasion was less than a riotous success. On 1 October he presided over his last staff meeting, and on 27 October he attended a dinner in his honour at Haberdashers' Hall, where he was served turtle soup with Madeira, trout accompanied by a 1977 Chassagne Montrachet, venison and Château du Port 1970, followed by an apricot sorbet and a 1963 Cockburn. Some 50 guests were headed by the recently installed Archbishop of Canterbury, Robert Runcie, who proposed the toast to Mervyn. He was followed, by all accounts with catastrophic consequences, by Frankie Howerd, who totally misjudged the occasion and, as they say in the theatre, died. But no matter, the next day a telegram arrived from Barbara Cartland: 'Marvellous party darling Mervyn you were wonderful my love for eternity Barbara.'

On the last day of September Mervyn had celebrated for the last time in the cathedral. In his autobiography, he describes the gift he received during the service from Michael Marshall as 'a token farewell present'. It was a double magnum of champagne, a drink he once described as overrated.[31] He also records that the service ended 'with the processional hymn "At the Name of Jesus", sung to Elgar's music for "Land of Hope and Glory"'. Alas, it did not.

Mervyn had especially requested the trio section from the first *Pomp and Circumstance March*, a request which apparently failed to reach the ears of the assistant organist, on duty that day, and out they all trooped to some tune no one, least of all Mervyn, had ever heard before. So deep had been his disappointment that in retirement Mervyn pretended to himself that all had gone according to plan.

Notes

1 Canon Hutt in conversation with the author.
2 Fr Lansdale in conversation with the author, *et seq.*
3 Canon Hutt, as above.
4 Giles Harcourt, in conversation with the author.
5 Canon Hutt, as above.
6 Giles Harcourt, as above.
7 David Sox, in conversation with the author.
8 Ibid.
9 Bishop Montefiore, in conversation with the author.
10 Hugh Montefiore, *Oh God, What Next?* (Hodder and Stoughton, 1995).
11 Memorandum, undated, from Eric James to the author.
12 Montefiore, *Oh God, What Next?*
13 'A few years ago Eric James was very keen to write a biography to be published after my Death. I was not enthusiastic as I had already written my autobiography "Chanctonbury Ring"': letter from MS to David Sox, 24 August 1993.
14 Eric James to the author, 18 January 1995.
15 David Faull, in conversation with the author.
16 Ibid.
17 Bishop Hugh Montefiore, in conversation with the author.
18 Rev. Giles Harcourt, in conversation with the author.
19 Letter from Lord Coggan to the author, 18 August 1995.
20 Tony Benn, *Against the Tide* (Hutchinson, 1989).
21 Information supplied by Lord Taverne.
22 David Faull, as above.
23 The Bishop of Liverpool, in conversation with the author.
24 Private information.
25 Bishop Marshall, in conversation with the author.
26 Giles Harcourt, in conversation with the author.

27 Ibid.

28 The Bishop of Lichfield, in conversation with the author.

29 Editor, *Church Times*, to MS, 15 August 1962.

30 Canon Paul Oestreicher, in conversation with the author.

31 In an article entitled 'Gaiters and Gastronomy' in Cyril Ray (ed.), *The Complete Imbiber*, No. 7 (Studio Vista, 1964).

Chapter 13

The best friend they had

For a man who suffered from chest problems all his life, Bath, straddling the north bank of the River Avon and so close to the sea, may seem a strange place to choose for retirement; the city is renowned, too, for its steep streets, and Mervyn Stockwood ended up in a house in a street requiring a steady climb, and with a garden running straight down to the Kennet and Avon Canal. But he probably reckoned that with the view and privacy the advantages far outweighed the disadvantages. As he had done when looking for a residence in Southwark, in anticipation of his retirement he sent a woman ahead to house-hunt: the mother of his former chaplain, Giles Harcourt. And never more so than now was he to benefit from the generosity of wealthy friends. He is said to have retired with savings of only £15,000, and a few years before he was due to leave Bishop's House, one of Mervyn's most generous patrons, Ronald Driver, purchased the house in Bath discovered by Mrs Harcourt, 15 Sydney Buildings, permitting Mervyn the free use of it for his lifetime.

Bath offered the best of two worlds. Had Mervyn opted for Cambridge he might have enjoyed the college chapels and high table dinners, but with Bristol only round the corner from Bath he was able to renew friendships made in his first parish while at the same time taking advantage of the pleasures offered by the shops and Georgian architecture of Bath. He was speedily enrolled as a patron of the Theatre Royal and as a member of the Council of Bath University, and the Bishop of Bath and Wells, John Bickersteth, his former curate, invited him to act as an assistant bishop in the diocese. Hence he continued to take confirmations. Yet to begin with he was far from settled. At ten o'clock each morning he would telephone Bishop's House in Southwark, with some lame excuse, to ask Peter McCrory where he had left a file, or to enquire if there had been any messages for him. After 44 years as priest and bishop, for almost all that time with his own show to run, and with an authoritarian temperament that liked to dictate and control events and people, he must have felt as though he scarcely existed. He had no immediate family, few if any intimate friends on whom to fall back, and no hobbies. He could not even cook, and had to set about learning. The mainstay of his menus were lobster, trout, roast pheasant, roast lamb and Stilton. 'When I think of Mervyn I automatically think of Stilton', one of his friends has said. Like many helpless gourmets, he developed harmless but expensive eccentricities, like sending to Paignton for frozen crab. But at least he knew how to draw a cork, and the wine racks at 15 Sydney Buildings were soon loaded with some very fine clarets indeed.

His new home was a modest early nineteenth-century terraced house, with a small study and a small sitting-room, a guest bedroom and a large bedroom for himself furnished with uninterrupted views across to Bath Abbey and the Mendip Hills. An attic boxroom adjacent to the bathroom was transformed into a chapel, with a crucifix in the window to advertise its purpose to strollers on the bank of the canal. The altar stood beneath the window; the walls were decorated in garish wallpaper in imitation of the House of Lords. Below, a narrow garden planted with cypress trees descended through gentle flights of steps to the canal.

One reason for Mervyn's initial loneliness was because he had left his cat Midge at Bishop's House, for he had feared she would stray from unfamiliar surroundings. But Midge fell out with the new Bishop of Southwark's cat, Pangur Ban, and as a result she fell foul of the Bishop and his wife too. It was not long before she was posted to Bath, living for the rest of her life on a diet of lobster and prawns. Mervyn inherited a recently widowed and very charming neighbour two doors away, Diana Cooke, whose younger son took care of Midge whenever Mervyn was away, and Midge was destined to outlive her master and was given a final home by Mrs Cooke.

Towards the end of his life Mervyn would complain that no one came to see him any more (which was not true; it was another way of saying his advice was no longer sought, that he had ceased to be at the centre of affairs), but by 7 November 1980 signatures were appearing in Mervyn's visitors' book in profusion. Charles Lansdale (who always referred to his visits to Mervyn as Bath duty) was there for four days in January 1981. Andrew Henderson, Dominic Walker, Bryan Green, David Sox (a frequent guest at Bath as he lived close by), Bill Skelton and David Diamond were among early and faithful callers. One of Mervyn's Boy Bishops, Roy Clevely, signed in on 20 September 1981. Mary Cryer was there in October. Stephen Spender turned up in November. And so it went on, although not everyone to whom Mervyn considered he had extended patronage rushed down to Bath to see him, and some, in consequence, were cut out of his will. Princess Margaret, who has an agreeable reputation for loyalty to old friends, paid Mervyn a visit on 18 November 1984, and whenever she was staying privately with friends in Bath she would slip into Mervyn's tiny chapel on Sunday morning to receive communion from him.

As Mervyn grew older and more garrulous some of his friends did begin to find 'Bath duty' a bit of a strain. On one memorable occasion Simon Phipps and his wife were instructed to arrive at a precise moment when the sun would be performing in a spectacular fashion above the Avon. As they were early, they dutifully circled round the outskirts of Bath until the appointed hour, eventually rang the bell, and were escorted into the garden. Champagne was poured, the sun conducted itself perfectly, and then, as it usually does, slowly sank in the west. More champagne appeared, but no sign of any dinner. Chill night air settled on the canal and the garden. By the time Mary Phipps was rather desperately wondering if she dared go indoors for her cardigan, Mervyn rose and announced that he would now repair to the kitchen and switch on the oven – in order to roast a leg of lamb, which duly appeared on the table one and a half hours later. 'Oh dear', Mrs Phipps has recalled, 'I really loved Mervyn but it *was* rather a trying visit!'

On 31 July 1981 Mervyn was writing to David Tankard to say 'I am very happy in my retirement. I adore Bath. I love my little bachelor's house on the canal and my boat. I am as busy as ever. I am deeply involved in the University of Bath and in the Bath theatre. I am writing my autobiography and I do a lot of church work. I have never been happier, and I cannot think why I did not resign years ago. I have no regrets for London.'

He went on: 'I am pretty hopeless at "greasy domesticity" and as I cannot cook I live on marmite on Bath Olivers. I have lost 1½ stone in six months and now am a slim ancient "young" man.' He said that now that he was on a 'miserable pension of £3,500 p.a.' he could not afford trips to London, and wondered if it would be possible for David to take the train to visit him. 'Although you may rarely hear from me, I never forget', Mervyn told him. 'I often say my prayers for you, especially on July 10.' 10 July was David's birthday, not withstanding that on 19 May 1980 Mervyn had written to him 'I have not forgotten that on July 2nd you will be 48'. By 30 June 1982, Mervyn was reporting to 'Dearest David' that he had lost two stone since he had been looking after himself, 'so I'm really quite slim'. He reiterated that he had no regrets about London 'apart from the House of Lords. Now that I am retired I could give adequate time to it which I never could when I was in office. But 22 years at Southwark [it had been 21½] was long enough. It is marvellous to be free from administration, and no longer a prisoner to a diary.'

Within a year of retirement, on 5 December 1981, in Trinity Cathedral, Newark, New Jersey, Mervyn managed to involve himself in a controversy. Despite his alleged misogyny Mervyn was a declared advocate of the ordination of women to the priesthood. In 1978 he had ordained Elizabeth Canham as a deacon in the Southwark diocese. Now Miss Canham was anxious to jump the gun (ordination of women to the priesthood in the Church of England was not sanctioned until 1992), and found no difficulty in persuading the radical Bishop of Newark, New Jersey, John Spong, to oblige, which was perfectly legal, for women priests were already accepted in the Protestant Episcopal Church in the United States of America. It was also perfectly legal for Mervyn, at the invitation of the Bishop of Newark, to assist at the ordination (he also preached), and this he was more than eager to do, because he would then become the first English bishop to ordain a woman. As it only requires the laying on of hands of one bishop in order to ordain, however, there could be no circumstances under which Mervyn's presence was other than provocative. Miss Canham had been serving as a non-stipendiary deacon at Tony Crowe's church, St Luke with Holy Trinity, Charlton, so Crowe accompanied Mervyn on his rackety flight to the States. Crowe says that Mervyn had no idea whether it was time to say Matins or Evensong, that by the time he arrived at Kennedy Airport he was exceedingly merry, and that by nightfall he was so drunk he fell out of bed.[1] The diocesan bishops back in England felt that Mervyn had stolen a march on them (after all, they could all have gone flying round the world ordaining women had they thought it a proper thing to do at the time). Mervyn managed to get his activities reported on the front page of the *New York Times*, and an invitation to preach at the traditionalist Anglo-Catholic church of St Thomas in New York was duly cancelled.

The following year Mervyn published his autobiography, *Chanctonbury Ring*. It received a cool reception from John Whale in the *Sunday Times*. Remarking that Mervyn's appointment to Southwark was shrewd and justified, he went on to say 'Yet from this point the tone of the autobiography becomes increasingly self-reassuring rather than self-examining. Sustained contact with other human lives seem to lessen: in their place are stories of brief encounters, broken friendships, bruising disputes about discipline and buildings, essays into spiritualism . . . '

Mervyn addressed the Oxford Union on 28 January 1983; supported by Norman St John-Stevas he was opposing the motion 'God Is Man's Most Dangerous Creation'. Shortly afterwards he had Hubert Chesshyre, at that time Chester Herald, to stay the night, when, according to Chesshyre's unpublished diary, they ate crab and trout and had 'far too much to drink'. In the end, both he and Mervyn retired to bed at 2.30 a.m. 'very drunk', and in the morning Chesshyre found himself on his knees, not in the chapel but the lavatory, trying to prevent himself from fainting.

In May 1984 Mervyn attended a 60th birthday party for Earl Spencer, father of the Princess of Wales, held at Althorp, the family's Northamptonshire seat. In the Hall, Alan Clark, at that time MP for Plymouth, found Barbara Cartland and Mervyn 'making stylised conversation, he complete with gaiters, waistcoat, much purple showing here and there, and various pendant charms and cruci-fixes'.[2] This was another good example of the kind of overblown impression Mervyn might give, but the fact remains he would have been 'showing' no more purple than any other bishop decked out in evening frock coat and apron, he was not wearing gaiters but stockings, and the likelihood of him wearing 'various pendant charms' or more than one pectoral cross was remote. It was a miracle that Lord Spencer was there at all, for some years previously he had suffered a massive stroke, his recovery being attributed, in part, to the ministrations of Mervyn. Informed that it was necessary for the earl to undergo some form of physical shock in order to emerge from his coma, Mervyn anointed him, then grabbed his arms, shook him violently, bellowed 'In the name of God, open your eyes' – and he did.

For both Lord and Lady Spencer, it was their second marriage, following divorce, and Mervyn blessed Spencer's marriage to the former Countess of Dartmouth. He conducted a service of thanks-giving for Lord Spencer's recovery, and was a frequent guest at

Althorp, where Lady Diana Spencer, before her marriage to the Prince of Wales, would take his breakfast to him in bed. 'I've just had a wonderful time at the royal wedding', Mervyn told David Tankard on 31 July 1981, having been invited by Prince Charles to St Paul's Cathedral two days previously. When Spencer died in 1992 Mervyn conducted the funeral service at St Mary the Virgin, Great Brington, and when Lady Spencer married Comte Jean-François de Chambrun, Mervyn took a clandestine role. Writing to 'Dearest Barbara' on 14 July 1993, Mervyn told the comtesse's mother, Dame Barbara Cartland, 'I am glad all went well. I am also glad that the press never discovered that I gave them the full marriage service and Holy Communion in my private chapel on the previous day! I hope things will turn out happily.' At a dance after the wedding, Dame Barbara's great-grandson Edward Legge was spotted gingerly sipping champagne with Mervyn.

Althorp was not the only grand house where Mervyn was a welcome guest. By coincidence, Raine Spencer had been educated at a lovely Elizabethan mansion, Longstowe Hall, ten miles west of Cambridge, when the house served as a school during the war. (So, by chance, had Lady Elizabeth Cavendish.) It was the home of Michael Bevan, Lord Lieutenant of Cambridgeshire, and his wife Mary. They and their children, who thought that Mervyn was really Merlin, had been frequent visitors to Bishop's House. Mervyn laid on a birthday party for young Jamie Bevan, for instance, on 6 December 1970, and a lunch party for six members of the family on Jamie's birthday three years later, when he provided tinned white peaches and custard for Jamie, with whom he particularly identified, for Jamie had confessed to hating his prep school. Mervyn told Mary Bevan he had once had a vision (in the Fens; so this may have occurred while he was an undergraduate). Mary noticed how Mervyn would be drawn to the lake at Longstowe, to feed the wildfowl, and she felt instinctively that here was an old man trying to envisage a happy childhood. He would visit Longstowe Hall sometimes twice a year, quite improperly (not being in his own parish or diocese) parading around in a cassock, and of course signing the visitors' book in purple ink.[3] Mary Bevan, like Lady Diana, would take Mervyn his breakfast to bed – orange juice and two kinds of tea – and she became so concerned about what she believed to be his parlous financial situation that she would tactfully slip him money to pay for his petrol. She was to receive quite a surprise after his death. When in 1983 Mervyn celebrated his 70th birthday Mary Bevan invited 100 guests to a dinner party for him. Ned Sherrin proposed a toast to Mervyn, but by the time it was Mervyn's turn to respond he was 'so drunk he just rambled on for ten minutes and no one had the faintest idea what he'd said'.[4]

In the year of his 70th birthday Mervyn paid a visit to New York. In January 1984 he went to Ethiopia, and in March that year he was in Dublin. May 1984 found him touring the vineyards of Bordeaux. The same year he was at St George's, Chichester, to preach at the Silver Jubilee Mass for David Brecknell, the designer of his Ordinals. He was also undertaking preaching engagements in Oxford. Despite feeling the pinch of a 'miserable' pension, there were days spent in London, 'and on Saturday I went to Gloucestershire to take a wedding', he reported to David Tankard on 18 June 1984. 'So you see, there are not many dull moments.' On 26 June 1985 he confirmed that 'Although I am now a geriatric I seem to remain as busy as ever. There has been a vacancy in the bishopric of Bristol for several months and the new bishop does not arrive until the autumn; for this reason I have been helping to fill the gap and I seem to be heavily booked most weeks. I am also helping the Bishop of Bath and Wells and the Bishop of Salisbury.' He said he still got invitations to go abroad but he was not too keen on accepting 'because I hate the delays and the inevitable security checks at airports. However, I am going to Ireland next year to give a series of lectures in Dublin. That is not too difficult an exercise because I can take an aeroplane from Bristol.' Mervyn's other varied engagements in retirement included, for example, an invitation to give an address in the Chapel Royal at Hampton Court Palace on Mothering Sunday in 1987 and a visit to All Saints', Royal Leamington Spa, in Lent the following year, to talk on 'Prayer and Spirituality'. 18 September 1994, only four months before his death, found him preaching at Blundell's, on the text 'Whoever shall compel you to go one mile, go with him two'. On 14 November he accepted an invitation to preach on 14 May 1995 at All Saints', Kingston upon Thames, at a Eucharist to celebrate the seventy-fifth birthday of Hugh Montefiore, an engagement he was fated not to keep.

It was probably in 1985 that Mervyn sent an undated round robin to men he had ordained to the priesthood 25 years before, and who would therefore be celebrating their silver jubilee. During his episcopate Mervyn ordained more than 700 priests. 'I hope', he wrote on this occasion,

Mervyn Stockwood

you are very happy in your work and that God will continue to bless you and give you all the gifts that are necessary for His service.

Here is the prayer I always say for you and for myself:

Jesus, confirm my heart's desire
To work, to speak, to think for Thee;
Still let me guard Thy Holy fire,
And still stir up Thy gift in me.

'If', he added, 'you should find yourself in Bath, I hope you will come and see me.'

The widespread affection in which Mervyn continued to be held can be gauged from the fact that in 1989 a card arrived, signed by the present Archbishop of Canterbury, then Bishop of Bath and Wells, who had extended Bickersteth's invitation to Mervyn to act as an assistant bishop (he was to serve under James Thompson too), and by a host of other signatories. It read: 'Congratulations & Best Wishes on the 30th Anniversary of your Consecration. From the Bishops & Clergy of the Diocese of Bath & Wells at their Conference in Swanwick, Derbyshire.'

It was the same year that Mervyn underwent an operation on his eyes. Other minor ailments afflicted him, but nothing desperately serious. In the garden he suffered a few falls, breaking his ankle in the winter of 1992, and on 'several occasions' during the summer of 1993 he had to pay visits to his doctor. 'He was', as his neighbour Diana Cooke kindly recalls, 'a fairly uncoordinated man, not at all dextrous. He once fell out of his chair, and certainly seemed to be rather accident prone.' He remained adept at recruiting voluntary helpers, in particular a self-employed builder and odd-job man, Neil Devereux, who also took to driving Mervyn around, and was rewarded with the largest legacy of anyone in Mervyn's will, £15,000. Mrs Cooke explains: 'Mervyn became rather a father to Neil, who telephoned most days to check that he was all right.'[5] A gardener called a few times a year, to plant spring bulbs and see to window-boxes and hanging baskets. Mrs Joanna Sleght would come in from Widcombe to help with the housework and carry out any necessary repairs. She received a legacy of £3,000. Mrs Jennie Cox, referred to in Mervyn's will as his secretary, was recruited on a part-time basis and worked from home; she was rewarded with £5,000.

Living only four miles from Bath was Rupert Legge, a grandson of Barbara Cartland, and his wife Victoria, a young couple of whom

236

Mervyn was particularly fond. He baptized their children, and was so alarmed to discover that both children suffered from asthma that he joined Victoria's campaign for cleaner air, much needed in Bath, where fumes tend to get trapped in a geographical basin. Quite by chance, Victoria Legge discovered she possessed remarkable healing powers; one day she gave some massage to a friend who had suffered a muscle spasm, and within half an hour her friend could walk again. Not knowing that Mervyn had broken his ankle, she experienced an 'incredibly strong feeling' that she should telephone him and ask how he was. Needless to say, she was treated to a pretty depressing tale of woe; he was on sticks and hardly able to move. She drove immediately to Mervyn's house and applied her healing powers to his ankle. Her hands, she says, went red and hot, and she could feel them vibrating on Mervyn's leg. The healing session was followed by prayer, and two days later Mervyn telephoned Victoria to say that he had cancelled an operation booked for the following January and had just walked unaided to the post office.

Victoria Legge believes that animals are even more susceptible to healing than humans, and 'had a go', as she puts it, on Midge, who was suffering from arthritis. Even in advanced old age, Victoria Legge found Mervyn 'an amazingly powerful man, with a fantastically powerful aura'. Again, her impression of him in old age was that 'he had an enormous personal struggle inside himself. He had a very good line to God but I'm sure he was battling with himself to stay on the straight and narrow.' She was impressed by how frequently he seemed to be called upon to comfort the dying and bereaved, and one of the attractions of Rupert and Victoria Legge, so far as Mervyn was concerned, was that they were happily married. 'Mervyn', Victoria says, 'was very interested in marriage because he thought it must be difficult for people. He used to re-bless people's marriages, to sort of reinforce them.'[6]

Mervyn could be very indiscreet, but he could be discreet too, never more so than on the subject of royalty. Asked in retirement about his relations with Prince Charles, he would reply 'My lips are sealed'. As the Prince's marriage began to fall apart (it was first seen publicly to be in trouble in 1992) he turned to Mervyn for advice and comfort, and Mervyn was often to be seen setting off for Highgrove. Over the years he accumulated a considerable correspondence with the Prince, and not wishing, presumably, to anticipate his death by destroying the prince's letters himself,

Mervyn left (or is alleged to have left) instructions that someone else should do the deed for him.[7] Two, however, survived.

In May 1993 Mervyn celebrated his 80th birthday. A card duly arrived from Midge, 'with the best purrs & love'. An invitation also arrived to preach at St Matthew, Moorfields, and on the eve of his birthday his former suffragans and chaplains gave a dinner party for him at the Athenaeum, when they enjoyed asparagus, grilled salmon and strawberries. Mervyn was writing to Roy Clevely on 17 June to say 'After a hectic fortnight with services and parties in many places the doctor has insisted on ten days of peace, with no engagements. The ban ends on June 26 when I go to Exeter to take part in an ordination.' This was an occasion when, very oddly, instead of signing himself 'Mervyn Stockwood' or '✠Mervyn' he did so '✠Bishop Mervyn'.

On 19 April 1988 Mervyn had told Roy 'I was very glad to be at the [funeral] service at St Matthews. I have such happy memories of your mother and she was a wonderful support to all of us in those early days. She was always such fun and much loved by a succession of curates.' This was just one way in which he kept in touch with the past. On 5 June that year he gave a party for his former servers, saying he regretted he could not ask their wives as well 'owing to lack of space'. He was to celebrate Holy Communion at noon, although how more than half a dozen people ever crammed into the chapel is a mystery, and he made as a stipulation of attendance at the lunch party 'no birthday presents!' On this occasion he was celebrating his 75th birthday. 'Inevitably', he wrote to his former parishioners, 'I shall soon be embarking upon a journey for which there are neither return tickets nor luggage vans. Hence the customs officer will reject all earthly possessions.'

Looking ahead to Mervyn's 80th birthday, Roy Clevely had evidently suggested a local party for Mervyn, who wrote on 7 December 1992 to say 'Nothing would give me greater pleasure than to meet my beloved Boy Bishops and former servers'. But he was somewhat strapped for dates. Finally they settled for 5 June, with a communion service at St Matthew followed by a reception and lunch in the church hall. Roy was especially requested not to serve any food with garlic. On 8 June Mervyn wrote to Roy to say 'It was a wonderful party and I am so grateful to you and others for all you did to make it such a happy occasion. It has been suggested to me that it would give great pleasure to the Boy Bishops if I were to give them a signed photograph of our collective gathering. Can you arrange this?' He offered to pay for a photograph for each of them. In a postscript he added: 'I do not know the name of the Head Server. Please tell him from me he did a superb job – and I greatly appreciate that he maintained a tradition of superb accuracy and devotion. You must all come here in the summer for a thanksgiving.'

By this time Bath had become thronged with beggars, and shortly before Christmas 1993 Mervyn received a cheque from Barbara Cartland. 'How very grateful I am', he told her on 16 December. 'Your gift is such a help as I am trying to raise funds for a few people who through no fault of their own are without work and for whom Christmas will be rather drab, especially for their children. So your gift will give much pleasure.' Dame Barbara sent another 'very generous' cheque a year later. Mervyn told her 'It will enable me to make Christmas a happier time for people known to me who are in sad or difficult circumstances. I know it will be greatly appreciated.'

It is not difficult to understand why Mervyn Stockwood and Barbara Cartland were mutually attracted. Both were in many ways eccentric, both certainly larger than life. Mervyn told one of Dame Barbara's biographers, Gwen Robyns, 'Barbara is one of the most generous people I have known. During my twenty years as Bishop of Southwark I had only to tell her of a parson's family that was in financial trouble and immediately a cheque would arrive, on condition that the name of the donor was not to be revealed . . . Barbara is indeed a colourful and expressive personality in more senses than one. In a dreary, bureaucratic and materialistic day her individuality stands out.'

It was in 1993 that Mervyn's mind seriously turned to posterity; it was the year he asked David Sox's advice about a biography, and the year he signed what turned out to be his last will and testament. As far as a biography was concerned, the only subjects on which Mervyn seemed able to focus his attention were his 'controversies with Geoffrey Fisher' and those over *Honest to God*. The idea that he might himself be worth writing about does not seem to have occurred to him; he told David Sox on 30 September 1993 'A few years ago I thought I would burn everything'. On 9 June 1995 Sox wrote to the present author to say

I don't know anything about the eventual deposit of those letters etc. I have the idea that somehow M. changed his mind – perhaps due to talking to someone else. I don't know. I did say I thought someone would be interested in doing a biography, but must admit I didn't give him the impression I was interested! One point to make in your biography is just *how difficult* it was for any of us to be his friends. It was always on his own terms & he wanted to be 'wooed.' At nearly 60, I wasn't in the mood ever to do that. He could be difficult to say the least.

The will which Mervyn signed on 30 November was an extraordinary document. It ran for eleven pages, and contained no fewer than 49 residuary beneficiaries, among them Battersea Dogs' Home, the RSPCA, the NSPCC, Age Concern, the Horses and Ponies Protection Association, Riverpoint Single Homeless Limited and the Friends of Claverton Down Cats & Dogs Home. Something called the Care for the Wild Trunk Paralysis Appeal had received a cheque from Mervyn for £50 in the summer of 1993, the trunks in question belonging not to trees but to elephants. Mervyn had no idea about business matters, and not much about time. It was fortunate that his solicitor, Ivor Seager, was an old friend. Mervyn would think nothing of telephoning Mr Seager at 10.30 at night, pretending to ask his advice but really to implore him to come round and keep him company. 'I shall always be haunted by the sense of his loneliness on occasions', Mr Seager says. 'He had not a clue about the value of money. He didn't realize he was a rich man, but leaving so many legacies gave him pleasure. And he gave money to charities in his lifetime.'[8] Many were the wills, later invalidated, that were circulated to executors before they received copies of the final one. Mary Cryer says she saw half a dozen. He must have had a pretty good idea how well off he was, for otherwise he would not have bequeathed so many sizeable legacies, and appointed so many residuary beneficiaries. Yet he never lived like a man who must have had an income from stocks and shares of £30,000 a year, especially bearing in mind he had no rent or mortgage to pay. He owed his wealth to the investment skills of his friends, who began nursing for him his small savings before he retired at a time when it was not too difficult to make money on the stock exchange. Yet the amount they accumulated for him was so considerable that there remains a strong likelihood he was given or bequeathed a substantial sum as well. When he died, Mervyn's estate (which did not of course include any property) amounted to £348,475. This came as a considerable surprise to everyone, and a shock to quite a few.

In June 1994 Canon Michael Hocking, whose wife had died a year before, went to stay with Mervyn. He has written:

Mervyn gave me a wonderful welcome and cooked a splendid dinner – smoked salmon and roast pheasant and a bottle of excellent claret. We talked and talked – and I found it most disturbing. Mervyn told me he had no living relatives, that he felt a complete non-person (his exact phrase), that few people called on him and that he found life lonely and depressing.

He told me he had a woman who came in once a week. He had been making his will. He had left her a substantial legacy and the remainder to charity. He wrote to the BBC asking for transcripts of the previous 25 good cause appeals, picked six of them and left his entire residue to them.[9]

If this is a faithful account of Mervyn's conversation with Canon Hocking (and there is absolutely no reason to think it is not) his mind was by now befuddled. Between 2 May and Canon Hocking's arrival on 17 June, 17 people signed the visitors' book. As to living relatives, he had a sister to whom only seven months previously he had bequeathed £12,000, two nephews, a niece and five great-nephews and nieces. The 'substantial legacy' left to 'the woman who came in once a week', Mrs Sleght, was, as we have seen, a modest £3,000. His 'former housekeeper', as Mervyn rather grandly referred to Mrs Enid Pike, received £4,000, plus £500 for every year she had spent in his service, and that amounted to a further £8,000. In total, cash went to 35 individuals and to 43 charities and institutions. Because of its Low Church tradition, Mervyn mischievously left his copes, chasubles and mitres to St Patrick's Cathedral, Dublin. His hairdresser and his wife were left £10,000. Two old friends, George and Joy McWatters, received the contents of his cellar 'on the unlikely assumption that there be any bottles left in it'. Surprisingly, there were.

A number of bizarre events occurred as Mervyn's life was drawing to a close. He had to evacuate the house when ceilings came down following a flood. Returning home from the theatre one night he was attacked by a gang of youths and was hit over the head by them with his own walking stick. He appeared as a guest in a recording of the BBC programme *This Is Your Life*, only to appear on the television screen posthumously. And at the Winter 1994 meeting of the General Synod at Church House, Westminster, the militant homosexual organization OutRage! decided to live up to their name by 'outing' ten bishops they claimed were homosexual. Among the placards displayed was one bearing the name of

Mervyn Stockwood, together with the words 'Tell the Truth'. In an attempt to justify his actions, Peter Tatchell wrote in the *Independent* on 24 August 1995 that OutRage! 'only named the bishops because of their hypocrisy and homophobia: they preached against homosexuality and supported anti-gay policies while leading secret gay lives ... we were seeking to defend the homosexual community against public figures who were abusing their influence to harm other lesbians and gay men.' Anyone less homophobic than Mervyn would be hard to discover. Far from supporting anti-gay policies, he spoke in favour of homosexual law reform and quietly supported gay clergy behind the scenes. As for conducting a secret gay life, all the evidence suggests he led a life of total celibacy. How anyone who had troubled to carry out an iota of research could have levelled OutRage!'s blanket charges at Mervyn Stockwood defies belief. His bishop, James Thompson, telephoned Mervyn to warn him what had happened. 'Jim', said Mervyn, 'I couldn't care tuppence. And if the press get on to you, tell them I've had a lot of women too!'[10]

It has been suggested that as Mervyn died only six weeks after the OutRage! action it somehow contributed to his death. There is no evidence, and it seems unlikely, but Mervyn's bravado on the telephone to the Bishop of Bath and Wells certainly belied his inner feelings. On 2 December an old friend, John Gough, and his wife arrived to stay for two nights. Mr Gough recalls that Mervyn was 'desperately upset by the outing. He felt really wounded by it.'[11] The last person to sign Mervyn's visitors' book, on Christmas Day, was Tony Gingell, once a diminutive boat boy who served at Mass when Mervyn was vicar of St Matthew. Tony called again, on 12 January, and again he was the last person to do so. It is most unlikely he had any idea that Mervyn had left him £10,000. It has been said of Mervyn's ministry in Moorfields that had it not been for Mervyn, Tony Gingell's family might not have known where their next meal was coming from. 'To many of his parishioners', says Diana Cooke, 'Mervyn was quite simply the best friend they had.'[12]

That evening, 12 January, Mervyn began to suffer an asthma attack, but by no means one of his worst. Unfortunately it had been a mild, damp winter, and the sort of weather that best suited Mervyn's condition was cold and frost. Hence his breathing difficulties had become chronic. A duty doctor was summoned, and because Mervyn was beginning to feel nauseated the doctor suggested that purely as a precaution he should go into hospital for the night rather than remain on his own at home. Mervyn was most reluctant to go, but eventually agreed, and a single room was found for him at St Martin's Hospital in Midford Road, Bath. Diana Cooke packed an overnight bag for Mervyn, gave her telephone number to the ambulance crew and waved him off. Although the crew had had to carry Mervyn downstairs, Mrs Cooke never dreamed she would not see him again, and she is quite sure that Mervyn, too, had no idea he was likely to die.

It was 11.40 p.m. when Mervyn was admitted to St Martin's Hospital. He died four hours later, at 3.45 a.m. on 13 January. He had lived to the age he did in spite of indifferent health, little sleep and too much to drink because, fundamentally, he had been blessed with the constitution of an ox. The end was swift, and mercifully Mervyn was spared any lingering and incapacitated old age. Following a post-mortem the cause of death was given as congestive cardiac failure, ischaemic heart disease, acute bronchitis and old age. Mervyn's body was taken to a chapel of rest at the Bristol Co-Op Funeral Service opposite St Matthew, Moorfields. On 25 January Vespers for the Dead were said at All Saints', Clifton, and here, two days later, nine bishops appeared robed in the sanctuary to honour him at his Requiem Mass. Back in 1987 Mervyn had asked Charles Lansdale, 'when the time comes', to dispatch him on his last journey 'and to scatter my ashes on Chanctonbury Ring'. Thus Fr Lansdale presided at the Mass, which was followed, as we can be absolutely certain Mervyn would have wished, by a champagne reception.

Self-evidently, Mervyn Stockwood was a great parish priest. Equally self-evidently, he was not a great man. Was he a great bishop? That question is harder to answer, for it begs so many ill-defined definitions of the role of a modern diocesan. The first duty of a bishop is to be a Father in God to his clergy, and the general consensus of those who knew him seems to be that despite serious lapses, his care for his clergy was outstanding, and his championship of controversial theological and ethical issues brave. He was not necessarily the best advocate of his own opinions, but the fact that most of the time he was on the side of the angels cannot be in doubt. His non-ecclesiastical failings were of the most human and forgivable kind; his virtues were more often hidden, except from those who benefited from his innate and private kindness, for they were shielded, surprisingly enough, behind a fairly thick cloak of shyness. His self-discipline, for a man with no obvious vocation to celibacy, was of an exceptional – indeed, heroic – nature. He brought much more fun, excitement, colour and hope into the life of his diocese than he did irritation, and the life of the Church at large, during the second half of the twentieth century, would have been a great deal duller and a great deal less creative without him. There would in all probability have been no explosive publicity for *Honest to God* and no Bishop Montefiore in Birmingham or Bishop Sheppard in Liverpool. It was Mervyn Stockwood's good fortune to have begun his ministry on an incoming tide, and hardly his fault that his consecration coincided with a general decline in church-going. But through all the years of stress and change, as the Bishop of Lichfield has clearly noted, he continued to give to his clergy a Godly pride in their vocation.

What of his personal faith? Significantly, among the few papers Mervyn Stockwood preserved was a well-rehearsed quotation from a Victorian canon of St Paul's, Henry Scott Holland. 'Death is nothing at all', it begins. 'I have only slipped away into the next room.'

Notes

1 Rev. Tony Crowe, in conversation with the author.

2 Alan Clark, *Diaries* (Weidenfeld & Nicolson, 1993).

3 MS often wore a cassock outside his own house or diocese; he did so in the last summer of his life when he went to lunch in Gloucestershire with one of his godsons.

4 Information supplied by two of the guests, not by Mary Bevan, who firmly declined to discuss the question of MS and drink.

5 Mrs Cooke, speaking to the author.

6 The Hon. Mrs Rupert Legge, in conversation with the author.

7 The author understands that MS's solicitor has destroyed letters to MS from various members of the Royal Family, including most of those from the Prince of Wales.

8 Mr Ivor Seager, in conversation with the author.

9 Canon Michael Hocking, letter to the author, 28 February 1995.

10 As related to the author by the Bishop of Bath and Wells.

11 John Gough, in conversation with the author.

12 Mrs Cooke, as above.

Major chronology

1913   Born 27 May, Bridgend, Glamorgan

1917   Moved to Clifton, Bristol

1919–26 The Downs School, Wraxall

(1923)   Bembridge School, Isle of Wight

1926–30 Kelly College, Tavistock

1931–32 Teacher at Kingsland Grange School, Shrewsbury

1932–35 Christ's College, Cambridge

1935–36 Westcott House, Cambridge

1936   Ordained deacon, and appointed assistant curate
St Matthew, Moorfields, Bristol. Missioner at Blundell's
School until 1941

1937   Ordained priest

1941–55 Vicar, St Matthew, Moorfields

1946–55 Member, Bristol City Council

1952–55 Honorary Canon of Bristol Cathedral

1955–59 Vicar, University Church of Great St Mary, Cambridge

1956–59 Member Cambridge City Council

1959   Consecrated Bishop of Southwark

1963   Takes seat in House of Lords

1976   Freedom of City of London

1980   Resigns see of Southwark and retires to 15 Sydney
Buildings, Bath. Appointed honorary assistant bishop,
Diocese of Bath and Wells

1995   Dies, 13 January, St Martin's Hospital, Bath
27 January: Requiem Mass, All Saints', Clifton, followed
by private cremation. Preacher: the Dean of Westminster
18 February: ashes scattered at Chanctonbury Ring
8 March: Memorial Service, Southwark Cathedral.
Preacher: the Rt Rev. and Rt Hon. Lord Runcie

Books by Mervyn Stockwood

1945 *There Is a Tide* (Allen & Unwin)
1945 *Services for Children* (SCM Press)
1948 *Whom They Pierced* (Longmans, Green)
1949 *Christianity and Marxism* (SPCK)
1955 *I Went to Moscow* (Epworth Press)
1959 *The Faith Today* (SPCK)
1959 *Cambridge Sermons* (Hodder & Stoughton)
1959 *Religion and the Scientists* (ed.) (SCM Press)
1964 *Bishop's Journal* (Mowbray)
1978 *The Cross and the Sickle* (Sheldon Press)
1980 *From Strength to Strength* (Sheldon Press)
1982 *Chanctonbury Ring* (Sheldon Press and Hodder & Stoughton)

INDEX